MW00619193

People, Power, Change

People, Power, Change

Organizing for Democratic Renewal

MARSHALL GANZ

OXFORD
UNIVERSITY PRESS

Oxford University Press is a department of the University of Oxford. It furthers
the University's objective of excellence in research, scholarship, and education
by publishing worldwide. Oxford is a registered trade mark of Oxford University
Press in the UK and certain other countries.

Published in the United States of America by Oxford University Press
198 Madison Avenue, New York, NY 10016, United States of America.

© Oxford University Press 2024

All rights reserved. No part of this publication may be reproduced, stored in
a retrieval system, or transmitted, in any form or by any means, without the
prior permission in writing of Oxford University Press, or as expressly permitted
by law, by license, or under terms agreed with the appropriate reproduction
rights organization. Inquiries concerning reproduction outside the scope of the
above should be sent to the Rights Department, Oxford University Press, at the
address above.

You must not circulate this work in any other form
and you must impose this same condition on any acquirer.

Library of Congress Cataloging-in-Publication Data
Names: Ganz, Marshall, 1943– author.
Title: People, power, change : organizing for democratic renewal / Marshall Ganz.
Description: New York, NY : Oxford University Press, [2024] |
Includes bibliographical references and index. |
Identifiers: LCCN 2023052233 (print) | LCCN 2023052234 (ebook) |
ISBN 9780197569009 (hardback) | ISBN 9780197569016 (epub) | ISBN 9780197569030
Subjects: LCSH: Community organization. | Power (Social sciences)
Classification: LCC HM766 .G36 2024 (print) | LCC HM766 (ebook) |
DDC 361.8—dc23/eng/20231214
LC record available at https://lccn.loc.gov/2023052233
LC ebook record available at https://lccn.loc.gov/2023052234

DOI: 10.1093/oso/9780197569009.001.0001

Printed by Sheridan Books, Inc., United States of America

Contents

List of Figures

Acknowledgments

I share this book with gratitude for the people with whom I've learned, experiences we have shared, commitments we have made, craft we have developed, and persistence without which there would be no book.

When Liz McKenna decided she would be the "doula" of this book in 2015, I knew it could become real: her belief in the value of our project; commitment to seeing it through; gift of bringing sustaining order to encroaching chaos; clarity and creativity of writing, co-writing, and editing; sharing of tough decisions; insight, intelligence, and thoughtfulness; and, perhaps most important of all, her spirit of humor, love, and hope. Liz, it's truly been nine years! Years during which it also has been my joy to accompany you on your journey from student to collaborator and, now to colleague, as you have accompanied me on mine.

Although I've aspired to this book at least since 1985, shortly after I left the farmworkers, I struggled to make it real. One reason I returned to school in 1991 was to structure my writing as a senior thesis (thank you, Margaret), master's thesis, and a dissertation (thank you, Theda, Richard, Andy, and Mark). This book only began to become "real-ish" after I finished my PhD in 2000; then, again, in 2009, after I published my first book; and, yet again, in the spring of 2015 when I took a leave with this purpose in *mind*, but not in *print*. This is when Liz took it on. We began work on a proposal and finding an agent, but, over the next three years, it still moved too slowly. So, in 2018, Liz made common cause with Hahrie Han, also a former student, collaborator, and colleague, then teaching at UC Santa Barbara. On the morning of June 19, they both knocked on the door to my hotel room in San Francisco, where I was to give a talk on organizing. It was what organizers call an "action"!: "So, are you going to do it or not? If not, let's drop it. But if so, show up in Santa Barbara on January 19, 2019, to face people with whom you have been working and who want you to commit to getting it done. Will you commit?"

It blew my mind. Like a drowning person, years of teaching, organizing, and coaching "flashed before my eyes." And on Friday, January 19, there they were: Hahrie, Liz, Nisreen Haj Ahmad (Zoom), Joy Cushman (Zoom),

Margaret Weir ("senior thesis advisor"), Art Reyes, Andy Andrews, Uyen Doan, Bernie and Roz Steinberg, Rune Baastrup, Liv Detlif, Uyen Doan, Kanoko Kamata, Ana Babovic, Kwesi Chapin, Ethan Frey, Dan Grandone, Nicholas Hayes, Tamara Kay, Jessica Mele, Scott Reed, Conrado Santos, Regina Schwartz, Chris Torres, Jake Waxman, Jyotswaroop Bawa, Hope Wood, and Sam Wohns.[1] They weren't just "there." They were there to offer support as both challenge and affirmation, to remind me of the learning we had done together, and they were organized: for each chapter and each deadline I was to be accountable to a specific chapter team.

Let me be clear. I did want to write this book! But I also think I would have failed the famous "marshmallow" test, unable to delay gratification because it always seems there is so much to get done now, given especially "fast" moments of danger and opportunity in the wake of the general election of 2016.

But it worked!

So now that the book is here, I'm grateful to many others who made the "end game" happen. At the Practicing Democracy Project, Emily Lin (who also joined me in figuring out how to launch our first online organizing class in 2010) made it a practical priority and Alyssa Ashcraft insistently managed the time. Thanks to Audra Wolfe, my hopeful, wise, and cheerfully "ruthless" editor; James Cook at Oxford who always kept hope alive; Jonah Evans, whose team contributed original graphics; Rosi Greenberg, artist, teacher, and coach—and designer of the cover of this book; "end game" editor Barbara Smith-Mandell; readers Danielle Allen, Rebecca Henderson, Kathryn Perera, Deb Roy, Doran Schrantz, and Margaret Levi. I'm grateful to my good friend and collaborator Sarah ElRaheb-Dagher, who brings pedagogical excellence (and imagination), empowering leadership, and the joy of learning in all she does. Thanks to David Weil for his helpful insights into the workings of American labor. The 400-some students with whom I work every year in my classes are a source of continual new learning, enabled by the leadership of my head teaching fellows, Kate Hilton, Hope Wood, Rawan Zeine, Shivani Kumar, Sachiko Osawa, Uyen Doan, Ashraf Hamzah, Abel Cano, Ana Babovic, Chuck Herman, Anita Krishnan, Vandinika Shukla, Toni Kokenis, Noor Masood, Markella Los, Celine Lebrun Shaath, Jake Waxman, Salma Sameh, and Lacey Connelly. Mais Irqsusi whose energetic leadership, backed by Board Members Jennifer McCrea and Ian Simmons, transformed the *Leading Change Network* into a source of inspiration, action, and learning.

Harvard

I'm also deeply grateful to those who contributed so much to my foundational learning: my good friend, teacher, collaborator, and colleague, the late Bernie Steinberg, with whom I learned so much about narrative, moral leadership, and my own traditions core to so much of this book; the late Richard Hackman, whose teaching, coaching, and mentoring transformed my pedagogy; Ruth Wageman, my partner in developing these powerful pedagogical frameworks, especially in how to enable real teams to work; Theda Skocpol, who offered such caring, strategic, and "relentless" support since I got here in 1991, including serving as my principal thesis advisor, friend, and collaborator; the wondrous Gerta Dhamo, who anchored all the moving parts; Adam Reich, with whom I reworked many of the core frameworks, including public narrative; Jane McAlevey, a kindred spirit and brilliant colleague, whose deep understanding of organizing—especially labor organizing—teaches and inspires; Joy Cushman, the committed developer of creative pedagogy in practice, campaign, and program design; Nisreen Haj Ahmad, a leader in the creative adaptation, innovation, and development of our pedagogy and practice including, but not limited to the Arab world; Dan Grandone for creating the foundation of what would become LCN. Don Berwick who saw the contribution our pedagogy and practice could make to the world of healing and health, initially built upon by Kate Hilton's work with Helen Bevan in the UK's NHS, and by Pedja Stojicic, now leading People, Power and Health, working to humanize health-care practice; Jorrit de Jong who enabled us to learn by training some forty mayors each year; Farhan Latif who invites us to work with American Muslim leaders each year; Jennifer Lerner who showed our pedagogy could yield empirically measurable improvements in leadership practice; Hahrie Han, not only for the Santa Barbara "intervention," but also for showing how excellent research can inform excellent practice; Mark Moore, Derek Bok, and Mary Jo Bane, without whose support I'd not have had the opportunity to develop this pedagogy year after year at the Kennedy School, nor to support the development of leadership, organizing, and action around the world; and my good friend Richard Parker not only for his love of purpose, energetic curiosity, stimulating debate, and unique insight, but also for keeping the sometimes bizarre context in which we work in some (even humorous) perspective, and who, with his wife Robin, have been of constant and profound personal support.

An utterly unexpected source of learning turned out to be supporting the leadership of former students moved to adapt our pedagogy to the organizing practice in their own worlds. This rich community of practice enables deeper understanding of one's own practice as well as that which is human across cultures and that which is particular with a specific culture. Along with Nisreen's above, this includes Kanoko Kamata in Japan; Ana Babovic in Serbia; Aprajita Pandey in India; Huang Hui in China; Ignacio Ibarzabal in Argentina; Anita Tang, Stephen Donnelly, and Nadia Montague in Australia; Olivia Chow in Toronto, where she was recently elected mayor; and Mariali Cardenas and Carlos Quintero in Mexico.

This whole learning journey at Harvard would not have happened without the loving partnership of my late wife, Susan Eaton, a partnership rooted in our appetite for learning, spirit of adventure, focus on practice, and belief in the dignity of all. After we shared a year earning our MPA's at the Kennedy School, her deep commitments to women's leadership, the work of caring, and the organization of people, moved her to do her own PhD at MIT. We both finished in 2000 and were hired to teach at the Kennedy School, a plan cut short when we lost her in late 2003. In fact, the whole idea of returning to Harvard took root in 1989 at what was my twenty-fifth reunion (without graduating) and her tenth reunion.

The In Between Years

The ten years between organizing with the farmworkers and returning to school, although challenging and uncertain, were also years of deep learning, especially about challenge and uncertainty. I'm grateful for the companionship of Jerry Cohen, former general counsel of the United Farm Workers (UFW), with whom I learned while processing the UFW experience. My good friend Chris Campbell, with whom I committed to learn ancient Greek, was an intellectual, emotional, and learning companion during some dark years. I'm grateful for learning to adapt my organizing craft to electoral politics with SF political consultant, Clint Reilly, and Jerry Brown, Nancy Pelosi, Maureen O'Connor, Alan Cranston, and others, including Alan's son, Kim Cranston, former UFW organizer Larry Tramutola, and Scott Washburn. Scott is a friend, colleague, and collaborator with whom I've realized the most creativity in action organizing, researching, or campaigning. I'm also grateful for the opportunity to continue learning with Miguel Contreras, who made his mark as the first Latino to lead the LA Federation of Labor. And I'm grateful to Carlos and Linda LeGarrette, colleagues in the UFW, who have always been there, good times and bad.

UFW

I'm grateful to Cesar Chavez, with whom I learned for sixteen years, not only about organizing, but about life, meaning, winning, and losing, culture, creativity, and leadership. I also learned of the dangers of isolation; the seduction of power; the reactiveness to fear; and the need for peers who can challenge as well as affirm. I'm grateful to Fred Ross with whom I learned the organizing "craft"—not only particular skills and practices, but how to imagine, learn, and develop new practices—and that organizing is a constant learning; to Teofilo Garcia, Adelina Gurrola, Jorge Zaragoza, and Juan and Maximina de la Cruz (Juan was murdered on a picket line in 1973), my movement "family" southeast of Bakersfield, with whom I learned the Spanish language—the real language, not just the words, but meaning embellished by gesture, tone of voice, emotional content, humor, and often seasoned with a good *dicho*; to LeRoy Chatfield, former Christian Brother, who introduced me to Cesar and became, with his wife Bonnie, a lifelong friend and collaborator. To Mike Miller, the SF organizer, my other connection with Cesar, who linked my work with SNCC (Student Nonviolent Coordinating Committee) with the UFW; to Hub Segur who taught me how numbers work.

Over the years with the UFW I'm grateful to Mack Lyons, the first farmworker leader I recruited and with whom I later served on the Board; to Rev. Jim Drake, whose real courage went well beyond standing up to armed growers and goons to their face, who knew when it was time to go, and with whom I reconnected when he came to Boston to organize Greater Boston Interfaith Organization. I'm especially grateful to farmworker leaders Mario Bustamante, Sabino López, Rosario Pelayo, Cleofás Guzmán, Aristeo Zambrano, Armando Ruiz, and Roberto García, with whom organizing, striking, campaigning each day was a new learning. I'm also deeply grateful to my colleagues with whom it was an honor to serve on our executive board including Mack Lyons, Eliseo Medina, Jessica Govea, Gilbert Padilla, Peter Velasco, and Phillip Veracruz.

When I was sent to Toronto to organize Canadians to boycott California grapes, it turned into an apprenticeship to Canadian labor, political, religious, and community leaders in a different—and more hopeful—way to make democracy work: Dennis McDermott, Terry Meagher, Lynn Williams, Keely Cummings, Iona Samis, Eamon Park, Bill Howes, Ed Seymore, Marilyn Landrus, Rebecca Hamilton, Fr. Bob Madden, Fr. Brad Massman, and many others especially my friend, colleague, and collaborator, the late Patty Park.

And I'm deeply grateful to my partner of eighteen years, Jessica Govea, and her entire family with whom I learned, loved, struggled, and flourished— my beloved companion, whose singing of "Cu Curu Cu Cu Paloma" rallied workers, organizers, and anyone within range (at the same time, covering for my weak guitar playing) on this challenging journey.

Mississippi

I'm deeply grateful to the mentors in Mississippi who set me on the organizing path to begin with: Hollis Watkins, Curtis Muhammad, and E. W. Steptoe. Without their understanding and support my organizing journey would have been a short one. Instead, it is with them that my real learning of race, power, and politics in America began. And with all due respect to Harvard, the most life changing moment there was meeting SNCC organizer, Dotty Zellner, who recruited me for the summer project.

In the Beginning

And going back to the beginning, I'm grateful to my mother, Sylvia, for her love of learning, teaching, curiosity, commitment to social justice, strength in leading the household, managing my inaccessible father, managing her ailing mother, managing me, and bringing her love to her students (and to me), her excitement of discovery, insistence on hope, and her precious life giving sense of humor (including puns). She had made up her mind that I would go to Harvard, the main reason it came to pass. Her realistic fear for me when I volunteered to go to Mississippi eventually turned into her leadership of a Bakersfield Friends of SNCC chapter, one of the least likely cities in California to support civil rights. I finally got to make good on her faith when she joined me for my Harvard College graduation at eighty-one.

It's been a rich journey—not of ease, to be sure, but one of struggle and celebration, losses and wins, betrayal and loyalty, of hurt and hope, disappointment and surprise, a journey shared with people, and most of all, a journey of learning. And, as Jaques concludes his Seven Ages of Man soliloquy in act 2, scene 7 of Shakespeare's *As You Like It*: "I would not change it."

And with that we return to the present.

Introduction

Why Me, Why Us, Why Now

Why Me?

The title of this book is *People, Power, Change*. It is a book about how to equip *people* with the capacity to build the *power* they need to get the *change* they seek. In other words, this is a book about organizing.

I was introduced to organizing in the summer of 1964 when I was finishing my junior year at Harvard College and volunteered for the Mississippi Summer Project. The project, also known as "Freedom Summer," was organized by a coalition of civil rights organizations, led by SNCC (Student Nonviolent Coordinating Committee), at a critical moment in the fight for a federal guarantee of the voting rights long denied Black Americans across the South, especially in Mississippi. The 1964 presidential election loomed large in the wake of the assassination of President Kennedy in November 1963. It was the culmination of a long hot summer that began with the assassination of Mississippi NAACP president Medgar Evers, the murder of four little girls in the bombing of their Birmingham church, assaults on peaceful protesters with police dogs and fire hoses, and a historic 250,000-person March on Washington for jobs and freedom. The plan was to organize a Mississippi Freedom Democratic Party (MFDP) that would send a delegation to the Democratic Convention in August and demand to be seated in lieu of an official segregated delegation. A critical challenge was that in Mississippi, the "law" did not protect the Black organizers, who were being arrested, beaten, or worse. The intent of the project was to support their work by bringing people, mostly white students from elite northern universities who, given who they were, might bring the "law" with them.

Some three hundred of us had gathered for training at a college in southern Ohio when, on June 24, 1964, the night before we were to leave for Mississippi, we got word that three of our party—James Chaney, Andrew Goodman, and Michael Schwerner—had disappeared. They had been dispatched to Meridian a week earlier and the day before had been sent to investigate the burning of a Black church in Philadelphia, Mississippi. They had not been heard from since.

Bob Moses, the soft-spoken lead organizer of the Summer Project, called us together in a college auditorium. He said, "Our three brothers have not been heard from. We don't *know* what happened, but we *think* we do know what happened. . . . We think they're gone."

Sure enough, two months later, their bullet-riddled and beaten bodies were found in a dirt levee where they had been buried by the Ku Klux Klan after executing them. The county sheriff had turned them over to the Klan with that intent.

"I'd like to tell you all to go home, that you're not needed, that it's okay," Bob said. "But I can't. I have to ask you to go. But I can't take the whole responsibility. Each of you must decide. And if you can't go, that's fine. There's no shame. But you must decide."

I sank into my seat in utter silence. Just like everyone else in the room. I asked myself: What am I doing here? Is this what I signed up for? What had I gotten myself into?

* * *

My father was a rabbi and my mother, a teacher. We had lived in Germany for three years after the Second World War, when he served as a chaplain in the American army. Much of his work was with Holocaust survivors: people whose lives had been shattered by that horror; people whom I had met in our home who were on their way trying to find some hope. My fifth birthday party was held in a DP (displaced persons) camp occupied only by children. At first I thought it was cool. But then I realized why it was only children. The parents were gone. And I had to give gifts, not receive them. At the same time my mother, a daughter of immigrants who had grown up in Virginia, had developed an acute awareness of the segregated world in which she lived. So, my parents interpreted the Holocaust to me as not only about anti-Semitism but about racism. And racism kills. The civil rights movement was challenging the institutionalized racism foundational to our country even before it became a country.

As an RK (rabbi's kid), I had to go to all the "stuff." I was also supposed to be perfect. But I did love the Passover seder, the telling of the story of the journey from slavery to freedom (with food): the exodus story. There was a moment in the seder when the leader would point to the children and declare, "You were slaves in Egypt." At first, I didn't get it. I hadn't been a slave, nor had I been to Egypt. But then I realized that that story is not the property of one people, one time, or one place. It is told generation after generation, and you have to figure out where you are in it. Are you with the warriors on their horses and their chariots, pursuing the people? Or are you with those people trying to find their way to a land of promise? Dr. Martin Luther King Jr. described the movement for civil rights as yet another chapter in the telling of that story.

Finding one's way to a "land of promise" became more challenging, and perhaps more urgent, as my father became afflicted by what would later be diagnosed as paranoid schizophrenia. He had become unavailable to me or to my mother by the time I was seven. When I was twelve he tried to beat me up. At the same time, I found myself unequipped to deal with the bullying a "new kid" in town often faces, especially a Jewish kid who can't go to Friday night football because he had to go hear his father give a sermon. My hurt at not being seen, not being heard, yet subject to arbitrary power—do it because I say so—grew into anger.

Now at twenty, I saw this abuse of power going on daily across the American South, but with Billy clubs, fire hoses, shotguns, bombings, and rope. And as I looked around the room, everyone seemed to be about my age: eighteen, nineteen, twenty-one, or twenty-two. The civil rights movement was a movement of young people. Dr. King had led the Montgomery Bus Boycott when he was twenty-five. Protestant theologian Walter Bruggeman argues that what he calls the "prophetic imagination" occurs at the intersection of criticality—a sense of the world's hurt, its pain—and hope—a sense of the world's possibilities, its promise.[1] Young people come of age with a critical eye on the world they find and, almost of necessity, with hopeful hearts. This creates a deep affinity between generational change and social change. So, it was for my generation—and, I believe, for this one as well.

As we sat in silence, each in our own thoughts, Jean Wheeler, a SNCC organizer, stood up in the back of the room. She began to sing:

> *They say that freedom is a constant struggle,*
> *They say that freedom is a constant struggle,*
> *They say that freedom is a constant struggle,*
> *Oh Lord, we've struggled so long we must be free.*

She continued:

> *They say that freedom is a constant dying,*
> *We've died too long; we must be free.*

As she got up and began to find her way out of the room, still singing, one by one, each person got up and followed her. The next day, we all went to Mississippi.

That moment in that auditorium would change my life. It was in Mississippi that I found what would become my "calling"—really for the rest of my life: enabling others to find the courage to lead, to build community, and to enable that community to turn resources it has into the power it needs to get what it wants. My career has changed many times since, but my calling has remained the same.

With all due respect to Harvard, my education about race, power, and politics in America also began in Mississippi. The inequalities in health care, education, and housing were so stark: whites were on the top and Blacks on the bottom. But I also learned that bringing a few books or medical supplies would not make much difference. That's when I began to learn the difference between justice and charity. Charity asks, "What's wrong? Let me help!" Justice asks, "Why is it happening? Let me change it!" When you ask these questions, you get pushback. Some people, it turns out, don't have enough because other people have too much—and they don't want to give it up. When you try to change that, you find yourself in a power struggle.

One of the most profound—and most useful—lessons I learned in Mississippi was the difference between resources and power. Many communities—and individuals—lack power. Black people in Mississippi had no real right to vote. They had been excluded from federal labor laws as agricultural or domestic workers since the 1930s. And I'd never had the experience of going up to someone twice my age who would stand up, offer me his chair, call me mister, introduce himself with his first name, and not look me in the eye, because he was Black and I was white. That happened thousands of times a day across the South.

But they did have resources: This was the lesson of the Montgomery Bus Boycott that sparked the modern civil rights movement. African Americans had to use the buses to go to work every day. But it was Blacks in the back, whites in the front, a no-man's-land in the middle, and an armed, deputized bus driver up front. If you were Black you got on the bus, deposited your bus fare, passed the armed bus driver, passed the rows of white people, and found a seat in the back, but if a white person wanted that seat you had to get up and give it to them—twice a day, every day, going to and coming home from work. There was a lot of anger in that community.[2]

When the US Supreme Court declared segregation unconstitutional in its 1954 *Brown v. Board of Education* decision, it sparked hope in Montgomery that the time to fix the buses had arrived. And when Rosa Parks, secretary of the local NAACP chapter, refused to give up her seat and move to the back of the bus, she was arrested and jailed. And after Parks went to jail, the women's committee at the local Black college decided it was wrong to let Parks go to jail by herself. They went to Dr. King and the others to propose that the community stay off the buses for a day in solidarity.

There's an account of Dr. King getting up early Monday morning to watch the buses go by—and there was not a single Black face on a single bus. At that moment that community saw itself differently. Powerlessness divides you. But that kind of solidarity empowers. That night, the community decided that if they had done it for one day, they could stay off the buses until they won.

It took a year, but they did win. During that struggle, the Black residents of Montgomery, Alabama, discovered that they did in fact have resources that they could turn into sources of power. Almost everyone had feet. If they used their feet to walk to work and deny the bus company their fare—and they all acted together—they could turn individual resources into collective power. They could turn individual dependency on the bus company into the bus company's dependency on a united community. In the end, their efforts not only desegregated the buses but perhaps even more importantly, empowered the community. The new leadership they developed would join in building a movement.

This was called organizing. In Mississippi, I discovered I could be good at it, and I got hooked. So, when it came time to go back to Harvard for my senior year, it seemed like the least relevant thing I could do. Instead, I wrote Harvard a letter asking how I could come back and study history when we were busy making history. Arrogant, to be sure, but also true.

Instead of going back to Cambridge, I returned home to Bakersfield, California, where we had lived since I was in the sixth grade. Bakersfield is an oil and agriculture town at the southern end of the San Joaquin Valley, made infamous by John Steinbeck's *Grapes of Wrath*. Cesar Chavez had just launched a grape strike there—a first step in organizing a union of the largely Mexican immigrant farmworkers. I had grown up in the midst of the farmworker world but had never seen it. I had to come back home with "Mississippi eyes" to see another community of people of color, also without political rights, also without labor law protections, and California with its own rich history of racial oppression, going back to its indigenous peoples, the Chinese, the Japanese, the Filipinos, and the Mexicans.[3] As late as the 1950s, movie theaters in Los Angeles sent Mexicans upstairs, reserving the downstairs for the whites. It turned out that Mississippi was not an exception in America. It was an example of the America we had to change.

That fall, I began to work with Cesar and what would become the United Farm Workers of America, better known as the UFW.[4] And in collaboration with my colleague, friend, and partner, Jessica Govea, I did so for the next sixteen years. In Mississippi I had found my calling, but it was with the farmworkers that I learned much of the craft I share in this book. We had to learn to organize in workplaces, communities, political campaigns, and boycotts. My first electoral campaign was Bobby Kennedy's California primary fight in 1968, when our team of some one hundred noncitizen farmworkers went to East LA to turn out the votes of Latino citizens. We won the primary for him, but we lost him to an assassin's bullets later the same night.

We also learned to work in many different ethnic communities. Although most of the workforce were Mexican immigrants, the Filipino immigrants started the strike. We also worked with Punjabis, Yemenis, the Azoreans— almost every ethnic group who at one time or another had been brought in to undermine the organizing efforts of the farmworkers already here.

I left the farmworkers in 1981 and did another ten years of electoral, labor, and issue organizing, training, and learning, mostly in California. But in 1989, I was invited to my twenty-fifth reunion at Harvard, even though I had never graduated. I didn't know they invited dropouts, although I could understand why they would invite a dropout who started a small software company up in Seattle. That wasn't me. But I had been working with Jerry Brown to rebuild the California Democratic Party, but we seemed to be stuck. So, in company with my wife-to-be, Susan Eaton, whose tenth reunion it was, I went.

Attending that reunion was like running into a twenty-year-old version of myself. "How's it going?" twenty-year-old me asked. "Not so great," I replied. "Reagan's been president for eight years and I'm feeling stuck. I need to find a way to go deeper and broader." "So why don't you come back and finish that senior year you left pending?" asked twenty-year-old me. "Well, I don't know if my synapses are up to it . . . and tuition has changed a bit." But a remarkable three-hour conversation with an Episcopal priest who was serving as a Harvard admissions person made it possible. If he'd laughed at me, it would have been all over. But we figured it out.

In 1991, after Susan and I were married, I returned to Harvard to finish my senior year. I wrote a senior thesis in history and government (having already done the fieldwork) and graduated class of '64–92. My eighty-year-old mother finally got to see her son become a college graduate. But that had only whetted my appetite for digging deeper. The following year, Susan and I did the mid-career MPA at the Kennedy School—making me the only person to go from undergrad to midcareer in one summer—and completed my PhD in sociology in 2000, the same year Susan completed hers at MIT. While I was working on my PhD, the Kennedy School asked if I would teach a course on organizing. That experience turned out to be a real gift for me. I could integrate my life experience with the social science I was learning in a pedagogical conversation with a rising generation. I got to go to class twice a week and have a conversation with the future. How cool was that?

I've been on the faculty full time since 2000, teaching organizing and public narrative both online and off. Susan was hired as an assistant professor at the same time to teach health care management and leadership, but in December 2003 we lost her to leukemia. Fortunately, perhaps, around the same time I got back into the world of practice through my students, beginning with Howard Dean's 2003/4 campaign for president in New Hampshire, organization work with the Sierra Club, and, in 2007/8, the Obama campaign. Since then, I've been blessed with the opportunity to work with individuals, organizations, and movements around the world, each trying to find ways to turn their values into the sources of power they need to shape a world in which they want to raise their children.

In the course of my journey, I did learn to bring people together, enable them to find common ground, and turn their resources into power. But exercising that power in a way that respects the equal, infinite worth and dignity of each individual requires rooting that power not in governing authorities, but in the people who authorize them to govern. That's called democracy.

When a person experiences a denial of their worth, of their family, or of their community, the dissonance can motivate action with access to sources of hope, solidarity, and self-efficacy, rooted in shared values. Turning that action into power, and that power into change, requires organizing. And organizing, in turn, requires leadership. The more leadership a community develops, the more power their community can grow. And the leadership it takes is not that of a single person like a Bob Moses or a Cesar Chavez but of many people who accept responsibility for enacting our country's most important social movements.

In other words, the craft of organizing drives the practice of democracy.

Why Us?

Many Americans only woke up to the fact that democracy was in trouble on November 9, 2016, the day after Donald J. Trump was elected president of the United States. Others, who had known trouble for much of their lives, in the United States and around the world, were less surprised but more directly threatened. The promise of democracy seemed to be at greater risk than at any time since the 1930s.[5] Although large majorities of the American public support far-reaching—and urgently needed—political, economic, and social reforms, their desires are held in check by our radically unrepresentative political institutions.[6]

But the motivation to renew, deepen, and broaden the democratic promise was also unmistakable in the wake of Trump's election: the Women's March, the airport protests of the Muslim ban, the emergence of Indivisible and thousands of pop-up groups, the youthful March for Our Lives mobilization against gun violence movement, the Sunrise mobilization for the "Green New Deal," and the Democratic wave of the 2018 midterm election.[7]

And then, just as the mobilizations were building momentum, COVID-19 disrupted everything. The pandemic confronted us with the radical vulnerability of those without the wealth or status to protect themselves in the absence of a responsive and effective government. Not unlike the 2008 economic crisis, the rich only got richer while the rest struggled to survive.[8] Many had to find the resilience to sustain the avoidable loss of parents, partners, children, friends, colleagues, and school days. Even as outrage at the murder of George Floyd mobilized millions—Black and white alike—to assert the value of Black lives, a hoped-for democratic renewal in the 2020 election fell short, as 74 million people voted for Trump, many of whom remain committed to scuttling democracy. Despite historic levels of mobilization since 2017—and key successes—organized constituencies with the depth, breadth, unity, and imagination to launch a movement capable not just of defending democracy, but of achieving it, remain more of an aspiration than a reality.

Democracy is not only a form of governance. It is a promise: a promise that we can live with one another in dignity, equality, solidarity, security, justice, and hope. Practicing democracy can enable us to grow, to learn, to care, and to act. Democracy promises "life, liberty, and the pursuit of happiness," but realizing this promise requires that a society commit to governance based on the equal value of each of our voices; discernment of our common interests through association, deliberation, and learning; and respect for the exercise of individual and collective agency.

In reality, however, this promise—problematic since our founding as a half-slave and half-free nation—has narrowed in the United States, especially since the 1970s. Despite real gains in the fight against racial, gender, and ethnic inequality, an accelerating concentration of wealth drives ever greater economic inequality. Public education deteriorates, even as access to higher education narrows. To access colleges, young people must mortgage their futures even before they have begun to live them. And most of us feel less safe, not more, driving those who can afford it to retreat behind gated walls and private security.

This deterioration of collective public capacity did not just happen. Beginning in the 1960s, right-wing reaction to the successes of the civil rights, women's, youth, anti-war, and environmental movements took root. In the 1970s, the economic crisis offered private sector leaders and their political and academic allies an opportunity to commit national elites to "free market" or neoliberal ideology, policies, and programs. Conservative organizers, advocates, and politicians blended these currents in a politics that delegitimized democratic government, marginalized public institutions, and lionized private wealth—all trends epitomized by Donald Trump. Eventually, this movement leveraged control of the Republican Party into control of the federal government,[9] the very institution they were hell-bent on ravaging. Trump may well be unique in the depth of his moral and empirical nihilism, his sociopathic focus on personal domination, and his dangerously erratic narcissism; but he and his wrecking crew were, and are, ugly symptoms rather than root causes of the current threat to democracy.

Worse still, the democratic political processes that movements had used to leverage the power to counter these threats have been commodified, monetized, and marketized.[10] After 1976, when the Supreme Court decided in *Buckley v. Valeo* that money equals speech, political spending could not be constrained. This launched the United States' powerful electoral marketing industry, a phenomenon almost unique among liberal democracies.[11] In 2020 alone, this industry earned $14 billion in the process of turning politics into marketing, campaigns into advertising, candidates into brands, voters into data points, and dialogic debate into one-way messaging. This transformation of the electoral "means of production" was driven by the new class of professionals who manage campaigns' polling, television, direct mail, computer targeting, and digital media.[12] Because their earnings depend on commissions, the more money they spend, the more money they make, transforming us from citizens into clients or customers.

Nor is this political pathology limited to electoral campaigns. Advocacy groups, many of whom depend more on philanthropic donors than on organized constituencies, became enthralled by similar, digitally driven marketing campaigns. They contract with the same firms, which are often active in both the electoral domain and the private sector. These firms' methods confuse numbers with impact, mobilizing with organizing, and top-down control with bottom-up representation.[13]

All this was brought into sharp relief by a pandemic that starkly revealed how a system that served the few failed to serve the many by almost any metric, in health, education, security, employment, income, and housing. The political, economic, and racial dividing lines were impossible to miss. Political failures in managing the triple challenges of globalization, financialization, and digitalization undermined democracy by facilitating concentrations of wealth; religious, racial, and class division; and the erosion of the civic infrastructure that Alexis de Tocqueville, reporting on American democracy in the 1830s described as "the great free schools of democracy."[14] This deterioration is particularly egregious in the United States, where archaic political institutions empower unrepresentative minorities to block action in majority interests, resulting in consistent, gross, and frustrating democratic dysfunction. This is not only an American problem. The promise of democracy is at equal or greater risk in countries around the world as authoritarian regimes become entrenched.

Why Now?

This is not how it was "supposed" to be. And it is not how it has to be.

Millions of Americans could strengthen our democracy by practicing it. Tocqueville argued that in a democracy, "knowledge of how to combine," is the "mother of all forms of knowledge." Yet it is precisely Americans' useful knowledge of the practices that enable purposeful collective action that we have allowed to atrophy. Many are out of practice at coming together, committing to one another in pursuit of a shared purpose, deliberating together, deciding together, and acting together—the essential practices of democracy in its most everyday form. The same goes for skills related to group decision-making, managing internal conflict, or holding one another accountable—the most basic democratic practices. We see, hear, and read about the major threats to democracy every day, but a closer look reveals the depth of the challenges we face in our everyday lives.

Effective public voice arising from commitment to common purpose—a political process—has become rare indeed. As philosopher Elizabeth Anderson argues in *Private Government*, people now live most of the time within private authoritarian bureaucracies or firms in which they own nothing, have no authority, and constantly must resist incursions in their private life.[15] Or they shop in markets that aggregate individual momentary preferences in what some purport to be the voice of the whole. Public voice grows quite faint.

Meanwhile proponents of market solutions argue they transform individual preferences efficiently into optimally beneficial common outcomes absent shared commitments, deliberation and decision making.[16] They have extended their well beyond economics into policy domains of all sorts, promoting market solutions to global warming, market solutions to health-care crises, market solutions to the deterioration of public schools, and, of course, market solutions to problems of the market itself![17] After all, it is far easier to mobilize individuals to send emails or to show up at a rally than it is to develop the leadership, organization, and constituency needed to strategize, sustain, and build power over the long haul.[18]

At the same time, young people since the 1960s had become increasingly suspicious of the power structures that they experienced as constraining their individual autonomy or freedom to do their own thing while also fearing the assumption of any collective obligation. Thus, despite their energy and commitment, sooner or later their power is crippled by what feminist sociologist Jo Freeman called the "tyranny of structurelessness." She argues that there is no such thing as an entirely "structureless group." The absence of a transparent formal structure only disguises opaque, informal, personalistic, and unaccountable structure, which ensures its dysfunction.[19] This collective disarray cannot begin to contest the power of increasingly concentrated wealth. And it is this erosion of our capacity for collective action that sapped our power to confront the sources of the inequality, creating a growing surplus at the top and deepening deficit at the bottom.

This in turn has enabled a "philanthropic" colonization of the civil society within which people-based politics and social movements had been rooted. Constituency-based power has thus been replaced by donor-based patronage, which expands the power of private wealth even more. Self-governing, bottom-up membership associations are replaced by donor-governed, top-down memberless "firms," NGOs barred from partisan politics lest they compromise their donors' tax benefits. Access to public power now depends far more on *ownership* than on *citizenship*.[20]

These approaches fail to enable democracy to work, because democracy is based on the equal value of each person's voice in making *collective* decisions about the good of the whole. Development economist Albert Hirschman described democratic governance as offering *voice* in return for *loyalty*. The right for one's voice to be heard politically (through voting, testifying, petitioning, etc.) is interdependent with the obligations that go with membership in the polity. Political voice is conditional on acceptance of one's obligations to honor the decisions thus made. By contrast, markets rely on *exit*—show up if the benefit outweighs the cost in the moment and don't show up if it doesn't. And structureless groups sooner or later fall into dysfunction.[21] *Voice* describes a political process in which commitment to the community (loyalty) goes with the right to make one's voice heard in community decisions. *Exit* operates like a transactional marketplace one enters and exits at will, no loyalty, no continuity, no commitment required. While the former can be a source of political power, the latter is, at best, a way to allocate goods based on the preferences of those most able to invest their resources in expressing them: a system in which value does not determine price, but price determines value.[22]

Organizing is how an inclusive, interdependent, and united citizenry can transform the desire to achieve change into the power to create change. Organizing is how we built the social movements that Americans have used throughout our history to achieve change. Temperance advocates, abolitionists, populists, suffragettes, the labor movement, the civil rights movement, the women's movement, the racial justice movement, the gender justice movements—all have relied on hopeful organizing.

But not all social movements strengthen democracy. Fear-based organizing undermines democracy: white supremacist, anti-immigrant, anti-government, pro-gun, and anti-gender equity movements may very well use organizing tools. But by stoking fears of a powerful—and hated—"other," everything comes to depend on its destruction, and action depends less on mindfully deliberate choices than on the dictates of a supreme leader with whom all can identify. Social movements based on hope can expand democratic access, even as social movements based on fear can constrain democratic access. It took movements of the latter to put us in this mess, and it will take movements of the former to get beyond it. So why don't we build one?

Unless we invest newfound energy with the urgency to build a more robust, inclusive, and responsive democratic infrastructure, we will miss the progressive possibilities of this moment. Can we turn the strength of our reaction to the rawness of this moment into commitments to each other to develop the moral, strategic, and organizational capacity we need to reclaim the democratic promise?

I've been blessed to work on this challenge since I was introduced to organizing in 1964 in the US civil rights movement. Over the course of nearly six decades of work in distinct parts of the world, I've learned that people can indeed find the courage to lead, the solidarity to engage with each other, and the imagination to turn the resources they have into the power they need to get what they want. This is possible because these practices are rooted in competencies we all have: relationship building, storytelling, strategizing, acting, and structuring. And we can get to scale by enabling learners to become leaders who in turn teach learners to lead. We call this process "practicing democracy." This is what this book is intended to teach.

1

Practicing Democracy

This is a book about the who, why, and how of democratic practice. It is about learning how we can practice democracy: a pedagogy of democratic practice. Practicing democracy is a craft that can be learned, improved upon, adapted, and sustained. And as a craft it is rooted in decades of practice, research, and teaching students and practitioners in online and offline classrooms, workshops, campaigns, and collaboration with colleagues.[1] Although one writes a book so it can be read, the value of this book can only be realized if it is used to scaffold learning how to work with others.

A pedagogy of practice is at the heart of learning to practice democracy: the way we learn is what we learn, and what we learn is the way we learn.[2] It is the difference between lessons *about* building relationships and lessons *in* building relationships. When my colleagues and I teach organizing in classrooms, workshops, or campaigns, we structure the learning of each practice in a four-step sequence: explaining, modeling, practicing, and debriefing. Debriefing facilitates the articulation of specific lessons so they stick. It's like learning to ride a bike. Often the first thing that happens when you get on the bike is that you fall off. This is the real moment of truth when you either go home and go to bed, or you find the courage to get back on the bike, knowing that you'll keep falling for a while because it is the only way to learn to keep your balance. In my experience, that's how we learn any practice—including how to practice democracy.

This way of learning requires constructing a holding environment or brave space in which people can respectfully give and receive critical, as well as affirming, feedback, thereby learning with and from each other.[3] Participants set their own norms or ground rules to facilitate their learning. These norms usually include practice mutual respect, assume good intent, appreciate impact, and the like. A time norm is especially important: gatherings should begin on time and end on time, and exercises should be completed within the given time frame. This underscores the fact that a person's most precious resource is their time. We can choose to accept responsibility for honoring each person's commitment of their time to learning together. This allows creation of a space within which everyone—not only the first, the loudest, or the tallest—can learn. It also requires agreement on a norm correction: what a person must do should they show up late. For example, do they sing a song? Do a dance? The point is not public shaming but rather shared responsibility.

Creating a culture of learning is important not only for learning specific practices like storytelling, and not only for enabling real-time improvement of practice in the field, but also because it is required for democracy itself to work.[4] Democracy can only be sustained if it has created the means for sustained renewal. Each session concludes with takeaways (lessons), pluses (what worked well), and deltas (things that can be improved). This not only models the value of candid evaluation; even more importantly, it builds in continual learning as a sustained—and expected—practice.

We introduced this approach with the launching of the grassroots organization of the 2008 Barack Obama campaign, beginning with a Camp Obama in Burbank in July 2007.[5] Since then, organizers, trainers, and educators have introduced and adapted this approach for diverse domains throughout the United States, including campaigns for gender equity, immigrant rights, climate change, gun control, economic justice, and politics. Practitioners of health care, education, and union representation have also used this approach in the reform, revitalization, and renewal of their institutions. And globally, local practitioners have adapted it to their use in countries as diverse as Australia, China, Denmark, Japan, Jordan, Kenya, Nepal, Senegal, Serbia, and Sweden.

This is also always a work in progress, needing adaptation, innovation, and continual learning. At the conclusion of my first workshop in Jordan, civic leader, artist, and educator Samar Dudin described our approach as a road map, not a blueprint: how to find the foundations in one's own culture, community, or institution in service of which these practices may be of value. Similarly, this book is an invitation to join us on a learning journey, a never-complete way to enable people to learn, grow, and develop their power to shape their own destinies: the work of democracy.

* * *

Organizing grows out of rich, diverse, and ancient traditions. For some it is rooted in the faith traditions telling the story of a people's arduous journey from slavery to freedom: the exodus story. For others it grows out of a civic tradition, rooted in decisions the Greeks made that they did not need kings but could govern themselves. People have also found ways to challenge the abuses of power exercised over them, such as the nineteenth-century Irish tenant farmers who held back their produce from their British landlord until he made promised repairs. The landlord's name was Captain Boycott.

Leadership, Organizing, and Action

Leadership: Who, What, and When

Learning organizing begins with learning to practice leadership rooted in three questions posed by Rabbi Hillel, the first-century Jerusalem sage (Figure 1.1). When asked what to do with one's life, Hillel responded with three questions to ask yourself.

If I am not for myself, who will be for me? This is not a *selfish* question. It is a *self-regarding* question. If we are to live—or lead—with integrity, clarity about our own values, resources, interests, and aspirations matters. It can be very hard for us to be fully present to others if we are not fully present to ourselves.

RABBI HILLEL'S 3 QUESTIONS

If I am not for myself,
who will be for me?

When I am for myself alone,
what am I?

If not now, when?

Figure 1.1 Rabbi Hillel's 3 Questions. *Source*: Steve Downer of the Difference

When I am for myself alone, what am I? To be a "who"—a human being—and not a "what"—a thing—is to recognize that we exist in relationship with others. We are relational creatures. And our capacity to realize our own objectives—or even shape them—is inextricably wrapped up with the capacity of others to realize theirs. Alas, most of us have moments in which we are "only for ourselves"—treating others, and even ourselves, as instruments, rather than as ends in ourselves.

If not now, when? This is not advice to jump into moving traffic. Rather, it is a recognition of the fact that we can rarely learn to do well what we hope to do without beginning to do it. It is a caution against what Jane Addams called "the snare of preparation": we'll do just another year of strategic planning, we'll have the perfect plan, so the world will totally conform to our expectations—except that never happens.[6] The reality is that understanding flows from action, rather than preceding it. And because we cannot know the future, action always entails risk, demanding the courage to take those risks.

Leadership, then, is about the interaction of the self, the other, and the action.

* * *

Why did Hillel respond with questions rather than answers?

What really is the domain of leadership? When things are going well, do we seek out the leadership to thank them? Or do we only ask "who's in charge here" when we run into problems, challenges, and dilemmas? If the system is working, why do we need leadership?

The reality is that the adaptive capacity of leadership is only of real value in the face of uncertainty, not certainty; the unexpected, not the expected; the challenging, not the routine.

This is what makes leadership itself so challenging.

One way to think about this challenge is in a "hands, head, and heart" way. When confronted by the unexpected, we may ask ourselves, "Do I have the skills to deal with it?" This is a challenge to the hands. We may ask ourselves, "Can I use the resources I have to deal with this new challenge?" This is a strategic challenge, a challenge to the head. When we ask, "How do I find the hope, the courage, the resilience to take risks often required to deal with real change?" or "How do I inspire that hope and courage in others?" we are posing a challenge to the heart. Leadership, then, is a hands, head, and heart practice (Figure 1.2) that I've come to define as follows:

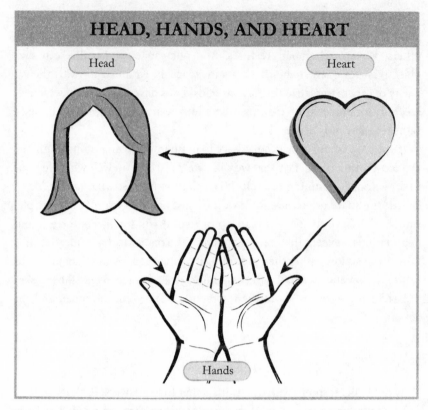

Figure 1.2 Head, Hands, and Heart. *Source*: Steve Downer of the Difference

> *Leadership is accepting responsibility (self) for enabling others (us) to achieve shared purpose under conditions of uncertainty (now).*

Leadership under conditions of uncertainty is therefore more about "learning" than about "knowing." No one can know the future, so leadership is less about having answers than it is about knowing how to find answers.

Enabling others to mindfully choose action requires entering into a relationship with them, not performing for them. During the massive 2020 protests of the murder of George Floyd—and of racially motivated police violence more broadly—a daily challenge arrived at the doorstep of every mayor. My colleague Sarah ElRaheb-Dagher and I were invited by the Bloomberg Harvard City Leadership Initiative to bring our practice of public narrative to a cohort of U.S. mayors grappling with this challenge. The greatest challenge these mayors faced in practicing leadership with protesters, the police, and the public was when they tried to fix the problem themselves. They put on a performance, only to find that performance alone couldn't solve the problem. Those who chose a wiser path asked for help, based on their relationships with all the parties, inviting them to become part of the solution rather than a source of the problem.

Finally, leadership is about *practice* rather than *position*. Most of us can easily think of examples of people who occupy positions of formal authority but turn out to be bad leaders. On the other hand, many of us meet people who are practicing leadership in the way I've defined it every day: at kitchen tables, in workplaces, neighborhoods, and elsewhere, without any formal authority, let alone a title, an office, or the CV to go with it.

Organizing: People, Power, and Change

Organizing is a particular form of leadership that asks three further questions:

First, **who are my people**? With whom am I entering into a leadership relationship (Figure 1.3)? Notice that the process does not start with identifying an issue. The people involved are both the source of the needed change and the resources that will be used to create that change. We listen, learn, and strategize with our people to identify the issues. Issue-based identities can fragment people; values-based identities can unite people.

Second, **what *change* do they want**? People's hurts and hopes are rooted in their lived experience. What hurts urgently needs healing: too small a check, a school that's failing my child, feeling unsafe in my home, abuse by a spouse, fear of the police? What would look different if we solved this problem: a bigger check (how much?), a better school (in what way?), a safe home (how?). And are these problems—as painful as they are—only symptoms of a deeper problem?

Third, **how can *people* work together to turn the *resources* they have into the *power* they need to win that change**? So, what is power? If you need

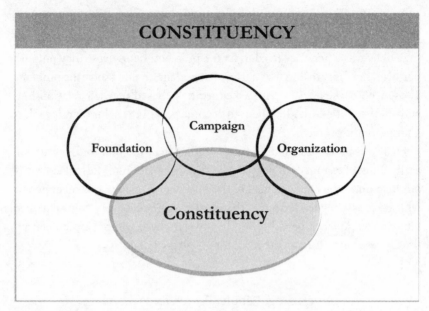

Figure 1.3 Constituency. *Source*: Steve Downer of the Difference

my resources more than I need your resources, who's got the power? I do. And if it is reversed, you do. That's how power works. It's not a thing you possess, but is an interdependent relationship based on the balance of needs and resources (Figure 1.4).[7]

An important distinction between creating power "with" others and exercising power "over" others is rooted in the work of management scholar Mary Parker Follett. If our interests converge and needs and resources are balanced, then we may find that through collaboration, we can create more "power with" each other than by going it alone, such as with a credit union, cooperative, or carpool. But if our interests diverge and I need your resources to meet my needs more than you, at present, need access to mine, I have to figure out how to challenge your "power over" me by learning what needs you have that depend on resources I have (Figure 1.5). In a word, how can I make it more costly for you to resist the change than accept it? A well-known Mexican saying explains why politicians only show up in the barrio before an election: "Al nopal no se

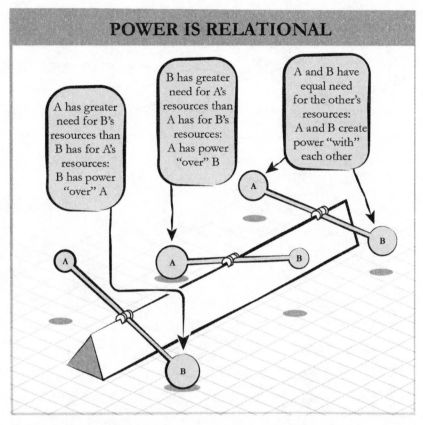

Figure 1.4 Power Is Relational. *Source*: Steve Downer of the Difference

viene a ver, solo cuando tiene tuna" (No one comes to visit the prickly pear except when it's bearing fruit).

Power also has three faces. The first face is obvious, as when someone gets arrested—we see who won and who lost. But who authorized the arrest, set the rules, enforces them? That's the second face: who decides. Then we may ask, why has nothing been done about this problem for years, or why do many of us just take for granted that this is the way things are? To figure that out, you must ask who is benefiting and who is losing: the third face. This is when the deep structural contours of power emerge. The strategic organizing challenge is how to engage with the urgent first face—the pain points—but in a way that builds our capacity to take on the third face.

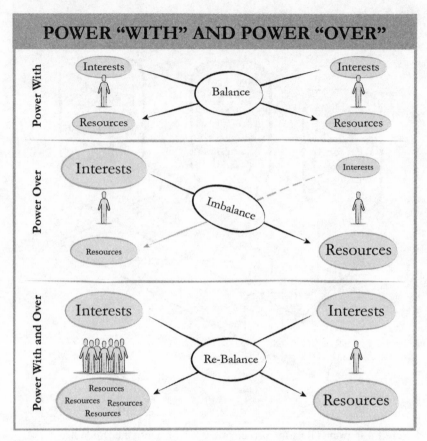

Figure 1.5 Power "With" and Power "Over." *Source*: Steve Downer of the Difference

The moral, political, and practical centrality of power in the work of organizing is most compellingly articulated by Pope Francis, in his most recent encyclical, *Fratelli tutti* (All brothers), where he writes,

If one person lacks what is necessary to live with dignity, it is because another person is detaining it. . . .

We are called to love everyone without exception; at the same time, loving an oppressor does not mean allowing him to keep oppressing us, or letting him think that what he does is acceptable. On the contrary, true love for an oppressor means seeking ways to make him cease his oppression; it means stripping him of a power that he does not know how to use, and that diminishes his own humanity and that of others.... Those who suffer injustice have to defend strenuously their own rights and those of their family, precisely because they must preserve the dignity they have received as a loving gift from God.[8]

Organizing is not about providing services to grateful clients. Nor is it about marketing products to paying customers. Organizing is not about advocacy on behalf of powerless beneficiaries. It is about enabling a community to become a *constituency*, from the Latin *con* (together) and *stare* (to stand)—a community that chooses to come together, stand together, learn together, decide together, act together, and in the end win together. It's also what democracy itself is all about.

The impact of an organizing campaign can be evaluated by asking another three questions:

Did we accomplish the goal we set out to accomplish? Did we win the election, pass the law, change the practice, improve the contract?

Did we grow stronger as a constituency than we were when we began? Did we empower our community, strengthen our organization, grow stronger? Did we learn how to use our resources to shift power held by others into our own hands? If we win a campaign but never want to see anyone involved ever again, our win likely won't stick. Who will get the law enforced, hold the elected accountable, grow stronger for the next round?

The strength of the constituency matters because most of the problems organizers are called on to solve are matters of structural power, not technical inefficiencies. My streets aren't cleaned because of poor sanitation technology. I live in a food desert because of problematic logistics. I can't find affordable housing because there's too much demand. No. These problems persist because something that is a big problem for many is no problem at all for the more powerful few.

Did we recruit, train, and develop the leadership to take our work forward? Did individual participants in the campaign grow, learn, and develop, especially in their leadership? The scale to which an organized movement can grow depends in large measure on the scale of the committed, skilled, and imaginative leadership it can develop. This is especially so if the movement aspires to make democracy work in neighborhoods, workplaces, schools, cities, states, and the nation.

Action: Hands, Head, and Heart

At the core of organizing are five practices rooted in our daily lives. Each practice is composed of three elements: values (heart), head (concepts), and skills (hands).

The **heart** is a way to describe the domain of emotion, *values* that motivate us and are implicit, if not explicit, in any practice. It is where we go to learn *why* we do what we do. It grounds the *storytelling* that can enable us to access, articulate, and share the motivational resources rooted in our values. It is less about what *is* in the world than about what *is good* in the world.

We use our **heads** to acquire a *conceptual* understanding of *how* to do what we do. Cognitively, it can ground *strategizing* in sustained, systematic, and critical reflection on what we are doing. We can thus improve upon our skills, adapt them to new contexts, and innovate new forms of skill. Conceptual understanding helps us avoid getting stuck in the rote, uncritical, and stagnant actions that only reproduce beliefs that shape the lens through which we discern what *is* in the world.

Our **hands** learn the *skills we need to do what we need to do as action:* it *is behavioral.* By making explicit how we build relationships, we can bring *craft,* intentionality, and purpose to achieve excellence in our work. We may have to unlearn some of the good-enough ways we built relationships in the past. Action is the place where what we do with our bodies enables learning, communication, and sense-making. I get a radically different and certainly richer understanding of what a strike is by walking on a picket line rather than by reading about it. My understanding of a movement differs if I use my body to join a highly disciplined military march, or if I use it to join an ever-evolving creative protest march. Each of these activities has its own rules, to be sure, but of a very different sort.

Five Practices of Democracy

Organizing is a learnable craft. Each chapter of this book offers a deep exploration of one of what I have identified as the five key practices of organizing (Figure 1.6): building relationships, telling stories, strategizing, acting, and structuring.

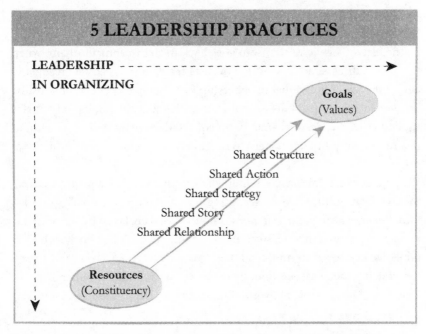

5 LEADERSHIP PRACTICES

LEADERSHIP
IN ORGANIZING

Goals
(Values)

Shared Structure
Shared Action
Shared Strategy
Shared Story
Shared Relationship

Resources
(Constituency)

Figure 1.6 5 Leadership Practices. *Source*: Steve Downer of the Difference

Relationship Building

Relationships grow out of the realization of mutual benefit, the creation of shared value, and the commitment to a shared future. They are the threads with which we weave our communities. We all build relationships, some good, some bad, some sustained, some not. Some are with family, some are with friends, some with colleagues, some with collaborators. Different kinds of communities are based on kinship, friendship, neighborhood, schooling, professional identity, the presence, or absence of children, and so on.

Democracy is a political community based on the civic relationships we build with each other. Civic relationships are based on a commitment to the shared purpose, values, norms, and practices of that community and respect for the individuals who constitute that community. Civic relationships, in other words, are a different kind of relationship than those based on kinship, status, wealth, or coercion.

Specifically, it is through civic association with one another that we can learn to turn narrow self-interests into common interests, forge the emotional bonds that enable our solidarity, and develop the skills we need not only to work together but also to govern ourselves. Tocqueville called these forms of association "great free schools of democracy." The civic relationships we build with one another, as human beings rather than as data points, are the fabric from which democracy is woven.

The idea of a civic relationship goes back to sixth-century Athens, when the Greeks discovered they could not sustain a *polis* (city) based on equality before the law if individual membership in the polis depended on kinship. They replaced unequal kinship affiliation with equal civic affiliation.[9] This is the source of the idea that I can be an equal citizen of a city or state without regard to family and, ultimately, to religious belief, gender, race, or national origin.

In our country, this has been more of an aspiration than a reality. Even so, the civic relationships have been eroding as we sort ourselves—or are sorted—into ever-narrowing race-, class-, and status-based enclaves. By learning and re-learning how to initiate, sustain, and renew civic relationships with each other, we can begin to transcend these manufactured enclaves by realizing the real interdependence underlying them, what Martin Luther King Jr. called our "inescapable network of mutuality, tied into a single garment of destiny."

Storytelling

Storytelling is how we can communicate why I care, why we care, and why we must choose to act now: a story of self, a story of us, and a story of now. It is how we can speak the language of the heart. Storytelling can create the experience of values and can equip us with the motivational resources to respond to disruptions hopefully, rather than react to them fearfully. Individuals, community organizations, and nations all respond to stories.

In recent years, critics of democracy seem to be telling a more powerful story than democracy's defenders. Why? Stories can evoke the experience of shared values. So, it is easier to tell a shared story rooted in the value of homogeneity: for example, racial homogeneity, gender homogeneity, or religious homogeneity. Any form of difference can be interpreted as a threat to the fundamental value. It can also be comforting to tell a story of real or imagined continuity from the past to the present: the ways of our fathers (usually), the comfortable good old days, and so on.

But democracy requires a commitment to equality, not to homogeneity. Democracy demands that we value each person equally, whatever their race, religion, gender, or class. This makes democracy about pluralism.

If the shared value is democracy, then difference is a positive value, not a threat. Democracy is about change, the future, and is enriched by diverse constituencies, generations, and classes. Democracy is also about broad-enough access to enough power to achieve change. Democracy's defenders must do the work of articulating the kinds of shared values that enable us to interpret diversity as an asset, rather than a liability.

Strategizing

Strategy is how we turn what we have (resources) into what we need (power) to get what we want (change). It too is something we know how to do. Any time you overslept, missed a bus, or had to take a sick child to the doctor, you strategized around the disruption. It is a verb, not a noun, something you do, rather than something you have. And just as we tell stories to access the emotional resources to respond to disruption, we strategize to access the cognitive resources to figure out how to respond to the disruption. We strategize by adapting to the obstacles that impede our progress to a valued goal, not by abandoning the goal but by reimagining how we can still get there.

Strategizing in the current context can be very challenging, given the disappearance of deliberative venues; the proliferation of narrow, issue-based mobilization; competition for funding; and an emphasis in many movements on tactical rather than strategic focus (e.g., how many calls did you make, rather than what difference did those calls make?). When we rely on a strategy that depends on access to outside money for organizing rather than on the resources of an inside constituency, we may get a win but fail to empower our people.

Unfortunately, the ease with which action can be digitally mobilized in re-action to motivating events often yields tactics devoid of strategy.[10] We protest because we have to do something. This claim, while heartfelt, is more expressive than strategic. In moments like the massive reaction to the murder of George Floyd, for example, less-visible organizational infrastructure, like that of Black Lives Matter (BLM), may surface as sources of strategic leadership, or with enough time, such leadership may emerge from the protests themselves. Or it may not.

When it comes to organizing, the strategic challenge is how to counter the far greater resources of the status quo with greater resourcefulness—much as David, the young shepherd, defeated the powerful Goliath, master of sword, shield, and helmet, with know-how learned protecting his flock from wolves and bears, a simple stone, a sling, some creativity, and a lot of courage. Good strategy is not a matter of genius, but it is a matter of who does the strategizing, with whom, what they bring to it, how committed they are to sustain it, and the process through which they create it.

Acting

The first time someone tells us they will show up and doesn't, we learn the difference between intention and action. In organizing, the purpose of action is to produce *observable change in the world by mobilizing individual resources and deploying them collectively*. An action might be a petition, a rally, a march, a public meeting, a picket line, a registered voter, a voter who voted, or something else. Close, specific, and sustained observation of the outcomes of one's actions, candid critical reflection on those outcomes, and identifying lessons for future action from that reflection, can, if systematic, turn one's own actions into a source of continued learning, growth, and development. We might think of it as "evidence-based organizing."

Whose resources are mobilized and by whom shapes who can deploy them and how—and vice versa. The most basic resources are money and time. Action today has come to rely far more on money than on time. These resources, in turn, are increasingly drawn from outside one's constituency than from within it.

This is a problem, as political scientist Sidney Verba argues, because time is far more widely distributed than money.[11] Relying on time, rather than money, strengthens democracy. Economist Albert Hirschman makes a similar distinction between moral resources that grow with use (commitment, skill, relationships) and economic resources (money, equipment, raw materials) that deplete with use.[12]

Similarly, resources contributed from within one's constituency—whether time or money—empower the constituency, whereas resources drawn from outside one's constituency—whether time or money—empower others. Perhaps the most serious challenges to democracy we face are the monetization of political mobilization and the transformation of much of civil society, including organizing, into the clients of philanthropic patronage.

Mobilizing and deploying people effectively requires motivation and commitment. We take our commitments seriously, which is why we avoid making them. Our motivation to commit is based more on the value we believe we can contribute than on the cost of the contribution. We invest more effort, initiative, and engagement in meaningful action for which we are responsible, and which is measurable as to the progress we are making than that for which we are not responsible.

Finally, action must be evaluated. When I was introduced to organizing I was told, "If you can't count it, it didn't happen." When it comes to changing facts on the ground, they happen or they don't happen. And that's what we're trying to do: create a different set of facts on the ground. And if we can't see what we're doing, how can you assess the effect, learn from the variation, and offer recognition or support to those who are doing it?

Structuring

Whenever two people share a commitment to meet at this place, on this date, and at this time, they are creating structure. They are building a possible future. That's what structure means: it comes from the Latin *struere*, to build. And building, because it is about the future, is an expression of hope. We create structure when we share commitment to how we work together, learn together, decide together, and act together. By structuring, we can make the future less uncertain, use our time more purposefully, and coordinate our work together more reliably. Structure is how we can create the space for creativity, learning, and deliberation. The opposite of structure is not space but chaos. This is why we invest our structures with authority, transparency, and accountability. We need rules, procedures, and processes through which we can govern ourselves.

Democratic structuring requires creating accessible ways for people to make their voices heard, consistent spaces in which deliberation and decision-making can take place, and transparent processes through which the work can get done. It is also true, however, that even democratic structure can constrain more than enable when we fail to adapt to change. Because the world is always changing, it can be more useful to think of structure as a verb than a noun.

Perhaps the most critical element of structure is time: our most unrenewable resource. Recognizing this, paleontologist Stephen Jay Gould noted two forms of time: time as a cycle, the rhythm of continuity, and time as an arrow, the rhythm of change.[13] Similarly, the Greeks distinguished between *chronos*, sequentially passing time, and *kairos,* the precise moment one must act. Campaigns embody time as an arrow: episodic, focused, and intense. Organizations embody time as a cycle: steady, deliberative, and substantial. Organizing involves both (Figure 1.7).

Campaigns are structured to achieve change by focusing attention, energy, and resources on the accomplishment of particular goals: for example, winning an election. They prioritize including as many people in the action as possible, but they are careful to bound decision-making and management to the qualified, however defined. They encourage diversity to facilitate creativity, innovation, and adaptation, but they require real unity in storytelling, campaign strategy, and effective action.

Organizations are structured to ensure continuity to grow in power, to develop expertise, and to secure sustained access to resources. They prioritize clear boundaries as to who is included as participants, managers, and decision-makers, but they also distribute responsibility, develop new leadership, and ensure accountability. And, like campaigns, they encourage diversity to facilitate creativity, innovation, and adaptation but require unity—or harmony—in storytelling, strategic focus, and effective action.

Organizing requires structuring continuity and change. Winning a single campaign—or even a series of campaigns—is a good thing. But rarely can one win shift the balance of power: wins are too easily reversed, promises not kept, and control reverts to the hands that held it before. Deep change requires sustained power to win it, keep it, and grow it. Individual campaign wins cannot be sustained in the absence of a vision of the organization we need to sustain those claims.

At the same time, maintaining power can too easily become a goal unto itself, supplanting the purpose for which the power was created in the first place. What was created to realize valued ends can become an end in itself. In the UFW, we were building a union, so each campaign, won or lost, could contribute the power built to that objective. Today, however, in many domains, after multiple campaign wins, power remains diffuse. The individuals who participated in the campaign may have changed, but that change hasn't been translated into sustained organization, much less structural change in politics, economics, or society.

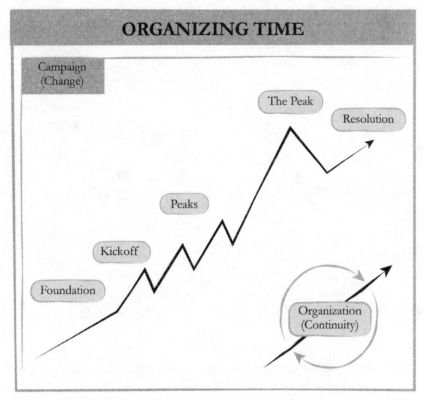

Figure 1.7 Organizing Time. *Source*: Steve Downer of the Difference

Democracy requires structuring continuity and change. Effective democracy requires the means to guarantee that each citizen's voice counts equally, the deliberative processes to transform individual interests into common interests, and executive processes through which individual resources can be transformed into collective power. At the same time, democracy requires the means to hold power accountable; ways in which new people, ideas, and needs can effectively assert themselves. Democracy requires ways of building on the past without becoming imprisoned by it.

Developmental Leadership

In the seventh chapter, I focus on developing the capacity needed to combine these five key practices of purposive organizing: leadership. Recall that our

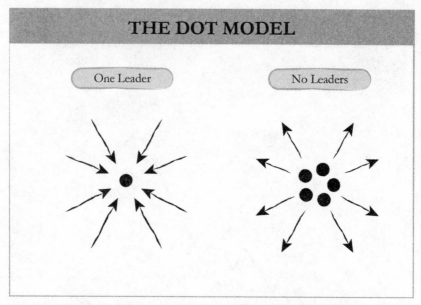

Figure 1.8 The Dot Model. *Source*: Steve Downer of the Difference

definition of leadership requires accepting responsibility for enabling others to achieve shared purpose in the face of uncertainty. The practice of democracy requires leadership that can integrate our five practices in pursuit of a shared purpose or common goal. Recall, too, that we distinguish leadership from authority in that leadership enables rather than commands.[14]

The reality is that no one person can really do all this, yet many think they can. Some people react by abandoning the idea of authoritative leadership entirely for a structure in which everyone leads. Neither structure lends itself to effective organizing (Figure 1.8).

Our first move, then, should be to focus on building "real" leadership teams, as opposed to single leaders. This too requires learning the craft of how to make it work. Our second move is to focus on how a leadership team can achieve scale by developing the leadership of others, an approach some people call a snowflake model of leadership: each team member reaches out to form their own team, and each member of that team reaches out to develop their own, and so forth (Figure 1.9).[15] We also tackle how we can identify leadership or potential leadership, how we can recruit them to lead, and how we can continue to support their development.

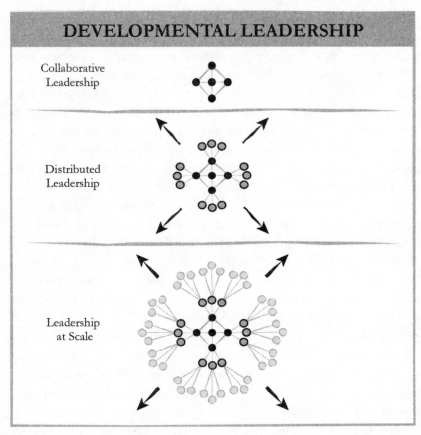

Figure 1.9 Developmental Leadership. *Source*: Steve Downer of the Difference

"The Promise of Democratic Practice"

The central argument of this book is simple: Redeeming the democratic promise from the clutches of oligarchic rule requires leadership, organizing, and action. It requires restoring people to the center of political processes, turning people's resources into the power they need to achieve real change in their day-to-day lives. This is a book about people, power, and change.

As stated above, leadership is the act of accepting responsibility (*self*) for enabling others to achieve shared purpose (*us*) under conditions of uncertainty (*now*). Organizers develop leadership, build community with that leadership, and create power from the resources of that community.

We can organize to do more than fix an immediate problem. We can enable people with the problem to build the power they need to challenge structures responsible for their problem in the first place. This requires ongoing leadership development, motivation, and learning. We do not have to be content with fixing bugs in the system. If we organize, we can change the features of the system itself.

The organizing craft is at the heart of successful community organizations, civic associations, advocacy groups, trade unions, social movements, and democracy itself. Social movements have driven transformational politics in America via their influence on the parties, policy, and political culture more generally.[16] And organizing can play a role in electoral politics, despite the political marketing business, as demonstrated by the 2008 Obama campaign or the more recent electoral insurgencies at local, state, and national levels.

Organizing brings us out of our narrow self-interests into broader understandings of the common good. It can create experiences of empathy that facilitate solidarity and enable us to learn basic skills of democratic self-government, just as Tocqueville said it would.

We need a better understanding of how the democratic promise is being betrayed, but perhaps even more important is what we decide to do about it. We must confront not only the immediate crisis of electoral politics, but also the lack of capacity for collective action on which our entire civic culture depends. Our challenge is to overcome the asymmetrical resources, the fractured electorate, the unequal voices, and the sclerotic political institutions that have enabled a recalcitrant minority to stifle the voices of our newly emergent majority—allowing the past to trump the future.

This is not a book of answers. Rather, it is an invitation to accept responsibility for joining with one another to forge answers. We must learn from the past as well as the present; from our failures as well as our successes; and we must learn to sustaining the effort in ongoing, resilient, and audaciously adaptive ways.

* * *

When Bob Moses called us into that auditorium in 1964, he was asking us to decide who we were going to be in the world. This book asks a similar question of its readership. This is a book about agency: my own, that of others with whom I have worked, and of those whom I have yet to meet but who find themselves asking questions of what they are called to do, what their community is called to do, and what they are must do now. It is another way of asking Hillel's three questions:

If I am not for myself, who will be for me?

If I am for myself alone, what am I?

If not now, when?

2

Relationships

Have you ever been in a relationship? Who decided to create the relationship? What did you bring to it? What did you take from it? What value did your relationship create?

Because most of us have been in relationships, we tend to take them for granted, like fish within the water in which it swims. But we are wise to pay attention. Relationships are the threads with which we weave our families, communities, and associations. Relationships, unlike transactions, require making commitments to a shared future. Relationships rooted in commitment to a common purpose, what I call "civic relationships," are also threads with which we weave organizations, movements, and democracy itself. Yet for the last fifty years, we've been engaging more in transactions than in relationships, especially civic relationships.[1] So if we are to renew our democracy, the foundation will be renewing our relationships with each other. In this chapter we begin learning how we can—and in more inclusive, equal, and authentic ways.

My Relational Challenge

Relationship building did not come naturally to me. I grew up in a relationally challenged home. My father, who struggled with the relational work his rabbinical calling required of him and was later diagnosed with paranoid schizophrenia, was emotionally unavailable to both my mother and me. Because of his difficulty keeping a post, I changed schools in the first, third, and fifth grades, each in a different location, with new classmates and teachers. My father could not teach me how to deal with bullies—or even how to throw a baseball without ridicule—so peer relationships were sources of anxiety for me. And I was a rabbi's son in communities in which it seemed like Friday night was about football, not prayer, for everyone except me.

It was in the civil rights movement that I found my way to relationship building—civic relationship building. Even before I got to Mississippi, it was clear that organizing, and my own safety, depended on others: SNCC organizers, my peers, local leadership, and members of the Black community in general. It was mind-bending to begin seeing white as threatening and Black as safe. But I was blessed with Hollis Watkins as a mentor. Hollis was twenty-two in chronological years, just two years older than I. But in organizer years he was far older than I could know.

Hollis grew up in Mississippi and in 1961, at nineteen, inspired by the Freedom Rides, he joined Bob Moses as an organizer in SNCC's first foray into Mississippi. In the three years since, he had been jailed multiple times, served time in the infamous penitentiary at Parchman, and comforted the families of persons murdered in the struggle. But he had also seen young people show the courage not only to challenge their elders but also to challenge Jim Crow itself and had earned a key leadership role in the Summer Project—even though he thought white students could be more trouble than they were worth.

All this made Hollis not harder, but wiser. He had also developed a gift for sharing his wisdom. On the second day of riding with him, I worked up the courage to ask how I, a Jewish white guy from Harvard, could connect with the people on whom I would depend, at times for my life. He stopped the car and said one word: "Respect." "Sure," I said a bit too quickly. "I have respect for everyone." "No," he said. "Respect is what you do, not what you have. First, listen, and hear; second, ask, and learn; third, show respect, and you will get it; and fourth, don't try to be anyone different from who you are. Be yourself." This turned out to be fundamental to every successful relationship I would build in my work, not only in Mississippi but also in my years with the farmworkers and, I'd like to think, with the students with whom I work with today.

I learned to build civic relationships in SNCC. It was our source of power. Critical of the flashy demonstrations favored by Dr. King, SNCC advocated long-term work in relationship with local people. One such example was organizing the Mississippi Freedom Democratic Party, locally rooted but coordinated at the district and state levels. Doing so required talking with people—lots of them—and under conditions far riskier for them than for me. Listening, asking questions, and learning really mattered. When I was assigned to Amite County, I was given a home by E. W. Steptoe and his family on his forty-acre farm about one mile from the Louisiana border. Mr. Steptoe was one of a band of courageous local leaders, including Medgar Evers, Amzie More, and others, who organized chapters of the NAACP in the

1950s and had lived to tell the tale—except for Evers, assassinated in 1963. Accompanying Mr. Steptoe to talk with people was very different from going on my own. New relationships were formed, connections made, and leaders identified. At times, relationships were built with the help of the pastors, deacons, or missionary society leaders in the churches. Other times, it was through local store or bar owners, like "Mama" Ayleen Quinn, who ran the Saturday-night juke joint in McComb and who seemed to know everyone. Sometimes it meant going door-to-door. But regardless of where or how or when it happened, relationship building was central to our organizing.

What Is a Relationship?

We all build relationships, and by building relationships we construct a shared future. When asked what it takes to build relationships, many point to trust, commonality, a shared purpose, and so forth. These factors are more likely to result from a relationship rather than motivate the formation of one. Relationships are motivated by differences, differences that can be exchanged (Figure 2.1): I have a resource you may need, and you have a resource I may need. This may sound cold unless we have a broader understanding of what can be a resource: understanding, empathy, courage, companionship, and collaboration. Needs may vary as well: a tennis partner, help with studies, someone to talk to, a chance at a job. If there's no exchange, there's no relationship—but exchange alone doesn't make a relationship.

Let's say you have had a great conversation with someone over coffee, but it's time to go. Eager to continue the conversation, you pull out your calendar. "Why don't we continue this next week?" "Err . . . I can't," you hear. "I have a project deadline on which I need to focus." "Oh," you say, "then how about the following week?" "Umm. I have some guests coming from out of town." "Then how about next week?" "Why don't I send you an email . . . ?"

What just happened? What was missing? A mutual decision to commit an hour of your time—your most valuable resource—to giving the relationship a chance: a chance to build a future, to acquire a past, to grow, to change, to become a resource itself.

Why would you risk committing your resources to an uncertain future? This is where values may come in, perhaps even not explicitly, because we may experience the emotional content of our values even when not artic- ulated This experience of shared values may motivate a person to take the

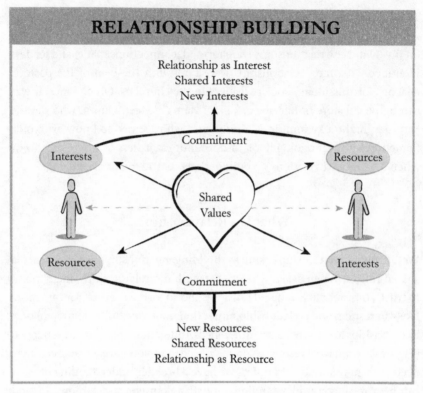

Figure 2.1 Relationship Building. *Source*: Steve Downer of the Difference

risk. If so, beginning a relationship takes courage, a leap of hope that trust may emerge later. Relationships, then, are about commonality and difference: commonality makes them possible; differences make them beneficial.

Relationships constitute the fabric of social life. It is through relationships that we construct ourselves, our communities, and our organizations.

Why Do Relationships Matter?

We all build relationships because humans are relational creatures. As long ago as the fifth century BCE, Aristotle spelled this out on one side of the world while Confucius spelled it out on the other. Although every culture abounds in wisdom about how to handle relationships, often distinguishing the instrumental from the authentic, the nature of relationships only came into question in the West around the time of the Protestant Reformation, with a shift in how the individual was viewed within a society.[2] An individual's opportunity to choose relationships with intentionality rather than limit themselves to the relationships into which they were born—along with their familial, caste, tribal, racial, religious, and gender constraints; inequalities; and other cruelties—was surely a good thing, but it was also disorienting. This led to struggles over the relationship of individual and collective, especially in the bloody religious wars of the sixteenth and seventeenth centuries. Views of the individual shifted again as industrialization transformed a person's labor, and thus the person, into a commodity.[3] In the nineteenth and twentieth centuries, both secular and religious movements continued to struggle with the right relationship of individual and community; some enhanced one's individual agency with collective agency in the form of democratic movements while others offered escape from the burdens of individual agency in collective submission to the will of a great leader, through authoritarian movements.[4]

Tocqueville, writing in the early nineteenth century in the context of his experience of revolution in his home country, linked equality with a radical individualism associated with the erosion of traditional authority. A focus on narrow self-interest could undermine governance on behalf of "self-interest properly understood," that is, "common interest." But he found promise in the associations he called America's "great free schools of democracy," writing,

> Americans of all ages, all conditions, and all dispositions, constantly form associations. . . . Wherever, at the head of some new undertaking, you see the government in France, or a man of rank in England, in the United States you will be sure to find an association.[5]

Civic associations remained a major element of American social life until the 1970s and 1980s when, as political sociologist Theda Skocpol shows, membership in associations gave way to the management of organizations better at control than at representation.[6] Older associations segregated by race, class, and gender went appropriately into the past. But because of political, economic, and technological choices, we have faced a whole new level of erosion in our relational fabric. Many imagine each person to be an isolated individual whose interests are best served through marketlike processes in which the successful survive and the unsuccessful disappear, all in the name of a purported well-being of all. Indeed, in much social science, the rationality of relational affiliation itself was problematized as the collective action problem.[7]

We have come to interact with one another more in instrumental one-off transactions rather than in sustainable relational commitments. This radical recasting of each person as a unit of human capital, utility, or preference not only consigns civic relationships to the past; it also robs us of our humanity. Whereas we used to take relational communities for granted, we now take incentive-driven, utility-maximizing individuals for granted.[8]

The reality that modern societies face is the fact that political scientist Robert Putnam brought to the nation's attention in the 1990s: a radical erosion of the relational capacity he describes as "social capital." He identified the phenomenon and linked it to various deleterious outcomes but made little progress on what was driving it.[9] One thing, however, is clear: a marketlike ideology of radical individualism, instrumental exchange, and competition does not help bring people together. This is especially true when this ideology's constituent parts can be amplified by using technology that makes it easier to share information and aggregate individual resources than to share commitment to one another to create collective capacity in pursuit of shared purpose. As one of my students put it, "I feel overconnected but undercommitted."

The fact that we begin with an argument that relationships matter reveals the depth of the challenge we face. Relationships do matter. Not only intimate relationships but also the far more fragile public, civic relationships on which the efficacy of democracy depends.

Why Do Civic Relationships Matter?

Civic relationships are the threads with which robust democracy is woven. Some relationships are private. We form them with our families, partners, and close friends, and they offer intimacy, love, and support. Other relationships are public, or civic. We form them with fellow citizens, colleagues, and collaborators, and they offer respect, commitment to shared purpose, and public trust. Organizing—and politics more generally—is about building civic relationships.[10]

As Tocqueville argued, civic relationships, or associations, are so important because they facilitate learning, solidarity, and self-governance.[11] They can be built with people not like us as well as with people like us, because they are based on commitment to a common purpose, not on kinship, friendship, or childhood. This enables a broader understanding of common interests, greater creativity, and genuine inclusiveness.

Building civic relationships is intentional. Among those who first recognized their value was the Athenian political reformer Cleisthenes (d. 508 BCE). Looking for ways to establish each person's equality before the law, he realized that if one's participation in the *polis* depended on one's standing within one of the four traditional, and hierarchically governed, kinship-based tribes, this wasn't going to happen. So he persuaded the Athenians to replace these four kinship-based tribes with ten geographically based and democratically governed civic tribes. In other words, he replaced kinship with citizenship as a new form of political identity.[12]

Civic relationships, like citizenship, are based on commitment to shared purpose or values as the moral foundation of a political community. The ties we inherit, those based on to whom we are born, where, and under what circumstances, matter for our life chances. But we can exercise agency with respect to the conditions under which we share the right to participate in public life.

The distinction between private and public—or civic—relationships is important. We enjoy private relationships with friends, acquaintances, and others. But when we organize to pursue common goals, we need to make our associational roles explicit. When friends become officers of an organization to which we belong, they may experience tension due to the formalization—publicness—of what had been a private, informal relationship. Teachers must negotiate a way to be in relationship with their students, true both to their own way of interacting with others and to the formal public role for which they are responsible; similar issues arise for lawyers, doctors, social workers, ministers, and organizers. We can distinguish the social interactions appropriate in private relationships from interactions appropriate in public relationships. Failure to distinguish between the two can come at great personal cost to us and to those with whom we work.

In *Roots for Radicals*, community organizer Ed Chambers makes the useful distinction between being liked in our private lives and being respected in our public lives:

> By acting publicly to be liked, people invariably violate their group or organization's self-interest, usually by failing to hold public power brokers accountable at critical moments. . . . What people need in public life is to

be respected, which is like, but different from, being liked. That is why it is crucial to learn to act for respect in public, to be disinterested in being liked there, to look for liking in the private realm. . . . Prophets, visionaries, and ordinary people who value justice and democracy can't be too concerned about being liked in the public realm, but they must insist on being respected there.[13]

Civic relationships are created by choices we make to link our own fate to that of another. Unlike momentary transactions, they sustain our engagement, succor us with support, and challenge us with growth. Some of our relationships—like our families—seem to be the result of chance. Other relationships—like our civic communities—are the result of choice. They only exist because the parties have chosen to give them life. In this way, we enable these relationships to shape our own lives, even as they shape the pathways along which we will live them.

Since we build civic relationships with intentionality, with whom do we build them? We can usefully distinguish between people like us and people not like us. Sociologist Mark Granovetter calls these strong ties and weak ties. Strong ties are homogeneous ties with people who are like us, and weak ties are heterogeneous, those with people unlike us.[14] It is easier to build relationships with people like us, but civic association may require that we build relationships with people not like us but with whom we can find common purpose. Relationships with people like us can be very supportive but can also close in on themselves, isolating us in echo chambers and limiting our creativity. Relationships with people not like us may require more work but can open us to diverse sources of information, a rich variety of perspectives, and greater creativity.

Granovetter's insight is that strong ties may inhibit our capacity to organize. This is because they quickly create a closed-in, limited circle of people and resources. A lot of weak ties, in contrast, may enhance our organizing capacity. This is because they create broader networks of resources by opening the circle outward—an important way people find jobs. As an example, he shows how the fragmentation of residents of Boston's West End into intense ethnically, religiously, familial, or culturally bounded "strong ties" inhibited their ability to combine and mobilize resources to resist urban renewal. On the other hand, diverse communities with weak ties found it easier to collaborate with each other and secure outside sources of support. For some purposes, especially those we share with people like us, strong ties may be very important. But for purposes that are broader and more inclusive, weak ties are the keys to success. Granovetter isn't arguing that strong ties are bad and weak ties are good—just that they are very different and contribute to common efforts in different ways.

Each of us has acquired values that inform the choices we make about specific interests. A resource is anything I can use to advance my interests. I may value good health, which gives me an interest in regular exercise, but I have a hard time sticking to it. You may be good at sticking to it but find the exercise boring. Despite other differences, we may both value good health enough to risk committing our time to building a public relationship with each other.

Commitment can turn a transactional exchange into a transformational relationship by giving it a future into which we can grow and a past from which we can learn. Relationships are beginnings, not endings. Unlike a contract that results from negotiations to protect our interests, relationships are open-ended, creating opportunity for our interests to grow, change, and develop. Our interactions may reveal interests of which we had not been aware: "Hmm . . . Before you asked me those questions, I didn't realize that I really wanted to be a doctor, but now . . ." We may discover common interests of which we were unaware: "After we started bowling together, we learned that we both like opera." Just as relationships can source new interests, they can also generate new resources: "Oh . . . you say I'm a good listener? I didn't know that." We may discover exchanges well beyond the original exchange: "I'll help you with your problem sets if you help me with my literature essay." And we may discover common resources: "Let's pool our funds to hire a tutor to work with both of us."

To the extent relationships become a shared resource, we develop a shared interest in doing the work to sustain them. This is why relational communities are capable of collaborative action of all kinds. Relationships among members are the foundation of any civic association. This can distinguish civic or political associations from civic or political firms that provide services to clients or market products to customers.

Relationship-Building Practice

Despite the importance of relational work, I didn't—nor did other SNCC volunteers—have any formal training in how to build relationships based on any theory of how to build them and why they worked or didn't. We followed, watched, listened, and learned. It was only when I got to the farmworkers that I began to learn that organizing was not only a matter of earnest, patient, and persistent work with the local people but was also a discipline, a craft, a practice to be learned, trained in, and adapted.

Organizers begin with a search for leaders or potential leaders. An organizing project grows via the identification, recruitment, and development of leaders who, in turn, can develop more. This search begins with relational work. Where might you find potential leaders? If you begin with recognized community leaders, it can be hard to know who is actually leading and who just holds a title. You might also begin by talking with other members of the community whom you meet at public events, at group meetings, or through door-to-door canvassing. You may start by canvassing, especially in an electoral setting, and following up on leads from a meeting or a rally. The point is that you are looking for persons with whom to get started, especially those who show signs of leadership.

One-on-Ones

The basic organizing practice is the one-on-one meeting, an intentional conversation in which we share stories, learn of each other's values, explore each other's interests and resources, and decide whether to commit to working together—or at least to meeting a second time. Their primary purpose is to decide whether to invest in building a relationship with this person within which deeper engagement and more possibilities may develop. A one-on-one meeting is successful if it ends either with a commitment to a next step—perhaps only another one-on-one meeting—or a decision that it would not be wise to invest further. This tactic can be very useful for building robust relationships among people who might not otherwise have formed them and has come into wide use well beyond the field of organizing. It is the most widely practiced skill associated with community organizing.

I only understood the real power of the one-on-one in 1984, after I had left the United Farm Workers (UFW), when at an Industrial Areas Foundation training in San Antonio, I observed veteran organizer Ernesto Cortes model one. I thought the purpose of a one-on-one (or personal visit) was to get a person to commit to coming to a rally, signing a petition, holding a house meeting, or something similar. It could be quite transactional. Ernie turned his meeting into a moment of real connection, learning, and value creation.

He enabled a moment of real self-discovery for his partner by using probing questions, genuine attention, and useful, if challenging, feedback, a technique organizers call "agitation." When well done, a one-on-one can enable each person to acquire an interest in sustaining the relationship itself, not simply as the means to some other end but as rooted in the experience of self-discovery, shared values, and the promise of new possibility, of hope.

One way we can discern values, as I discuss in the next chapter, is by sharing stories of self: those narrative moments in which we learned to care, which are often moments of hurt, and moments in which we learned to hope. Sharing these moments can enable the other person to get us in a way a resume, interview, or question-and-answer cannot. We grow up, we encounter challenges, large and small, we figure out what to do, and we learn from them. These are moments of challenge, choice, and outcome. So one of the most direct forms of exploration is to learn each other's stories, focusing on choice points. Why did you go to school here rather than there? Why did you study this rather than that? Why did you decide to emigrate rather than remain at home? As we begin learning each other's answers to these questions, we learn more about each other, what moves us, and what we can contribute. An organizer who can elicit another person's story of self shows real interest, attention, and engagement that few of us experience in our daily interactions.

Similarly, a person who shares a story of self enables another to access their value sources in a real way. An organizer might begin with a simple version of their own story of self, just enough to give the other person some sense of who they are and why they want to talk with them, and then show interest in them by probing for their story of self. Most people will not find this offensive, but rather engaging. We all seem to be interested in people who are interested in us. Then you can share more about your own story, noting points of convergent value where you may find them. But this is only the beginning. To the extent that we can locate shared values within which to embed a potential relationship, the relationship may grow.

It is important to distinguish between a lead—someone who shows interest—and a recruit. A person is not a recruit until a relationship has been built that anchors their sustained engagement. Community leaders—religious leaders, labor leaders, parent leaders—can be very important, especially if you are trying to build an organization of organizations. Even if they are too busy, they may refer you to people within their network with leadership potential. This is how Fred Ross found Cesar Chavez in San Jose, based on a referral from the local priest. It can be more challenging if you're approaching a local leader or leaders who don't want any competition. There is a Mexican saying: "Entre menos burros, mas elotes," the fewer the donkeys, the more the corn. Sometimes we fool ourselves that we can co-opt community leaders into leadership roles in our organization when the reality is that they already have more than enough to do and are unlikely to drop everything and join our cause.

The challenge is to find good leads, so you don't use all your time on random contacts. When building political organizations in campaigns, we may start with people who have already volunteered. We can also go door-to-door in a neighborhood we need to organize until we find persons with whom we can have a one-on-one and, perhaps using house meetings, go from there. This can be especially important if you are trying to build an organization from scratch. By identifying potential community leaders—those who can hold a successful house meeting—you need not rely on existing organizations that may be resistant to change. That's how we found the people with whom to organize the Get Out the Vote campaign for Bobby Kennedy in East LA. In the 1983 mayoral election in San Diego, we also learned to target people identified as "always" voters, whom we could then recruit to take responsibility for turning out the "occasional" voters among their neighbors.

How do we begin a one-on-one (Figure 2.2)? First we must catch the attention of the other. If I call someone up to set up a meeting, it will help get their attention if I can say I was referred by someone they know. If I'm calling a potential volunteer on the phone, it will be important for me to use their name and explain how I got it. We may be related to a common institution, or across a room full of people, we may just make eye contact.

Once we have gotten the other's attention, we need to establish an interest in taking the time to have a conversation. I may mention, for example, how I was told they were interested in doing something about domestic violence and that's what I'd appreciate their advice on. Or I was told they are the key person from whom to get advice about what is really going on in the parish. Or since we happen to be working on the same project, maybe we should talk about how we can help each other. Be transparent about who you are, who you're working for, and why you want to have a conversation. "Hiding the ball" or withholding information can create serious trust issues that can undermine the whole thing.

There usually follows a period of exploration, of asking and answering each other's questions, of probing for areas of common interest, of testing whether the other has anything to contribute to us and whether we have anything to

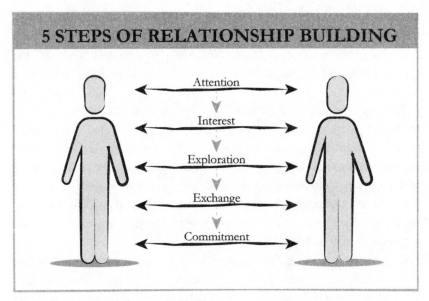

5 STEPS OF RELATIONSHIP BUILDING

Attention

Interest

Exploration

Exchange

Commitment

Figure 2.2 5 Steps of Relationship Building. *Source*: Steve Downer of the Difference

contribute to the other. The key here is learning to ask good questions, such as why a person has made the choices they have. This is where the story of self can be most useful.

As a result of our exploration, we may begin to make exchanges—not just in the future, but then and there within the conversation. We may turn out to be a good listener for someone who needs to be heard. We may find we are learning a great deal from the interaction. We may find we can challenge the other person in ways that may bring them new insight ("agitation"). We may find we can offer the other person some understanding, support, or recognition they find valuable. We may discover a basis for future exchanges—such as going to see a movie we both want to see, deciding to come to a meeting the other has told us about, taking responsibility to help pass out some leaflets, or just deciding to have another conversation.

Implicitly, one-on-ones explore three questions: Do I have resources in which you have an interest? Do you have resources in which I have an interest? Do we share values that may motivate us to work together that go beyond a single exchange or moment in pursuit of shared interests?

And if we've determined a basis may exist for a relationship, we may commit to meeting again and to continuing the conversation. We can turn an exchange into a relationship by committing to each other. People often err by going right to a commitment without having first created a relational basis for it. We may identify shared values and experience fruitful exchanges, but only commitment can transform an exchange, even a promising one, into a relationship.

Although one-on-ones are not the only way in which organizers build relationships, they are fundamental to the craft. They can also be used to get to scale. We can hold numerous one-on-ones to recruit a fresh network of individuals whom we can organize to work together to create a mass meeting of hundreds of interested people. We can hold one-on-ones to identify leaders who can launch committees in multiple locations. We can meet one-on-one with representatives of diverse groups who join to create a coalition to pursue their common interests.

One example of the use of one-on-ones was when my friend and former colleague Jim Drake came to town to organize the Greater Boston Interfaith Organization (GBIO), which at present links sixty dues-paying member churches, synagogues, mosques, community development corporations, unions, and other groups and represents over 107,000 people.[15] Jim devoted his first two *years* of work almost entirely to one-on-one meetings— a practice that has achieved almost ritual quality in an organization that operates across many traditional boundaries. When GBIO launched, it was at a 1,700-person public meeting, the most diverse in Boston memory. On May 27, 2008, GBIO, which deserves major credit for health-care reform in Massachusetts, celebrated its tenth anniversary with an assembly of some 4,000 people drawn from all these communities, attended by the mayor of Boston, the Speaker of the Massachusetts House of Representatives, and the governor of the state.[16] This example offers some insight into how the challenges of associating across lines of race, class, culture, generation, and ethnicity can be surmounted. It took work on a firm ground of respect . . . and many, many one-on-one meetings.

House Meetings

One-on-one meetings can lead to house meetings, where the host invites a network of their acquaintances to attend, some of whom will commit to hosting their own house meetings, activating social networks that weave their way through every community. House meetings are designed to make use of these networks.

In the UFW, our basic training was in house meeting organizing, a method Fred Ross devised when organizing the Community Service Organization (CSO) in East LA in the late 1940s. Unlike in Chicago, where Ross's employer, Saul Alinsky, had developed a form of community organizing by organizing organizations, in East LA, there were few organizations to be organized. Even the Roman Catholic Church viewed the Latino community as more appropriately served by missions than conventional parishes. So Ross reached out to a with a small number of local leaders who in 1947 had failed in attempt to elect Edward Roybal as the first Latino to serve on the Los Angeles City Council since it was formed inn 1889. They worked with Ross to organize house meetings to expand their relational networks to build the organization. In the 1949 election they succeeded not only in electing Roybal by organizing an historic Latino voter registration and turnout effort. They also succeeded in launching the Community Service Organization which was to become the Latino civic association that developed the leadership, organized the local chapters, and, by acting on a statewide, play a significant role in California public life.[17] Four years later Cesar Chavez was not only trained in this approach but was in fact recruited in a house meeting—a key moment in his own story.[18]

House meetings work because they begin with a civic relationship between an organizer and a person who commits to becoming a host. The host invites fifty people they know—not only close friends and family—to come to their house in a few days for a one- or two-hour meeting. The host convenes the meeting, explains its purpose, and invites guests to share stories, thoughts, and feelings about their challenges, sources of hope, and places of connection. They then discuss pathways to action. They are asked not only to commit to an action program but also to host their own house meeting within a few days. New relationships are built from old ones, new leaders (hosts) can emerge, and scaling up begins.

I was introduced to my first house meeting—a meeting in which my lack of Spanish drove me to do what I had to do to achieve fluency—in Bakersfield by Cesar's cousin Manuel Chavez. Manuel's method of training consisted of not showing up and expecting you to sink or swim. It wasn't until I worked directly with Cesar in a six-week campaign in Earlimart early in 1968 that I really got it. You did as many one-on-one meetings as you could to find a person who would commit to hosting a meeting. This required being careful not to box yourself into a corner by avoiding people you thought might not be interested. Or by recruiting the wrong person. The organizer would follow through, make reminders, and show up to make a presentation, engage the attendees, make asks, and recruit as many people as possible to host their own meetings, creating a cascade of meetings through which more people could be recruited, not unlike the well-known Tupperware parties.

We used this approach in the Howard Dean presidential primary campaign in New Hampshire, in which we asked each potential host to make a list of fifty people with whom they were acquainted. This helped ensure more heterogeneous connections. It turned out almost everyone could, with the organizers' help, make such a list. The organizer then coached the person on how to get the people there successfully: practicing a phone call, an in-person ask, and so on. In this way, we quickly met with a large number of people in conversational settings and identified a corps of potential leaders from among the house meeting hosts.

In the 1987 Pelosi for Congress campaign in San Francisco, our team of six organizers held eighty-seven house meetings attended by six hundred people in just three weeks. In addition to being asked to host another meeting, attendees were asked to volunteer on a phone bank. At the end of the house meeting drive, the eighty-seven hosts and another fifty very active volunteers were invited to a meeting at which they were asked to become precinct leaders. In this way, four weeks into the campaign, we had recruited proven leaders for 110 of the 150 precincts we needed to organize to cover the entire congressional district. Each also had its own corps of volunteers with whom to work.

This approach is so useful because you can start almost from scratch in any setting and identify potential leaders from among house meeting hosts. The host, not the organizer, does the recruiting, coached by the organizer. The organizer turns informal private and public relationships into the formal public relationships with which to build an organization. And if done well, it can grow geometrically. During the first Obama campaign, by October 2007, organizers in South Carolina had held some four hundred house meetings, attended by some four thousand people. This became the foundation for the deployment of fifteen thousand Election Day volunteers—most of them active politically for the first time.[19]

Emergency Meetings

On occasion, we simply do not have the time or the numbers to begin as above. The less time we have, the more organizers we need; the more time we have, the fewer organizers we need. An emergency meeting can be one way to mobilize within limited time, but to do so in a more relational way. This is often the case in last-minute electoral campaigns. In the 1986 US Senate campaign of Senator Alan Cranston, we had to organize a Get Out the Vote in some twelve hundred precincts in African American and Latino districts of South-Central LA, East LA, San Diego, San Jose, and Oakland. We recruited fifty organizers who accepted responsibility for recruiting fifteen precinct leaders each. Since we had very little time—the whole campaign was done in five weeks—we built on what we had learned in the San Diego mayoral campaign: we got registered voter lists for each precinct that were coded as to who "always" voted, who "occasionally" voted, and who "never" voted. The organizers called the "always" voters in their turf to recruit them for an emergency meeting that afternoon or evening at campaign headquarters. From among those who attended, the organizers recruited precinct leaders who agreed to contact the "occasional" voters in their precinct and to take the day off work on Election Day to help us get them out to vote. We turned out an additional 160,000 voters this way. Cranston won by 110,000 votes.

Relationships are the glue of any organizing effort. And like any other relationship, they require ongoing maintenance work. Old relationships need to be renewed and new relationships developed. If this ongoing work is not done—and if the relationships unravel—it becomes harder and harder to accomplish the tasks that must be accomplished. We also may remain ignorant of who the people are that make up our organizations and what they have to contribute. In the absence of solid relationships, the kinds of political difficulties and factions with which we are all familiar develop, undermining our collective capacity.

Building Relationships Online

Although the tactics we've looked at so far vary in setting and in scale, what they all have in common is that they develop direct relationships among people we hope to involve in the work of the organization. These tactics do not rely on flyers, phone calls, or email, because relationships are about commitment and co-creation, as well as information. Initially, online media was used mainly for sharing information, not for building committed relationships. Similarly, the idea that technology alone can enable people to self-organize doesn't work. Meetup, for example, one of the key platforms the Dean campaign used for organizing in 2004, facilitated thousands of meetings between people looking for others with similar interests but suffered from a very high mortality rate because it offered no training, structure, or coaching that could enable these new groups to succeed.

A more promising route for relationship building is at the intersection of online and offline organizing. Tech has long been used to make it far easier for people who want to become involved to do so—for them to become leads and find leads. In the summer of 2007, some one hundred thousand potential volunteers had signed up for the Obama campaign online, but the campaign did not yet have the capacity to engage them. Once this capacity was built, however, these records became a very important way to grow the movement. Similarly, use of online tech can put tools in the hands of people who are motivated to use them to find others who are interested in them, to reach out to others who may be interested, and, as in the phone bank operations during the campaign, to reach out to individuals in other states whom they could contact by phone. The relative ease with which information can be shared greatly facilitates reporting, coordination, analysis, and, in general, transparency, as when the Obama campaign decided to share the VAN, or Democratic Party Voter Activation List—what had until then been closely guarded voter file information—with volunteer leadership teams.[20]

More recently, especially in the wake of COVID-19, we all got a crash course in how to use Zoom to initiate, cultivate, and develop committed relationships. Visual technology like this enables people to see and interact with each other in real time so that they can build relationships and share learning, motivation, and interaction at a very low cost and in a way that goes far beyond what was possible in writing or over the phone. The closer we can get to face-to-face visual interaction, the more we can harness the power of new tech to the work we do through relationship building. I experienced this potential when I took my practice-based organizing class online in 2010. It has grown annually to about 140 students from some thirty countries and a team of seven teaching fellows who each work with some twenty students, creating an online learning community through one-on-one meetings, establishing shared purposes, adopting group norms, and so forth. As with good organizing practice, these sessions include the scaffolding, coaching, and peer-learning necessary for sustained engagement.[21]

In the summer of 2018, I led an organizing workshop in Silicon Valley with young people eager to apply their technical skills to solving social problems. One challenge that became evident during this workshop was that many of the participants seemed to be thinking of human beings as users—individual customers whom one must incentivize or disincentivize to do the right thing and not the wrong thing —rather than people whom one can engage in learning, reflection, or moral and political judgment. Tim Berners-Lee, the inventor of the World Wide Web, once commented to me that while machines can make decisions based on this or that algorithm. But only human beings could exercise the judgment to make choices.

A second challenge is to distinguish information sharing—or awareness facilitated by digital communication—from relationship building. Digital information sharing is usually anonymous, unidirectional, individual, and almost always devoid of commitment. Relationship building, on the other hand, is based on making commitments to other people with whom I share a common purpose.

A third challenge was enabling workshop participants to recognize the difference between *aggregating* individual resources and *organizing* collective capacity. Mobilizing individuals to send an email, contribute, or show up at a rally without building relationships among them creates no collective capacity. It spends down resources we have rather than generating new resources. This approach also realizes none of the benefits of association, which include learning, solidarity, collaboration, and leadership development. It substitutes mobilizing for organizing, as well documented by sociologist Zeynep Tufekci in *Twitter and Teargas* and political scientist Hahrie Han in *How Organizations Develop Activists*.

Because social media dramatically reduced the cost of sharing information in real time, many now decide to skip organizing and go straight to mobilizing. They count on crisis events to generate reactions, choices made by individuals who command the media, and the ability to generate big numbers of clicks, even if the impact is no greater than that of counting sheep in the clouds—and not as beautiful.[22] Unless we build the organizational capacity—lateral committed relationships, decision-making venues, and leadership structures—to do the mobilizing, not only will the resources dry up, but mobilization will turn out to have been nothing more than tactics in search of a strategy.

Happily, we have begun to learn to distinguish between carpenters and tools. The best hammer in the world won't build a house. It takes a skilled carpenter, with a vision of what a house can look like, command of the craft of building houses, and a readiness to use new tools to get the job done better. Effective organizers are distinguished by the craft of turning the new energy and connections made possible by digital tools into a successful organization or movement. We all build relationships, but excellence depends on doing the work to master the craft that can become an art.

Conclusion

How leaders practice relationship-building in any given campaign depends on their role in the overall campaign strategy. In the examples I've discussed here, these skills were used to build an organization from scratch (as with the farmworkers), create a campaign organization (Pelosi, Dean, Obama), and build an organization of organizations (GBIO). In an electoral setting, even if the organization is abandoned after the election is over, relational organizers may have created quite a bit of civic capital that can be of value in subsequent campaigns. Most organizations employ some combination of relational organizing through individuals, networks, and organizations. But the claim that "we can't do relational organizing because it will take too long, and our situation is urgent" is belied by many of the examples I've cited here. Urgency can motivate going deep very fast, or it can be used to justify remaining shallow to invest in other priorities.

We can begin with brand-new relationships based on leads recruited at tables, street corners, sign-ups at rallies, or other gatherings. We can begin by drawing people in through relational networks of which they are already part. Sometimes networks are recruited from old organizations that act as incubators for a new effort. This was the role of many of the southern Black churches and colleges in the civil rights movement, which some scholars referred to as "indigenous mobilizing structures."[23] We can also build relationships with leaders of existing organizations, bringing them into relationship with each other to make a new organization possible. This makes use of organizational resources that already exist, but it also requires accommodating the new organization to meet the interests of existing organizational leaders. This was Alinsky's approach and is that of the Greater Boston Interfaith Organization.

Regardless of the chosen approach, organizers create collective capacity through the purposeful formation of civic relationships to enable democracy to work. I focused on relational tactics first because the devil is in the details. Far too often, organizing campaigns fall short and then say organizing didn't work, when it failed because they didn't invest resources—time, people, and money—in the training needed to achieve excellence. What really matters is not the amount of time in weeks, months, or years but rather the value placed on relational organizing, the quality of the initial training, and a commitment to sustained coaching.

In sum, relationships are the threads with which community—and constituency—are woven. We form them to create the social context within which we engage in numerous social transactions every day. They construct the context within which we articulate our individual and collective narratives, develop our creative strategy, situate our collective action, and build structures that enable us to work with others. This is why the instrumentalization of our relational worlds is so deeply disorienting and, at the same time, creates the necessity for their reconstruction. This is what organizing does. And it is what makes democracy work—or not.

3

Storytelling

I grew up in an ancient story: the story of a people—my people. The story is told every year at the Passover seder. I recently found a photo of our Passover seder in Germany in 1948. My father, the chaplain, is leading the seder in uniform at a mic; my mother, seated to his left, is looking glowingly at me: as the youngest person there (all of five), I had just finished asking the Four Questions about why this particular night is different from all other nights and to which the rest of the seder is a response. The prayer book for the seder is called, quite simply, the Haggadah, "the story."

When I began to work in Mississippi, I found myself within the telling of yet another chapter of the same story: the arduous journey from slavery to freedom. As Dr. King declared the night before his assassination:

> I would watch God's children in their magnificent trek from the dark dungeons of Egypt through, or rather across, the Red Sea, through the wilderness on toward the promised land. . . . I just want to do God's will. And He's allowed me to go up to the mountain. And I've looked over. And I've seen the promised land. I may not get there with you. But I want you to know tonight, that we, as a people, will get to the promised land.[1]

Like the story in which I grew up, this story wasn't just told. It was celebrated—in church, in mass meetings, in song. Although the Christian narrative of the Black church was new to me, the religious sensibility with which I grew up helped me get it better than some of my secular companions. To "testify" in church was to tell a story linking one's personal redemption with that of one's church and one's faith. In movement mass meetings, testimony linked one's personal freedom story to that of the community and the movement.

The farmworker movement told its story as well, a story deeply rooted in Mexican culture, in the Mexican Catholic tradition, in its revolutionary tradition, and in the traditions of everyday life. Values central to Catholic social teaching, renewed by Vatican II, interwove with strands of the civil rights movement and American labor history. We celebrated this story in a

Eucharistic mass, on picket lines that became *vigilias*, on marches that became *peregrinaciones*, and in mass meetings rich in song, theater, and solidarity. By the time I left the farmworkers, I had learned that to try organizing without a story is to try organizing without a heart—the emotional resources we need not only to launch a struggle but also to sustain it, and in the end, to win.

By the time I began teaching here in 1994, I had learned that without a story of hope, not much would happen. Grievances may abound, but few would act without a spark of hope—real hope. In 1997, when I joined a doctoral seminar on the neurophysiology of myth, I began to understand the link between how stories work and how our brains work.[2] I explored this connection further with my colleague Bernie Steinberg, director of Harvard Hillel. Guided by his teaching I discovered whole new depths of meaning in the familiar Bible stories with which I grew up, if we read them as the stories they are, not as theology. When I finished my dissertation—having identified the critical role of narrative motivation in strategy—I committed to deeper study of how narrative works, its role in organizing, and how to teach it. In 2005, while on leave after the death of my wife, Susan, and doing narrative work of my own, Adam Reich and I came up with a way to do it. I called it "public narrative" and tried it out in a course at Harvard Kennedy School, a project with Sierra Club chapters, and at Camp Obama sessions in 2007/8. It turned out that it worked—not because it came from the academy but because everyone tells stories.

What Is Public Narrative?

In the first seven minutes of his keynote address to the 2004 Democratic Convention, Barack Obama begins by sharing his story: the choices that shaped his life and the values driving those choices. He then reminds us of our own shared stories: the values that unite us, the choices we have made, our sources of hope. He then confronts us with challenges to those values, enlivens our sources of hope, and inspires us with hope: he describes for us the America that could be, but only if we step up, accept responsibility, and make it happen: a story of now. He wasn't calling us to choose what *he* wanted. He was calling us to find the courage to choose what *we* wanted. He shared a "story of self," a "story of us," and a "story of now." Although he didn't call it that, this was his public narrative, a talk with which he introduced himself to America.

Public narrative wasn't invented at Harvard. In fact, it's more of a discovery than an invention. An early instance of which I'm aware is recounted in Exodus 8. Moses—the Jew who is an Egyptian, of the oppressed but raised in the house of the oppressor—at once was confronted with this identity conflict. He sees a slave being abused by a taskmaster and kills the taskmaster, an action that earns him not the support of the captive Israelites but rather their fearful condemnation of him for "rocking the boat." So, he flees into the desert, which is where, in the Bible, you go to figure things out. He finds a spouse, a family, and a job as a shepherd. One day he's walking along with his sheep and sees a glow off to the side of the road; he's a curious fellow, so he steps off the road only to find a bush that is burning but not being consumed. At that point he hears the voice, the timbre of which is uncertain, "Moses, you are called to free your people."

For those familiar with the text, how does Moses respond? "Wait a second! Why me? You've got the wrong guy! I can't even give a speech. I've got an impediment," then, "And who exactly are you and these people of yours who won't accept me?" And then, "Couldn't this wait?" To which God responds with the promise of help from Moses's brother Aaron, as well as a staff that can turn into a snake to spook Pharoah's magicians.

Why me? Why us? Why now? These are ancient questions. And I've yet to find a culture in which people don't ask themselves these questions. They give different answers, to be sure, but the questions are the same.

Public narrative, then, is a way we can harness the power of narrative to the work of leadership: accepting responsibility for enabling others to achieve shared purpose under conditions of uncertainty. I can tell a story of self to enable others to "get" me by sharing my moments of hurt (why I care) and moments of hope (why I can) and the values motivating how I chose to respond to them. I can tell a story of us to enable others to "get" each other by recalling shared moments of hurt and of hope and how we responded to them, expressing values we share. We can tell a story of now to access sources of courage to transform a current moment of disruption from a threat from which I flee fearfully into a challenge with which I can engage hopefully: from thoughtless reaction into mindful response—the exercise of agency.

In this way we can use narrative to construct an empathetic bridge with others to enable them to respond mindfully to the disruptive impact of loss, difference, domination, and change. By weaving articulation of these moments into a coherent story, we can share a motivational experience of our individual and collective values. Through the coherent articulation of narrative moments, we can mutually construct our individual and collective identities.

The dynamics of narrative, emotion, and values grow out of the work of Jerome Bruner, the twentieth-century cultural psychologist who taught for many years at the Harvard Graduate School of Education. Bruner argued that we interpret the world in distinct paradigmatic and narrative modes.[3] The paradigmatic mode relies primarily on a cognitive mapping of the world, within which we identify patterns, discern connections, hypothesize empirical claims and test them, and construct explanatory frames based on what we've come to believe about what *is* in the world. The narrative mode relies primarily on an affective mapping of the world, through which we valorize experiences, objects, symbols, and people as fearful or safe, hopeful or depressing, soothing or unsettling. We construct narratives based on what we have come to believe *is good* in the world.[4]

We use the paradigmatic mode to answer the question of how: How can we efficiently and effectively achieve our goals? We use the narrative mode to answer the question of why: Why are these our goals, why do we care, why can we be hopeful, why must we choose, why must we act?

The Power of Stories

Where did you hear your first stories? Who told them to you? Most of us hear them from our parents, grandparents, aunts, uncles, and other caregivers who told them to us in our early years, even as we began learning how to tell our own stories. Those stories shape a child's formation of their understanding of the world, themselves, and the relationship between the two. Why so many stories? To instruct? What is it that stories do that a list of dos and don'ts cannot?

All stories have a plot, a character, and a moral. Stories have a *plot:* they begin with a disruption, narrate a response, and yield an outcome. We experience the emotional content of these moment by identifying with the *character*, the protagonist. This experience then teaches an experiential *moral* that teaches not only the head but, more importantly, the heart, in this way our experience of the story can become part of our own experience, an experience we can draw on when we face challenges of our own.

Because our stories, like all stories, begin in the beginning, by sharing our "origin stories" we can most effectively, and accessibly, communicate our values sources: moments early in life when we learned to care—often moments of hurt—and moments in which we experienced our worth, our value—often moments of hope. Because everyone tells stories, and because our beginnings are often fraught with similar challenges, sharing our origin stories can communicate shared values surprisingly well across the cultural, racial, class, and gender boundaries that separate us.

And because a well-told story moment can bring a felt experience of the past into the present, we become emotionally present as well, thus communicating the emotional meaning of this unique moment. The specificity of a particular moment can thus become, like a poem, a portal to the transcendent. In this chapter I show how we can link the power of story to the work of leadership as *public narrative*: a story of self, a story of us, and a story of now.

Public narrative is a *framework* not a *formula*, so the order of the stories (self, us, now) can be varied and played with, as long as they make sense and flow together in a clear, cohesive way. In a linked narrative, the three elements (self, us, now) are told through story moments with all the elements of the craft present: challenge, choice, outcome, and hope. You are *telling* the stories, not telling *about* the stories.

We all learn to tell stories, implicitly if not explicitly.[5] So by making the implicit explicit, we can learn to practice storytelling as a craft with intentionality, skill, and sustained learning. We will look first at the emotional dimension of storytelling; then, at the structural dimension; and then, how they come together in the leadership practice of public narrative.

Emotion, Values, and Leadership

When we tell stories, we speak in the language of emotion. Speaking the language of emotion is not irrational, reactive, or thoughtless. Music speaks the language of emotion, as do worship, poetry, theater, and sports. Emotions inform us of what we value in ourselves, in others, and in the world. The emotional information we experience as feelings is partly physiological, as when our respiration or body temperature changes; partly behavioral, as when we are moved to advance or to flee, to stand up or to sit down; and partly cognitive, as we describe what we feel as fear, love, desire, or joy.

Emotions provide us with vital information about how to live our lives. This emotional information is not better than analytic reasoning but more of a precondition for it.[6] Decisions are ultimately based on value judgments, and value judgments require emotional information. In fact, moral philosopher Martha Nussbaum cites research on people afflicted with lesions on the amygdala, an element of the brain central to emotional experience. When called upon to solve problems, they can reason multiple options but cannot decide on which to act. But relying on emotional information is not consigning ourselves to the realm of the irrational. On the contrary, as Blaise Pascal observed, "The heart has its reasons, which reason does not know."[7] Some of our emotions enable intentional, mindful, and agentic action, while other emotions inhibit it.

When it comes to public leadership, the emotional challenge is how to enable others to experience a disruption as real enough to motivate action (Figure 3.1). At the same time, it is to enable others to encounter disruption courageously enough to choose a mindful response rather than a fearful reaction in lieu of making a choice.

Most of the time, we rely on habit, often reinforced by feelings of inertia and apathy. This can be efficient. I don't have to relearn how to drive my car each time I want to go somewhere. But when something unexpected happens, like a truck suddenly pulling out in front of me, my surveillance system compares what I'm expecting with what is actually happening and signals me with anxiety. Without this emotional cue, political psychologist George Marcus argues, we may remain on autopilot.[8] This anxiety is beneficial because it confronts us with the reality that we are not in a business-as-usual moment but are in one that may require a strategic or agentic response. This is constructive because humans are very good at screening out data that conflict with our cognitive frames or assumptions—a consistency bias—and because a comforting sense of inertia (it's always worked out this way) or resigned apathy (nothing we do works anyway) reinforces an inaction bias. An emotional shock or disruption can penetrate habit enough to enable recognition of a novel disruption that demands a strategic response. Anxiety tells us, "Hey! Pay attention!"

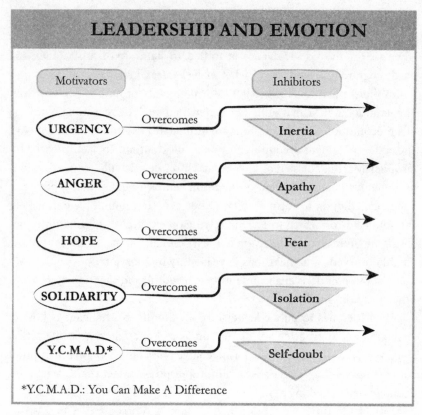

Figure 3.1 Leadership and Emotion. *Source*: Steve Downer of the Difference

Urgency and Anger

Our leadership challenge may be to awaken people to an urgent need for intentional action in response to a disruption, not yet experienced as immediately proximate or threatening. It often involves challenging people with the contradictions in what we may assume to be the case and our own lived experience—a technique organizers describe as agitation.[9] The climate change movement has long struggled with the fact that carbon parts per million only became urgent when floods and fires forcefully intruded on daily lives.

Urgency establishes priorities. I may need to decide on my future vocation, but I have an exam in the morning so, especially if unprepared, I must study tonight. I may need to study tonight but they're coming to evict our family first thing in the morning, so I'd better start packing. There are two kinds of urgency: *urgency of need* and *urgency of opportunity*. Urgency of need can be created by a condition so intolerable that it demands immediate action: a child is ripped from its parent's arms at a border crossing; a young Black man is murdered in public view by a police officer; a ban on Muslims entering the United States is announced; another mass shooting demands a protest. Urgency of opportunity is created by a deadline by which action must be taken if it is to have any effect at all: the vote on restricting reproductive choice is in just three days; if I don't find my rent money by next week, I'm out on the street.

Balancing the important and the urgent can be challenging. Those trying to mobilize a vitally important response to climate change must also make it urgent. The urgent can displace the important when a critical volunteer training that has been in the making for three months is suddenly cancelled in reaction to a small shift in the polling numbers. Two weeks before the election, the call goes out, "Where are our volunteers?"

Sometimes social movements can mobilize a caring public, as well as their own constituency, in response to the "moral urgency" of their cause. In 1960, for example, in Greensboro, North Carolina, Black students denied service at a segregated lunch counter polarized the moment by refusing to leave. They're being spit on, beaten, jailed. We can't wait any longer. We must act now. The Occupy Wall Street movement set up shop in New York's Zuccotti Park in 2011 and refused to leave; they too created a moment of "moral urgency" that moved much of the public to recognize, if not act on, the challenges of economic inequality. When the Dreamers risked deportation by "coming out" to claim their undocumented status in public, it also created "moral urgency" among their supporters. And the widespread protests in response to the televised police murder of George Floyd in Minneapolis in 2020 responded to the "moral urgency" created by what the nation had seen, had witnessed.[10]

Anger can also counter habitual apathy or inertia not as rage but as outrage: the experience of the dissonance between the world as it is and the world as it ought to be. As individuals we may become angry if someone or something robs us of our dignity or self-respect: the experience of moments of domination, discrimination, bullying, violation, or neglect, regardless of attempts to legitimate them. Communities may react with anger not only to the foregoing but also to violations of their "moral order," evident in the culture wars dominating US politics.[11] People rarely mobilize to protest inequality or even low wages as such, as inconvenient as these may be. They do mobilize to protest "unjust" inequality or low wages, a kind of moral dissonance that crosses the line.[12] In other words, assaults on our values, our moral traditions, or our personal or community dignity can function as critical sources of the anger that can motivate action.

Fear and Hope and Choice

If anger or urgency can create critical experiences of disruptive anxiety, whether they spark courage or aggression depends on whether they partner with fear or with hope.[13] Unfortunately, fear is often our default reaction to any disruption. We're all well acquainted with fear, one of the first emotions we experience, provocative of all the crying for comfort. Fear is a hardwired reaction to perceived threat: flight, fight, or freeze. This was an adaptive response when the disruption may have taken the form of a saber-toothed tiger. But especially as we began to live in larger communities, reacting to any source of disruption with fear could be deeply destructive. And when combined with anger, it often leads to hateful aggression toward an identified source threat—the "dangerous other." And if anchored in isolation and self-doubt, the more a yearning for safety abounds, at times accompanied by despair.

We began finding the emotional resources with which we could manage our fears—principal among them is hope. Hope, unlike optimism, sees clearly what can be a fearsome reality but responds to it in a spirit of "could be" or "possibility," a space between certainty and fantasy.[14] The twelfth-century philosopher Maimonides understood hope as belief in the plausibility of the possible as opposed to the necessity of the probable.[15] We live in a world in which it is always probable Goliath will win, but sometimes David does. It was highly improbable we would elect a Black man president of the United States, but it happened.

When anger combines with hope, it can become a source of the courage we need to transform a threat from which we must flee into a challenge with which we can engage. In concert with the experience of self-worth ("you can make a difference") and solidarity (love, empathy), hope can move us to act.

So where do we go to get hope? Many people draw hope from the stories expressive of their faith, cultural, and moral traditions, often accompanied by the experiences of transcendence or "awe."[16] The American civil rights movement, the Polish Solidarity movement, and Gandhi's Swaraj movement for Indian independence directly or indirectly drew strength from religious traditions. Indeed, much of the community organizing going on in the United States today is rooted in faith communities. Another source of hope is our own experiences of self-efficacy—a small success, an overcoming of the odds—and solidarity—a parent who believed in us, a friend who stood up for us, a person in whose life we made a difference. And we all know people who simply inspire hopefulness in others—a form of "charisma" rooted not in hero worship but in their enabling others to experience their own value, their belovedness, their possibilities. Cultivating a sense of possibility—not certainty—is to cultivate sources of hope.[17]

Feelings of isolation can both result from and contribute to fear. We counter isolation with experiences of belovedness or solidarity or community. Mass meetings during the civil rights movement were not only shows of strength or reports on progress but also celebrations of community, solidarity, and love. Singing was an embodiment of that love. Group activities like singing help individuals experience the values shared by the community.

Leaders counter self-doubt by enabling people to experience a sense of self-efficacy, that *you* can make a difference. Leaders can contribute to this sense of worth by enabling the experience of respect. Most of us experience disrespect, as well as respect, in very similar ways. The heart of the experience of respect is being seen, being heard, and being valued. Most of us get a pretty good sense of whether we're being seen or just being looked at. We also know if we are being heard or being observed. And we know if we are being valued or being used. The starting point to building self-efficacy is being fully present to each other.

Exercising leadership, then, requires engaging in an emotional conversation that draws on positive emotions grounded in one set of experiences to counter negative emotions grounded in different experiences or circumstances—a dialogue of the heart. This kind of dialogue can restore the hope for change that had been abandoned in despair.

Craft, Values, and Leadership

The Story Moment

Stories teach through story moments. A story moment is a specific event in which we are confronted with an anxiety-creating disruption to which we must react or respond. To the extent we experience it as a threat, we are likely to react fearfully, to retreat. To the extent we experience it as a challenge, we are likely to respond thoughtfully, to explore. The outcome teaches a moral not so much to the head as to the heart. This is so because we can identify empathetically with the person of the protagonist, feel the fear as if it were our own, feel the hope as if it were our own. And most importantly, we can feel the source of value on which the protagonist draws to respond with solidarity, dignity, faith, compassion, loyalty, and so on. The moral is not only a set of words but an emotional experience, an experience of the heart, an experience that can become our own.

A story moment encompasses a challenge, a choice, and an outcome (Figure 3.2). It is not simply the description of a scene, like that of a beautiful sunset. It is dynamic, an experience of change. For example, I was watching the beautiful sunset with my partner when it began to rain. As I turned to go, she reached out and took my arm. "It's only rain," she said. "We'll be fine as long as we're together." Something happened. A challenge elicited a choice that yielded an outcome. And we are offered a moral: love can conquer adversity.

Story moments are nested. Story educator Robert McKee describes this moment as a "beat" (challenge, choice, outcome), each one of which is nested within a larger story moment, a scene; each scene is nested within a still larger story moment, an act; and each act is nested within a much larger story moment, a play.[18]

The story begins. A character is moving toward a desired goal. But then, suddenly, there is a disruption, a threat. Now what? All plans are off. All eyes are on the character who must figure out what to do, who must make a choice. Now we get interested. Do they react fearfully? Are they scared? Do they get a grip? Do they respond thoughtfully? They choose. It works! It doesn't work. There's an outcome.

The Character (Protagonist)

When we identify empathetically with a character, the protagonist of the story, we can experience the emotional content of their experience almost as if it were our own. We can experience the fear. We can experience the hope. We can experience the sources of that hope—often the hard-earned values of the character. We understand now that the mechanism of mirror

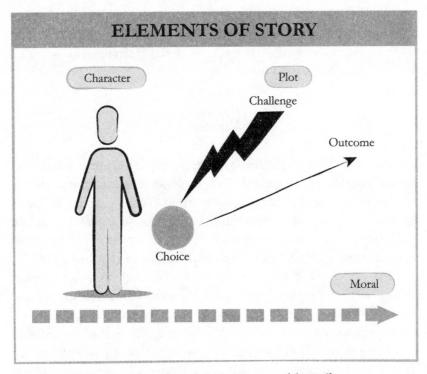

Figure 3.2 Elements of Story. *Source*: Steve Downer of the Difference

neurons enables us to experience the actions of another we can observe almost as if they were our own, knowledge held by storytellers for literally thousands of years.[19] What we hope to learn, then, is not so much the tactics of accomplishing the goal. This is emotional learning—where the character finds the hope, the courage, the persistence, and the creativity to persist. As Aristotle wrote of Greek tragedy, this is how the protagonist's experience can touch us and, perhaps, open our eyes.[20]

Sometimes we identify with protagonists who are only vaguely like us—like Road Runner (if not Wile E. Coyote) in the cartoons. Other times, we identify with protagonists who are very much like us, as in stories about friends, relatives, or neighbors. Sometimes the protagonists of a story are *us*, as when we find ourselves in the midst of an unfolding story, in which we are the authors of the outcome.

Why do we care?

Is it because someday I may face the same challenge and I want to be prepared? If I watch closely, might I learn what to do, learn the skills I need to be ready? Maybe I'm just curious: I want to see what happens. But why do I care how it turns out? The fact is that we spend billions of dollars a year on movies, books, plays, songs, and sports, all structured in the same way. And they pretty much all start in the same way.

The Plot

Think about it for a moment. How many times a day do we have to deal, in ways little and big, with the unexpected? They're sold out of tickets at the movie theater. There's no place to park. Marriages break up. People lose their jobs. We all lose loved ones—losses for which almost by definition we cannot be prepared. Isn't having to deal with the unexpected, with the disruptive, a core dimension of human experience? And we seem infinitely curious to learn how.

The power of a story moment depends on our ability to make the past, present, or the distant nearby. We can tell stories because our species, unlike most others, is capable of episodic memory, to recall not only semantic data, but an event, an episode.[21] So we can bring the moment alive by telling it in the present tense, for example, by drawing on very specific sensory details: sounds, smells, textures, and especially visuals. This is what good storytellers have known for thousands of years, the dynamics of which modern science is only just catching up to.

We link story moments that tell of the challenge, the change, the outcome, and hope to tell our story of self, story of us, and story of now. And all of these elements combine to form our public narrative. The experience of these stories becomes a part of our own experience. Bruner describes this as *agency training*: a way we learn to make mindful choices in the face of uncertainty. Stories thus teach us how to engage our emotions, not to repress them, so we can act with agency to face our own challenges.

The Moral

Story moments thus teach the heart as well as the head. Stories can instruct us what to value, how to choose, how to respond. They can also inspire, enabling us to act. They are not simply examples and illustrations. When they are well told, we experience *the point*. It is that experience, not the words as such, that enable us to learn, to choose, and to act.

A story is like a poem. It moves not by how long it is, nor how eloquent or complicated. It moves by offering the experience of specific moments through which we grasp the feeling or insight the poet communicates. The more specific the details we choose to recount, the more we can move our listeners, the more powerfully we can articulate our values, what moral philosopher Charles Taylor calls our "moral sources."[22] Like a poem, the particularity of a story moment can open a portal to the experience of the transcendent. Stories teach a moral—an experiential moral. We've all heard the ending—"and that is the moral of the story." Have you ever been at a party where someone starts telling a story and they go on . . . and on . . . and on . . . and on? Someone may finally shout, "Get to the point!" We deploy stories to *make a point*, to elicit a response.

The moral of a successful story is an emotional experience, not only a cognitive takeaway. It is a lesson for the heart, not only for the head. Saying haste makes waste does not communicate how haste making waste feels, what it's like to lose it all because I moved too fast. Nor does a moral provide detailed tactical information. We do not retell the story of David and Goliath to learn how to use a slingshot. We learn that the little guy—with courage, resourcefulness, and imagination—can beat the big guy, especially one with Goliath's arrogance. We can feel David's outrage, courage, and resourcefulness. We can be hopeful in dealing with apparently overwhelming challenges of our own. Stories thus teach us how to engage our emotions, not to repress them, so we can act with agency to face our own challenges.

This is why we tell stories—to instruct, to share values, and to inspire. This is why our faith traditions teach through stories, our cultural traditions teach through stories, and our families teach through stories. Where did you hear your first stories? From a parent, a grandparent, an aunt, an uncle?

Let me tell you about Uncle Charlie. He had everything going for him: good at sports, good school, good job. But then he took a wrong turn . . . and it was all downhill. You don't want to be like Uncle Charlie, do you? So let me tell you about Aunt Harriet. Now she got it right. . . .

Families across the world tell versions of this story. Bruner reported that 85 percent of parents' time with young children is spent in storytelling.[23] You may have children of your own. So why all the stories? To keep them busy, no doubt. But isn't it also to instruct? Why not just read a list of rules? Do this and don't do that? It doesn't work, does it? It's all in the head. Stories teach what it feels like to deal with adversity, temptation, and arrogance, what it feels like to choose well—or poorly—in response, and where to go to get the courage to choose well—the values. The experience of these stories then becomes a part of the child's own experience—a moral resource. Bruner describes this as *agency training*: a way we learn to make mindful choices in the face of uncertainty.

Authoring Your Public Narrative

Recall our definition of leadership: accepting responsibility for enabling others to achieve shared purpose under conditions of uncertainty. As a leader, I'm not trying to compel people to choose what I want; rather, I'm enabling them to choose what they want. Leadership enables the exercise of individual and collective agency, the ability to choose well. The telling of public narrative works in three ways: a story of self, a story of us, and a story of now (Figure 3.3). This framework was inspired by Rabbi Hillel's three questions, on which our whole approach to leadership is based. I tell a story of *self* to evoke experience of values that called me to accept leadership. I tell a story of *us* to evoke shared values that can enable agency in choosing a response. I tell a story of *now* to evoke experience of the urgent challenge to those values that demands a response now, the sources of hope to enable the agency to choose well, and clarity as to the choices we must make to respond. Public narrative can also be understood in terms of Aristotle's definition of the three components of rhetoric. The *logos* is the logic of the argument. The *pathos* is the emotional content. The *ethos* is the listeners' experience of the storyteller, the credibility of the person who makes the argument—their story of self.

Stories of Self

If I am not for myself, who will be for me? You tell a story of self to share values that have called you to leadership—not as abstract principles but as lived experience. You construct your story of self from moments to which you had to respond, when you faced a challenge, made a choice, experienced an outcome, and learned a moral. You can communicate your motivating values by selecting particular story moments and recounting what happened as if it were happening now. Because storytelling is a social interaction, you engage

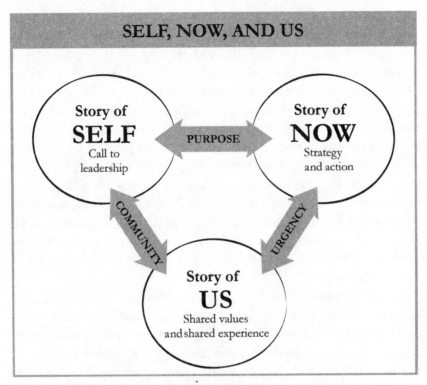

SELF, NOW, AND US

Story of
SELF
Call to
leadership

PURPOSE

Story of
NOW
Strategy
and action

COMMUNITY

URGENCY

Story of
US
Shared values
and shared experience

Figure 3.3 Self, Now, and Us. *Source*: Steve Downer of the Difference

your listeners' memories as well as your own. The experience occurs at the intersection of the moments you share and the moments your listeners recall. In fact, we construct our identities by telling our story. What is utterly unique about each of us is not a combination of the categories—race, gender, class, profession, marital status—that include us, but rather the meaning we give to our own journey, our way through life, our personal text from which each of us can teach.

We may think our personal stories don't matter, that others won't care, or that we shouldn't talk about ourselves so much. On the contrary, if we do public work, we have a responsibility to give a public account of ourselves— where we came from, why we do what we do, and where we think we're going. This is one way we can acquire the moral authority to be heard by others. The truth is that if we choose public leadership, we don't have a choice about telling our story of self. If we don't author our story, others will—and they may tell our story in ways that we may not like. This was the hard lesson learned by John Kerry, the 2004 Democratic presidential nominee. When Kerry was unable to tell his own story, his opponents seized ownership of it. Something similar happened to Hillary Clinton in 2016. This outcome is not necessarily a product of malevolence: others try to make sense of who we are by relying on their experience of people they consider to be like us.

Stories of self can be challenging because people are often moved to participate in social change through a prophetic combination of criticality and hope. In personal terms, this means that most people called to social movements have lived stories of the world's hurt and the world's hope. If we hadn't felt the hurt, we wouldn't think the world needs fixing. If we hadn't felt the hope, we wouldn't think we could. And if we haven't talked about our stories of pain very much, it can take a while to learn to manage it. But if others try to make sense of why we are doing what we are doing, but we have left this piece out, our account will lack authenticity, raising questions about the rest of the story.

Social movements are often the crucibles within which participants learn to tell new stories of self as we interact with other participants. In the early days of the women's movement, people participated in consciousness-raising sessions: group conversations that mediated changes in their stories of self, in their stories of who they were, as women. Women shared stories of pain, but also stories of hope. In the civil rights movement, African Americans living in the Deep South who feared claiming the right to vote had to encourage one another to find the courage to make that claim, which, once made, began to alter how they thought of themselves and how they could interact with their children, with white people, and with each other.

Stories of Us

When I am for myself alone, what am I? We tell stories of us more often than any other kind of story. At a family dinner, for example, stories of us begin with "remember the time that . . ." or "remember when. . . ." The storyteller then recounts a familiar story moment through which they experience values they share—courage, resilience, or foolishness.[24] Or after an athletic event, fans may gather over beers to recall when so-and-so threw the winning pass or when so-and-so fumbled the ball. In this way we celebrate the values that make "us" an "us": courage, coming through in the crunch, persistence, and so on.

When it comes to leadership, our intent is to enable our "us" to respond with hope rather than to react with fear: to exercise the agency to choose our actions well. The "us" we are constructing is experiential, not categorical. We build a categorical "us" defined by ascriptive characteristics a group may share, such as everyone with brown hair. We build an experiential "us" defined by values we share. We can experience shared values by recalling specific story moments in which we felt them: when we all stood up at the meeting to volunteer; when we all rushed onto the field when our team won the crucial game; when we all first met and were uncertain about our relationship to one another, but when someone's baby began to cry, we all rushed over to offer support. That's when we knew who we are.

Some story moments may be shared by an entire generation, such as the moment we heard JFK had been shot or the moment we saw the planes crash into the Twin Towers. Our cultures are repositories of story moments: stories of the challenges we have faced, how we stood up to them, and how we survived are woven into the fabric of our political cultures and our faith traditions. We tell and retell these stories as folk sayings, songs, religious practice, and celebrations (Easter, Holi, Passover, Fourth of July, Eid). And like individual stories, stories of us can inspire, teach, offer hope, or advise caution. We often adapt old stories to new challenges. The Puritans retold the Exodus story as a source of courage and justification when they colonized North America; African Americans told it again when they fought for their civil rights in the freedom movement.

We can bound an "us" very broadly, extending membership to people with few shared values and experiences, as when a president begins a speech with "my fellow Americans." Alternatively, we can narrow the "us" to those with specific shared values and experiences, as at a family meeting or among workmates or day care partners. Broad bounding can be inclusive, narrow bounding, exclusive. The appropriateness of either depends on the purpose for which the "us" is created, the values they share, and the agency those values enable. A story of us may articulate values that transcend one's community, but it must be included, shared by the community. A story of us can also be told to distinguish our community from another, reducing uncertainty about what to expect from those with whom we interact. Social scientists often describe a story of us as a collective identity.[25]

For a collection of people to become an "us" requires an interpreter of shared experience, a storyteller. In a social movement, the interpretation of the movement's new experience is a critical leadership function. And like the story of self, the story of us is built from the founding, the choices made, the challenges faced, the outcomes experienced, the lessons learned.

Stories of us also bring attention to the sources of hope, and often power, that those in the group share. Classic eve-of-battle speeches by generals, such as in Shakespeare's *Henry V*, and halftime speeches by coaches, such as Al Pacino's in *Any Given Sunday*, don't promise victory, and most don't even mention the opposition. Rather they focus on enabling people to experience the creation of real value that is within their hands, win or lose. Shakespeare's King Henry V, for example, stirs hope in his men's hearts by offering them a different view of themselves. No longer are they a few bedraggled soldiers led by a young and inexperienced king in an obscure corner of France, about to be wiped out by an overwhelming force. Now they are a "happy few," united with their king in solidarity, holding an opportunity to grasp immortality in their hands, to become legends in their own time, a legacy for their children and grandchildren.[26] This is their time!

Stories of Now

If not now, when? On August 23, 1963, when Dr. King delivered the speech known as "I Have a Dream" to some 250,000 at the Capitol Mall, and to the nation, he described the purpose to be,

> to remind America of the fierce urgency of Now. This is no time to engage in the luxury of cooling off or to take the tranquilizing drug of gradualism. Now is the time to make real the promises of democracy. Now is the time to rise from the dark and desolate valley of segregation to the sunlit path of racial justice. Now is the time to lift our nation from the quicksand of racial injustice to the solid rock of brotherhood. Now is the time to make justice a reality for all of God's children.

When we recall this as the "I Have a Dream" speech, we misremember the prophetic voice in which it was given with its proper title: "The Fierce Urgency of Now." Prophets don't make people comfortable. They make people uncomfortable. Before bringing alive the dream, Dr. King brought alive the nightmare. He confronted us with the nightmare of "whites only" signs across the South for water fountains, lunch counters, hotels, and poll booths. That summer, Mississippi NAACP president Medgar Evers had been assassinated.

Four little girls had been murdered when their Birmingham church was dynamited. And in the same city, police dogs and fire hoses had been turned on children marching to demand their rights. The favored chant of the movement had changed from "Freedom" sometime to "Freedom Now!"

This is the experience a story of now is intended to create. And unlike stories of self and stories of us that bring experiences of moments in the past into the present, a story of now is in the present: it is a challenge we face, a choice we can make, and an outcome that may result. In fact, a story of now is when story and strategy come together—when the *why* we need to do what we need to do (story) joins the *how* we could do what we need to do (strategy). I discuss strategy more fully in the next chapter, but a key element in hope is a plausible vision of how we could get from here to there.

We spell out the urgent challenge or threat to values we hold, that we share. It may be urgent because of need, or it may be urgent because of opportunity. We ask people to make a choice—an ask that also must be specific, not any one of fifty-three things that you would be comfortable doing. The reality is that people will commit their most precious resource—their time— not because it's easy but because it's valuable, because they can do something that could make a real difference to the desired outcome. A choice is something like, "Can we commit to boycotting every single bus in Montgomery, Alabama, until we win? Yes or no?"

The story of now is that moment in which story (why) and strategy (how) overlap and in which, as poet Seamus Heaney writes, "Justice can rise up, and hope and history rhyme."[27] For the claim to be credible, the action must begin right here, right now, in this room, with action each one of us can take. It's the story of a credible strategy, with an account of how starting with who and where we are, and how we can, step-by-step, get to where we want to go. Our action can call forth the actions of others, and their actions can call others, and together these actions can carry the day.

Linking Self, Us, and Now

Public narrative only becomes a leadership practice when we link all three stories together into a coherent, cohesive, and compelling values-based narrative. A linked narrative communicates why you care (story of self), why we care (story of us), and why we are called to respond to threats to those values (story of now). The goal is to create an experience of your values (story of self) and the values of the people you hope will join you in collective action (story of us) with the values being threatened by the urgent challenge(s) you're facing that require hopeful action (story of now).

All three stories are interdependent in practice, much like a three-legged stool, because each story part must be strong for the linked story to stand. Imagine that you have strong stories of self and now but a weak story of us: your listeners may understand what you care about and what you hope to do about it, but if they don't feel connected to the story and to each other, why would they join you? If you have strong stories of us and now with a weak story of self, the group may feel connected to each other and compelled to take collective action, but what reason do they have to trust and join *you*? As a leader, you've failed to offer a sense of who you are and why you care, or to establish any kind of moral authority. Finally, if you have strong stories of self and us but a weak story of now, then you've succeeded in bringing a group together—one that feels connected and hopeful about itself! But then what? If you're not drawing people together for a *shared purpose*—to act and face a challenge of some kind—then it may be a fun time, but it's not *leadership*.

In a linked narrative, the story of self, story of us, and story of now are woven together by values. This narrative communicates the speaker's values through the story of self, lifts up the values that connect members of the "us" with each other, and that are challenged by the story of now. This is called "values coherence": when the same or similar values are experienced in all three stories.

When people first try to link their narrative together, it's not uncommon for one or more of the stories to deteriorate, to be given very little time, or to drop out completely. This can be for several reasons (e.g., time, lack of understanding of the craft, wanting to share less vulnerability). But the story of self is foundational to a linked narrative: it's where the values running through the story are rooted. If a narrative has a strong self, it can potentially ground a weaker us and now; however, a weak self affects the strength of a narrative and can make it ineffective. It's in the story of self that a leader establishes their moral authority, helping people understand who they are and why they care. While every story of self may not be an origin story, we find that origin stories are the most powerful in enabling people to connect with the speaker; when we know how, where, and when they learned to care about their values, that foundation connects the rest of the narrative too. It is also sometimes easier for people to articulate their sources of hurt than their sources of hope, yet it's from the story of hope that they have so much to teach us.

As we noted earlier, public narrative is a *framework* not a formula, so the order of the stories (self, us, now) can be varied and played with, just as long as they make sense and flow together in a clear, cohesive way. Nor is public narrative a way of asking people to do you a favor or manipulating people to do what you want; rather, it's about communicating what's important to you, calling on people who share those values, and offering them a *choice* and an *opportunity* to act on those values to take hopeful and meaningful action in the face of an urgent challenge. An effective linked narrative should answer the following questions for the audience (the "us") whom the speaker is trying to call to action:

> *Story of Self:* Do we get what this person is all about? Do we know what they value and care about and why? When did they learn to care?
>
> *Story of Us:* Do we get what we're about? Do people in this room share that same value? How do we know that? Did the story make us feel more connected to each other? What moments did they share about the group that show we care?
>
> *Story of Now:* Do we know what challenge they're asking us to act on? Is it clear what they want us to do and what impact it will have? Do we feel compelled to act because something we hold dear is threatened? Do we know what happens if we don't act (*the nightmare*)? What could the future look like if we do act (*the dream*)? Is there a sense of urgency? Must we act now?

The Challenge of Narrative Leadership

The Empathetic Bridge

Although every "now" moment could be an opportunity to practice leadership by enabling others—their "us"—to respond to the disruption with agency as opposed to reacting with fear, we can use an "empathetic bridge" to focus specifically on the interaction between "self" and "us." We pay particular attention to the actual words used to communicate in such moments, planned or not—words do matter. We do this by focusing on four particularly challenging and, at the same time, most widely experienced moments: loss, difference, domination, and change. This approach is grounded in a respectful engagement. We know how it feels to be respected: it is to be seen, to be heard, and to be valued—not to be pitied or rescued. We use the empathetic bridge with respect, drawing on our own resources to enable others to draw on theirs.

The empathetic bridge has four elements (Figure 3.4):

- **Acknowledge the challenge.** Do not ignore it, deny its importance, or tell the other person not to feel bad. These words dismiss or belittle real pain, fear, or anger. Respect requires recognizing the hurt of others.
- **Offer empathy, but do not claim it.** Do not say, "I know just how you feel," because you don't. Speak rather from your own experience. People often respond to a friend's news that a loved one got diagnosed with cancer by sharing a story from their own experience. Making yourself

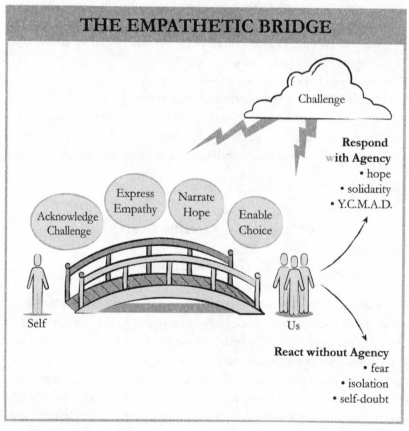

Figure 3.4 The Empathetic Bridge. *Source*: Steve Downer of the Difference

empathetically available can create a brave space within which others can experience validation for their own feelings.

- **Narrate hope.** Don't promise everything will be okay. It may not be. And you can't promise it anyway. Don't promise that something or someone will miraculously save the day. In our own lives and the life of our community, we have sources of hope that have enabled us to get this far: in our faith, our relationships, our improbable life experiences. As Maimonides suggested, hope lives in the space between certainty and fantasy: the possible if not the probable.[28] We can elicit sources of hope from within our own life experiences and those of others.

- **Offer a choice.** When we experience a deeply disruptive blow, we can lose our sense of agency or our ability to choose our future. The last step in the empathetic bridge is to restore choice. It is not by telling others what they should do, must do, or will do. Instead, it is in offering possible choices to your "us" that they can make now. It may be a choice of how to respond emotionally to what has happened. Do we let it overwhelm us so much that we must hide, or do we discover that we can find the sources of courage and solidarity to face it?

Although these elements are evident in Robert F. Kennedy's speech delivering the news of Dr. Martin Luther King Jr.'s assassination to a Black audience in Indianapolis, Indiana, on April 4, 1968, a more recent example is the address by Jacinda Ardern, the prime minister of New Zealand, to the nation on March 29, 2019, following the murder of fifty Muslim men, women, and children in Christ Church on March 15.

In this way we can draw on the empathetic bridge to equip leaders to enable their "us" to respond to these four challenges. Each of the conceptual frameworks we use, however, is only a lens through which we may choose to look at a complex reality to the extent it proves useful. A single moment of disruption can be looked at through multiple lenses, each suggesting different ways to respond. Change, for example, often involves loss; difference often involves power. Using different lenses to understand a moment of disruption can illuminate perspectives, nuances, and connections that you may not have noticed before and that can turn out to have critical bearing on the problem you're trying to solve.

Leadership Challenges: How to Restore Agency

Loss

We begin with the challenge of loss. Narrative psychologist Dan McAdams identifies two ways people may interpret the experience of loss. One is *contaminative*: the experience of loss is so hurtful that it becomes predictive—good things will always go bad, I will always be a victim, etc. McAdams calls the other way to respond *redemptive*: the loss is real, painful, and lonely, but it can also become a source of learning, growth, discovery, and resilience.[29]

Difference

We then turn to the challenge of difference: how widely or narrowly to bound the *us* with whom we engage. The leadership challenge is to approach bounding strategically based on the core values that members share and the agency to be enabled. Narrow bounding is rooted more in multiple kinds of shared experiences, as with members of a particular team. Broad bounding is rooted in fewer kinds of shared experience but may be more inclusive, as with an entire school. Neither is good or bad. The objective is to evoke values shared by the "us" to enable it to act with agency. We may also consider the depth of the shared experience in which our "us" is rooted. We may experience moments of parenting, for example, quite deeply no matter how widely shared. We may also experience neighborliness quite lightly, even though many of these experiences are shared.

Domination

The challenge of domination occurs in any moment in which a dominant and a subordinate meet. Drawing on the work of political scientist James Scott,[30] we can distinguish among four different stories being told in such a moment: the public and hidden stories of the subordinate and the public and hidden stories of the dominant. The question is how to use narrative to enable the agency of the subordinate and, at times, even the dominant on a continuum from compliance to resistance. When and how do we choose to comply or resist?

Choosing is a matter of responding with agency rather than reacting. Power depends on strategy—can we turn the resources we have into the power we need to win? Similar choices can be made on the dominant side as well.

Change

Finally, with the challenge of unexpected change, we ask how leaders can enable their "us" to respond mindfully to this disruptive change. This does not refer to the change we seek but rather to change that is thrust upon us. We consider four positions: (1) deny the reality of change by insisting on the old story, (2) deny the reality of the old story, insisting on an entirely new story, (3) accept elements of change to the extent they can be accommodated within the old story, or (4) accept elements of the old story to the extent they can be adapted to a new story.

These four leadership challenges describe the kinds of disruptions many of us have experienced in our own lives. Here we look at them as leadership challenges: how can we enable others—and not just ourselves—to respond with agency?

Practicing Public Narrative

As we learn to practice public narrative, we can also turn moments that have been influences on us—some of which we may have forgotten—into resources for us. When asked why we do what we do, we often respond, "I always wanted to be a teacher." Always? But unless you came out of the womb with a book in your hands, you discovered your calling primarily through experiences like those we have discussed in this chapter.

When it comes to stories of self, origin stories really matter. Our own stories, like any story, begin in the beginning. We begin forming our values early in life through the challenges we face growing up, engaging with others, dealing with stress, and experiencing our own value—or not. These experiences often occur with siblings, parents, grandparents, aunts and uncles, teachers, and classmates. When we are recognized, experience being loved, or otherwise experience success, these encounters may be very affirming, or they may be negative. We may have been excluded, required to shoulder responsibility beyond our years, or experienced abuse in many forms. Although our experience of our formative years may have been quite hurtful, it is unlikely our origin story would stop there. Most of us have had moments of hurt or we wouldn't believe the world needs fixing. But if we hadn't had moments of hope, we wouldn't be trying to fix it.

A mom comforts us, a teacher sees us, a sibling supports us, the natural world heals us, our faith uplifts us, or we find sources of resilience that surprise us. It is often in these experiences of hurt and hope, of wounds and scars, that we learn to find value and create value with others. While life may not unfold in a straight line, these moments are nevertheless where we begin. Astronauts, surgeons, carpenters, and organizers all have origin stories. These stories are the kind of experience that can find the deepest resonance with the experience of others, and we may discover values we share despite sharply different occupations, nationalities, political preferences, or faith traditions. This can be a very empowering discovery.

Telling about a story is different from telling a story. When we tell a story, we bring the past into the present or the distant into the proximate. We enable the listener to enter its time and place with us, see what we see, hear what we hear, feel what we feel. An actor friend once told me the key was to speak entirely in the present tense and avoid using the word "and." I step into the room. It is dark. I hear a sound.

You cannot learn to practice public narrative looking into the mirror. We need coaching. A Yiddish riddle asks, "Who discovered water?" The answer is, "I don't know, but it wasn't a fish." We are all fish in the water of our own stories, so we need a coach or an interlocutor to ask us the probing questions that can enable us to recall specific moments in which we learned to care and learned to hope, moments we may even have forgotten about. This can be uncomfortable, even scary, but the reality is that learning is often uncomfortable because we are setting out beyond our comfort zones. Pedagogical scholar Lev Vygotsky's insight into the role of discomfort in the social nature of learning describes what he calls the "zone of proximal development."[31] For a child to move beyond their comfort zone, the affirmation and challenge that can be offered by another person is critical for the child's development— often the role of a parent. And it isn't only children who hesitate to take a step beyond their comfort zone.

A coach can motivate us to step out of the comfort zone into a zone of proximal development and by offering us challenge and support. A coach may connect the dots we haven't connected because we are so within our own story that we have not learned to articulate them.

As I shared in my introduction, you can't learn to practice public narrative, or any other practice, simply by reading about it. Like learning to ride a bike, it requires getting on, falling off, learning, and getting back on again. You've been reading lots of explanations about how it works, so now it's time to observe a model, debrief it, and then you may be ready to go practice with a partner yourself.

James Croft crafted this five-minute public narrative when he was a student. His story calls us to respond to the crisis of suicide among gay youth.[32] As you read James's story, or watch it, ask yourself these questions: When is he telling a story of self, a story of us, and a story of now? Why does he choose the moments that he chooses? Why all the details? What are the values this story evokes?

James Croft: Modeling Public Narrative

6.12 seconds. That's about how long it takes to fall 604 feet. And 604 feet is about how far Tyler Clemente fell after he jumped off the George Washington Bridge. Now as we know, he took his own life because live video footage of him having a romantic encounter with another man was streamed live on the Internet by his college roommate. Just one on a very long list of young people who have taken their lives because of anti-LGBT bullying in the past few weeks.

Now I never experienced anything like what Tyler went through when I was at school, but I was bullied for being gay. You see, when I was a kid, I was a ballet dancer, and every week I squeezed into a leotard and blue shiny hot pants. It was, uh, quite an outfit, and I spent an evening practicing demi-pliés and pirouettes, and I loved it. I loved the discipline, the music played on the old piano, the feel of the wood beneath my feet. I even secretly quite liked the outfit.

But my schoolmates and some of my teachers didn't like ballet as much as I did, and one of my teachers, a PE teacher, used to make fun of me. He used to say how girly I was, how dancing is not something that boys should do. I remember the sneer on his face as I walked past, and I remember that he was the first person to call me a fag, which at seven years old, I didn't really understand. I remember in high school how "gay" was only ever used as a term of abuse, and I remember one cold morning sitting in assembly while the principal intoned, "Homosexuals deserve our pity and our prayers." And I sat among hundreds of other boys thinking that I was alone in the world, and that I was the only one who had this . . . problem.

Now not everyone may have experienced something like that, but we all know, I think, what it means to feel alone—to feel like there's no one on our side. Perhaps you were too tall, and the short kids made fun of you. Or perhaps you were too short, and you got it from the taller ones. Or perhaps you were too smart, or too dumb, or from the wrong side of town, or the wrong race. We all know, I think, even if just for a moment, what it feels like to think that there's no one on your side. To think that no one has your back . . .

And all of us, if there are young people in our lives that we care about, can agree that we don't want this to happen to them. Imagine, if you can, what it must be like to come home and see a strange shape hanging from a tree in your backyard, twisting in the wind, the creak of the branch that bends beneath the weight, and that feeling in your gut as you get closer and you realize what it is hanging there, who it is—who it was. Because that was Seth Walsh, 13, who hung himself from a tree in his backyard. It was Billy Lucas who hung himself at his grandmother's house, and it was Raymond Chase who hung himself in his dorm, and it could have been your brother, your sister, your son, your daughter, or your friend. It could have been one of us . . . .

So, I know—I—I only came out in March this year, after ten years, ten years after I first told my parents I thought I was gay. And in those ten years I lost a lot of opportunities to make a difference. I was a high school teacher, and every day I wasn't out was a day I deprived a gay student of a positive role model. And I'm not willing to waste any more time. I have to act now. We have to act now. Because it isn't enough to let these things happen and then mourn them afterwards. We need to capture these kids before they jump.

And there is something we can do to help, as a start. Journalist Dan Savage just started a campaign, the It Gets Better Campaign, to send messages of hope to teenagers who are being bullied because they're gay, or for whatever reason, that they should have hope for their future, that they do have something to live for. And I think that if we made such a video, as Harvard students with glittering careers ahead of us and sparkling degrees, that we could make a difference.

So, we need people to hold a camera, to share their stories, to do editing and sound, to stand in a big group, and say it gets better. No contribution is too small. And if you want to get involved, and you're an undergraduate, talk to Tevin, and he'll tell you how to get involved. If you're a graduate student, or if you just wanna come along, from 5 to 7 p.m. in the Elliott Lyman room in Longfellow Hall at the Education School's campus . . .

Stand up and say, we're standing with these kids. We've got your back. Let's catch them before they jump.

Debriefing James Croft

When is he telling a story of self, a story of us, a story of now? He begins with a story-of-now moment: "6.12 seconds. That's about how long it takes to fall 604 feet. And 604 feet is about how far Tyler Clemente fell after he jumped off the George Washington Bridge."

Why is this a story of now? He confronts us with an urgent challenge: the 6.12 seconds it took for this young man to fall from the bridge. We react to this image in ways that make the challenge feel real, urgent, and compelling. We are shown, rather than told about the reality of suicide among gay youth. Stories move by replacing adjectives with images. We begin to get it.

Where does he go next? The ballet. As vivid as it is, why does he begin his story of self with that moment? He is determined not to become an iconic victim, so he starts by taking us to a moment of joy, a joy we feel. It's as if he were saying, "Look, I'm a real human being, capable of joy, delight in colors, sounds, love for what I do, for who I am."

Then, in sharp contrast, he takes us to the moment when he was seven and his gym teacher hurls the insult at him. We flinch. We experience the insult. See the impact. And we react most likely with a flash of anger—or, at the very least, concern. We begin to get why he is doing what he's doing.

We then see him in the moment when he is sitting in the auditorium among hundreds. Yet he is all alone in his reaction to specifically demeaning words of the principal. What if all we had heard was "the principal spoke derogatorily of gay people"? He's showing us, not telling us.

Then he makes a shift. He begins to shift to a story of us. We may not have had the identical experience, but he asks, have we never felt alone, isolated, fearful, without support? In this way he calls to mind those moments of our own, how they felt, how much someone on your side matters. We begin to become a broadly yet deeply bounded "us," connected with each other.

Now that Croft has us, he takes us to another more intense now moment, a moment we experience together: a body hangs from a tree, the branch creaks, the wind blows. We feel dread, heartsick, sorrow as we realize "what it was . . . who it was." These are not data points. They are human beings with names—Seth Walsh, Billy Lucas, Raymond Chase. They could have been our brother, or sister, they could have been one of us.

And isn't that image of bodies hanging from trees a familiar one, at least in the United States? Between 1882 and 1968, 3,446 African Americans were lynched in the United States, an image we are shown in Billie Holiday's singing of "Strange Fruit" with "blood at the leaf and blood at the root."[33]

Croft doesn't have to say a word about injustice. He confronts us with the image of injustice. He shows. He doesn't have to tell.

Croft then returns to his story of self. He has more work to do. We haven't heard much about hope so far. He begins by referring to the moment he came out only a few months before. Although he had told his parents he was gay ten years before, he had not publicly come out during his time as a high school teacher, thus depriving gay kids of a role model. In part, his failure to act then is why he needs to act now, and that is exactly what he is doing.

But wait a moment. As a leader he's calling us to act now, something he didn't do for ten years. Why confess his failure, his vulnerability? Won't we lose confidence in him as a leader? To the contrary, despite his failure to act then, he has found the courage to act now. Because he failed before, we can find hope in the fact he found the courage to act now. Because he found the courage, so can we. By owning his vulnerability, we can learn from his courage—a critical dynamic when it comes to leadership.

What can we learn from a perfect person? To be perfect? Where do I start? This is one reason I've learned so much from the story of Moses. He is so flawed, yet his struggles to overcome those flaws teach us so much.

We have experienced the challenge, we have experienced the hope, so what is the ask?

Croft gets us there through a story of now: "We must catch these kids before they jump!" He offers us a path to action we can take, should we choose to. We can join the It Gets Better campaign by making videos of hope and solidarity for gay youth feeling isolated and hopeless. It is specific, something we can do, and suited for his "us" with their "sparkling degrees." There is nothing generic in his ask—he's not saying that someone can make a difference, but that you can make a difference. And his ask is part of a larger campaign, encouraging people to join an effort they believe really could make a difference.

Croft accepts the strategic responsibility that comes with leadership to offer us a specific way forward. We know where to meet, when to meet, with whom to meet, and how we can contribute. We can catch these kids before they jump.

What are the values that link the parts of this public narrative into a coherent whole—values that link Croft's story of self, story of us, and story of now? Remember, values are experiential. We experience values of respect, solidarity, inclusion, compassion, and responsibility. We experience moments in which these values were challenged or threatened, or when their opposites were present (e.g., isolation, exclusion, scorn, cowardice), and these moments contrast with moments of hope, when these values were present, powerful, and motivating.

Finally, by looking at Croft's public narrative, we can see how it's a framework, not a formula. Unlike Obama's 2004 talk, the first seven minutes are not a linear self, us, and now. Instead, Croft moves back and forth between them. He begins with a story of now (6.12 seconds, Tyler Clemente jumping off the bridge, the reality of gay teens committing suicide), moves to a story of self that shares his own experiences (ballet dancer, gym teacher, moment in the auditorium). He then goes to a story of us (asking the audience to recall their experience of bullying, isolation, and exclusion), then goes back to the story of now (finding bodies hanging from trees), touches on the us (imagine if it were your son, daughter, friend, etc.), then briefly returns to the self (his late coming-out and depriving students of a role model) before moving into his call to action (story of now), asking people to join with him to become a part of the It Gets Better campaign.

Conclusion

My first teaching foray outside the English-speaking world was in Amman, Jordan, in an organizing workshop with some fifty NGO leaders in collaboration with my colleague Nisreen Haj Ahmad. I was warned that, in this world, people would never tell a story of self. This was despite the rich Arab tradition of *hakawatis* or storytellers famous for leaving listeners hanging so they would return the next night to the coffeehouse to learn what happened next. Especially, I was told, men would not do this.

Indeed, one of the men insisted firmly that he had no story to tell about why he had become an environmental activist, despite work by our best coach, community leader Samar Dudin. But the next morning, this man arrived with the news that he had indeed found his story. He shared with the whole workshop:

> I grew up in a village where my father had olive trees. He loved his trees. They were his pride and joy. The Qur'an tells us that even in combat one is to spare the innocent and the trees. Trees are sources of life. Then, one day, the bulldozers came, tore out all the trees, and my father fell on the ground on his back, tears in his eyes. And that's when I knew I had to save the trees.

He received a standing ovation.

I was back in Amman about a year ago, where Nisreen and her colleagues have been doing great work for the last ten years. I was to give a talk about organizing to what turned out to be a paying audience of some four hundred. In my talk I told this story, and a hand went up. "That's me. That's my story! Just as it is!"

Leadership is a relational practice. And as Rabbi Hillel observed, we must make ourselves—our full selves—accessible to others for anyone to enter a relationship with us. Our story of self gives our identity coherence—a past, a present, a possible future—as we evolve our self dynamically over the course of our lives. But we do not constitute ourselves by ourselves. Instead, we articulate ourselves in relationship to others, how they see us, how they interact with us and us with them. Leadership requires enabling others to work together. So we tell a story of us. Leadership also requires action—not in the distant future—but in the present. So we tell a story of now.

We turn now to strategy, story's partner, to learn how we can enable others to respond to challenge by turning what we have into what we need to get what we want.

4

Strategizing

In the last chapter, on narrative, I focused on the "why" question: why we feel the way we do about things, a matter of the heart. In the next chapter, on action, I focus on the "what" question: what we do about things, a matter of the hands. In this chapter, on strategy, I focus on the "how" question: how we think about things, a matter of the head.

Although I grew up like many, I suspect, strategizing to get what I wanted, I only began to learn strategic craft when I began to do it: in the civil rights movement, in the UFW, and in the world of electoral politics. Sometimes it worked, other times it didn't, but learning from success and failure informs the craft of strategizing.

As I recounted in the Introduction, one goal of the Mississippi Summer Project was to support the organizing of the Mississippi Freedom Democratic Party (MFDP). We would go to the Democratic National Convention in Atlantic City in August to demand that the Freedom Democrats be seated to replace the segregated—and all-white—delegation sent by the racist Mississippi Democratic Party.

Our focus was clear: organize in Mississippi, mobilize for Atlantic City, and impact our politics nationally. We could win the freedom to organize in Mississippi at the same time. The leadership of the Summer Project had linked who we were, what we would do, and the outcome we could achieve—strategy! Even though the summer began tragically with the murders of Chaney, Schwerner, and Goodman—and much other violence—we achieved our initial objective: we organized 80,000 people to register with the MFDP. By August, thirty-eight local chapters had held precinct caucuses, county caucuses, and a state convention where they elected a slate of sixty-eight delegates headed by Ms. Fannie Lou Hamer. Ms. Hamer was a courageous, passionate, and powerfully eloquent organizer from the Mississippi Delta who had endured unspeakable violence at the hands of the local authorities when she tried to register to vote.

For support, we had organized sympathetic Democratic convention delegates from California, Wisconsin, and across the country. Our outreach to the nation began with Ms. Hamer's widely televised testimony before the Credentials Committee. But she only got halfway through her riveting account when the cameras shut down. President Lyndon Johnson, who had been watching her testimony, suddenly called an emergency press conference in the White House Rose Garden. Despite the righteousness of our cause, the president, fearful of alienating Southern Democrats in November, had decided to stop the MFDP. After the press conference, he assigned vice presidential nominee Senator Hubert Humphrey, a very well-credentialed liberal, to disorganize our support. Within hours, our allies began to withdraw one by one. They had been threatened with political reprisals, loss of their jobs, and exclusion from subsequent Democratic Party activities.

We lost.

Despite an MFDP sit-in on the convention floor with borrowed credentials, some organizers gave in to despair. Others gave over to rage. Affirmed in their cynicism, some were content to denounce the system with greater vehemence. But others—me included, along with most of the MFDP delegation—learned a critical lesson about power: Just as might doesn't make right, right doesn't make might. Enabling right to make might is what strategy can be all about. Or as theologian Paul Tillich taught, power without love can never be just, but love without power can never achieve justice.[1]

What Is Strategy?

Strategy is how you turn what you have into what you need to get what you want. We all know how to do this. If you have ever overslept, missed your bus, and needed to get to work or school on time, you crafted a plan B or a workaround. Whether you called a Lyft, borrowed a bike, called on a friend with a car, or something else, you were strategizing—figuring out how to turn the resources you had into the power, or capacity, you needed to get what you want. Like storytelling, we strategize every day. We are purposeful creatures who come up with plans for the next few minutes, the next hour, the next day, and the next year. Because the world is a contingent place, a place of continual change, some intended, some not, some random, some not, reality often disrupts our plans. It's not that the plan was bad (unless it didn't allow for change), but the future is uncertain. So implicitly, if not explicitly, we learn to strategize throughout our lives.

The word "strategy" comes from the Greek *stratos*—the word for army based on *strateo,* spreading out, like on a field of battle—and *agein*—the word for leading. The general was called *strategos,* an army leader. The *strategos* would go to the top of a hill and evaluate the resources on both sides; reflect on opportunities and constraints imposed by the battlefield, the time of day, the strengths and limitations of his own troops and those of his opponent; and consider how to deploy his troops in ways most likely to achieve victory. The *strategos* needed a good overview of the field, as well as intimate knowledge of each army's capacities, and details of the streams, bridges, forests, trees, and overall terrain. Another way to describe what the *strategos* does is to hypothesize a theory of change: how to get from here, a moment of uncertainty, to where we need to be, which is winning.

The soldiers down on the field were described as *taktikos,* skilled in the art of arrangement, putting things in order, or deployment. They were the ones who had to translate the theory of the *strategos* into action (Figure 4.1).

Figure 4.1 Strategy and Tactics. *Source*: Steve Downer of the Difference

Tactics are the specific actions through which strategy is embodied and enacted. An activity, from shooting an arrow to hosting a house meeting, to organizing a rally, is not a tactic unless it is strategic: implementing and at the same time testing a theory of change. Launching a petition, for example, or any action done because "that's what we always do" is not a tactic because it is not strategic. When people describe recent mobilizations as tactics in search of a strategy, they are describing habitual or reactive activities uninformed by any theory of change.

Strategy is not big or tactics, small. They are different. We strategize to develop a hypothesis about how we could use our resources to achieve valued change: a "theory of change." A theory of change, in turn, can guide our choices about targeting, timing, and tactics. On what do we focus, targeting deployment of our resources to get the most leverage: a strategic goal? How can we harmonize the temporal rhythm of our campaign with that of the world around us, as well as our personal rhythms? When do we start, when do we stop, do we go fast or slow, short term or long term? How do we deploy tactics to implement our theory of change and, at the same time, test it, adapt it, or even change it based on new learning?

Strategizing is also highly contextualized in a unique way. It requires seeing trees and forest at the same time. The *strategos* on the hilltop has a great overview. The *taktikos* in the valley has an intimate view of the field of battle. The problem is when a fog may settle between the hilltop and the valley. The *strategos* imagines he knows the whole truth. The *taktikos* imagines that he knows the whole truth. Strategizing requires both truths—intimate knowledge of the context along with a capacity to put the context in context.

Learning to Strategize

Having learned the importance of strategy, my real training in strategic craft began in the UFW. One of Cesar Chavez's real gifts—rooted in the street smarts that came with needing to do a lot with a little—was his ability to strategize. I was in awe of it. But this gift only became a strength of the UFW because Cesar shared it, engaged others in it, and challenged others to learn it. So, the UFW became a venue in which many of us learned to strategize. Cesar blended his street smarts with study of the lives of the saints, ten years of organizing with Fred Ross and Saul Alinsky, Gandhi's teachings evident in the civil rights movement, a mastery of cultural resources, and a commitment to constant adaptive learning. If civic associations were, according to Tocqueville, "great free schools of democracy," then the UFW was a great free school of strategy.

The question of power was central to our work, a legacy of Alinsky's focus on power. But this was power based on people, not money. We strategized within four venues: strikes, boycotts, politics, and the law. We contested the growers for power in each venue. Our primary source of power was our constituency, their depth of commitment, their hopefulness, and their readiness to sacrifice. We organized a secondary source of power in our urban supporters who could organize grape boycotts by stopping supermarkets from selling them. We learned to manage alliances within the labor movement, the churches, liberals, and the Latino world without losing our own autonomy: we drew resources from each of them without falling into dependency on any one of them. My own assignment from 1968 to 1970 and 1973 to 1975 was to organize Canadians to stop buying California grapes in Toronto and Montreal, the third- and fifth-largest grape markets in North America, respectively. Organizing in Canada also gave me a uniquely valuable opportunity to learn how unions, politics, and democratic government could work far better than they did here at home.

Although the challenges were great, figuring out how to turn lemons into lemonade can also be fun. Cesar used to love carom shots—as in pool, when you hit one ball to move another—and enjoyed talking about "killing two birds with one stone and keeping the stone." My school of strategizing was in this setting of widely diverse cultural, political, and economic contexts. We learned to do community organizing, workplace organizing, urban boycott organizing, and electoral organizing.

Our Pilgrimage to Sacramento was timed to coincide with the Schenley boycott, and with a visit to the city of Delano by Senator Bobby Kennedy, inspired by Dr. King's Selma-to-Montgomery march, and aligned with the Lenten season and resulted in our first contract. Cesar's fast for nonviolence defanged growers' claims of union violence, gave our grape boycott a critical boost, and recommitted everyone in the movement to a longer, deeper, and more disciplined struggle. The grape boycott itself enabled supporters across North America to translate their moral support into real economic power. Learning how this worked was my second school of strategy.

After I left the UFW in 1981, I found a third school of strategy in the world of California electoral politics. I was introduced to electoral organizing in the 1968 Robert Kennedy for President campaign and had worked on three of Jerry Brown's campaigns (one gubernatorial [1978] and two presidential [1976 and 1980]), but my technical learning began with San Francisco political consultant Clint Reilly. Clint had entered and dropped out of a Roman Catholic seminary, and his first campaign was trying to elect a Bay Area peace candidate, the priest who had been his mentor. He had also supported the UFW in a 1972 campaign to recall the governor of Arizona. By 1982, Clint had emerged as a Bay Area campaign pro who also recognized that organizing skills—volunteer recruitment, leadership development, and voter mobilization—could be of real value in campaigns. His experiment with organizing tactics began by working with former UFW organizers Larry Tramutola, Scott Washburn, and Fred Ross, Jr. to conduct a house meeting drive that thwarted an attempt to recall then-mayor Dianne Feinstein and, instead, solidified her political base.

"Studying" with Clint, I learned to set vote goals, distinguish motivation from persuasion, segment the electorate by likelihood of voting, and use digital technology to enhance the effectiveness of electoral organizing. California was far ahead of the rest of the country in digitizing voter information. This had contributed to a narrowed focus on most-likely voters—who tended to be older, whiter, and richer—while marginalizing everyone else. But in the 1983 San Diego mayoral election, we devised an "occasional voter" strategy. We could identify the people who always voted and recruit them to join us in organizing their neighbors who were identified as only voting occasionally. We could provide them with lists of the names, addresses, and phone numbers of each occasional voter in their precinct. Instead of having us try to motivate four hundred or five hundred people in a precinct, these precinct leaders could focus on eighty or ninety voters for whom it might make a real difference. We could focus on Latino and Black precincts where voters generally supported our candidates but voter turnout was low. Instead of persuasion, we would focus on motivation. This approach to combining sophisticated digital targeting with solid grassroots organizing would, years later, inform the Obama campaign.

Years later in the 1990s when working on my PhD in sociology, I was happy to find that a study of the farmworker movement had become part of the social movement canon. But I was shocked to find that this then-classic article by J. Craig Jenkins and Charles Perrow argued that the UFW's victories—victories in which I had played a part—could be explained by the conditions (opportunities, resources) at the time, not by anything we had done![2]

This turned out to be a microcosm of a much larger problem in the social movement literature, which focused mainly on conditions that made movements probable rather than on leadership who finds ways to figure out how to make the improbable possible. Yet this move, of making the improbable possible, is at the heart of strategic leadership practice, especially in highly volatile social movement settings. How this imaginative process works became the focus of my master's thesis, my first academic article, called "Resources and Resourcefulness" (2000), and eventually, my dissertation, and finally my book *Why David Sometimes Wins* (2009).

How Strategy Works

Strategizing, like storytelling, is a verb. We strategize in the present, relying on what we've learned from the past and imagining a future that remains unknown. Strategizing is the practice of adapting to unexpected opportunities and challenges far more than it is planning and implementing the plan. As organization scholar Henry Mintzberg describes it, strategy is like a potter interacting with the clay on the wheel.[3] Although our goal remains clear, we are (or should be) constantly adapting to new information: sudden opportunities or obstacles, change in the resource in the environment, the actions and reactions of others, discoveries about our own limitations and capabilities.

Strategy, like music, only exists in time. That's what makes strategy dynamic: opportunities—or obstacles—may occur suddenly. The same resources may acquire greater or lesser value not because of anything we do but because of a change in the context. A full granary, for example, acquires greater value in a famine, affording greater power for its owner. A close election creates opportunity for political leaders who can influence swing voters. A labor shortage creates opportunities for workers to get more for their labor.

Strategy, finally, is dynamic because the actions and reactions of others, especially when oppositional, alter the environment. In contexts where rules, resources, and interests are fixed, we may use analytic tools such as game theory to inform our strategizing. But in settings where rules, resources, and interests are emergent, ambiguous and contested—such as social movements—strategizing becomes more of an exercise in creative, yet grounded, imagination. Strategizing is a creative, dynamic, and agile process of adapting intentional action in response to ever changing conditions. It is a motivated, intentional, proactive, creative, and nested practice.

Strategy Is Motivated

We strategize, as with storytelling, in response to immediate or anticipated disruption. Stories provide the emotional resources to meet the challenge of responding hopefully rather than reacting fearfully. We strategize in response to the cognitive challenge of learning how to turn the resources at hand into the power we need to achieve our goals. Because we are creatures of habit, we are usually only motivated to tell stories or devise strategy when there is a problem to be solved. Only then, because we must, do we pay attention, look around, and decide what we must do. Storytelling facilitates our emotional response by reminding us of our "why." Strategizing facilitates our cognitive response by opening a pathway to our "how."

Strategy Is Intentional

We strategize to respond to disruption with intentionality. Our purpose may be, for instance, to achieve educational equity. But how can we do it? Finding possible answers requires analysis and a deeply rooted understanding of context: who we are, where we are, and when we are. The challenge is specific: figuring how our specific "us" can turn specific resources into the specific power we need to achieve specific goals aligned with our purpose. We may learn of a suitable program but also learn that enacting it would require funds from our school board that, even if they supported it, they don't have. In that case, the first step may be to organize voters to approve a school bond, but to do that we may need the support of the school board. Both may depend on organizing the broader community to show visible support early on. To do that, we'll have to engage with parents who may want greater equity for their kids—for those who have less as well as those who have more. So we would be wise to base our campaign on well-organized, vocal, and diverse community support, which may, in turn, require developing new leadership who can give this cause the attention it needs. This practice is intentional because it is grounded in deep understanding of the entire context, including ourselves.

Strategy Is Proactive

There are two common ways we operate in the world: we can be reactive, as many organizations are, or we can be proactive. Even when we are strategizing in response to a new challenge, we can be proactive by sequencing the timing of our campaign goals to retain the initiative, enhance our capacity, build momentum, and take advantage of moments of opportunity. Initial tactics can be chosen to yield resources in the beginning that can be deployed toward the end. As we reach a peak—a point at which we've created a new capacity—we can begin to employ new tactics. Most campaigns must devote an initial chunk of time to recruiting enough volunteers to create the critical mass needed to recruit supporters on a large enough scale. This is what builds momentum. Each success contributes new resources, which make the next success more achievable.

When we strategize, we give a voice to a possible future, enabling it to make claims on the present. This requires the courage to say no to current demands to commit to an uncertain future. When we must choose how to invest scarce resources, voices of present constituencies speak loudly, even though they were created by choices in the past. The voices of future constituencies are silent. Trying to shape the future may require choices that could involve substantial risk in the present. The first step in shaping the future, however, is to engage others in imagining it—and then to find the courage to act on our imagination.

Strategy Is Creative

Strategy is a form of street smarts: figuring out how to do a lot with a little, adapting to disruptions or the moves of your opponent, and doing so quickly, imaginatively, and effectively. In virtually every culture there is a story of how, against all the odds, the "little guy" beat the "big guy." Defeating an opponent by deploying overwhelming force stirs little interest or lessons in strategy—unless we ask how that overwhelming force was assembled or how the force was positioned in a spot where it could be overwhelming. Classic strategists include Odysseus in Greece, Momotarō in Japan, Zhou Yu in China, and many others. In the West, pride of place goes to the biblical story of David and Goliath.[4]

When Goliath, veteran warrior and victor of many battles, challenges the Israelites in full battle gear, their military leaders cower in fear. It is David, the young shepherd boy whom God has anointed, who finds the courage to face the giant. David's success begins with his motivation, commitment, and courage, but it takes more than courage to bring David success. The king's advice is to use the conventional tools of battle—sword, shield, and helmet—of which Goliath, not David, is master. David, showing proper respect for the king, takes the advice. But the sword, shield, and helmet are too heavy for him. He can't move.

That's when David begins to see the battle through different eyes: his eyes, the eyes of a shepherd, not those of a warrior. Noticing five small stones in a wadi at his feet, he reflects on previous challenges protecting his flock from bears and lions. Realizing Goliath might be "just another bear, just another lion," he reframes the battle in a new way that gives him an advantage based on resources he does have—five smooth stones and his skill with a sling— as well as his opponent's self-satisfied arrogance. "Am I a dog," Goliath says, "that you send a boy with a stick?" And at that moment, he gets David's stone in his forehead . . . and it's the end of Goliath. Surely it is not a story about nonviolence, but it is a story about strategy, the difference between resources and power, and the way the creative use of novel resources can compensate for the business-as-usual use of conventional resources. In other words, one way to compensate for imbalance in resources is with greater resourcefulness, like moving the fulcrum on which the balance, or imbalance, rests. Good strategists learn to get more leverage from resources that are available. Power is thus not simply a matter of resources, but also of the resourcefulness with which those resources are used.[5]

Strategy Is Nested

Although our goals to change the world—restructure US health care to make it cheap, accessible, and of quality by 2030; create a carbon-neutral world by 2050; visibly reverse the galloping economic inequality by 2025—may be (necessarily) ambitious, rarely do we have the power to achieve them at this moment. We may be wise to persuade the local mayor and city council to commit to a less ambitious goal on their own. If we do the same thing in twenty other cities within our state, we are not only broadening our political support, but we are also building a statewide organization that can enhance our power by many times (Figure 4.2).

To elect a president of the United States, we will need 270 electoral votes to win. How can we get them? In which states must we campaign to get those votes? Some states will go for us or for our opponent, no matter what. If only about eight states could go either way, we need to figure out how to win those states. We must look at each state and ask very similar questions: which counties, towns, or even precincts do we need to win? Just as each goal is nested within a larger goal, we must look at our resources and our goal, and figure out how we can use our resources to achieve that goal. It works the same way with time. How many voters do we need to get out to vote on Election Day? To get that number, how many commitments do I need to have two weeks before Election Day, and so on?

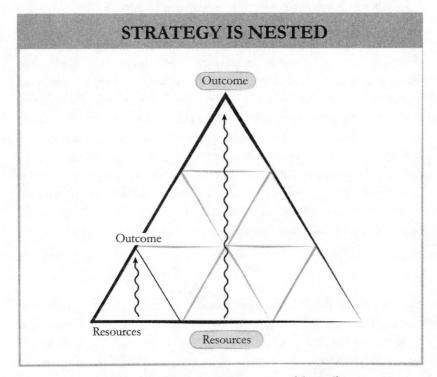

Figure 4.2 Strategy Is Nested. *Source*: Steve Downer of the Difference

Although the scale (space) and scope (time) vary for different goals, the strategic process is the same, whether I want to have a great first meeting or elect a new president: turning what I have into what I need to get what I want.

Practicing Strategy: Who, When, and How?

Who Strategizes?

Because strategizing is sustained creative work that particular people do in particular contexts at particular moments, who strategizes matters. It matters as much as the musicians playing a jazz set, the players on the soccer field, or Kierkegaard's pilot traversing a stormy sea. It also matters because particular people are responsible for leading the creative adaptation that strategizing requires. Yet most observers focus more on what a good strategy is, rather than how good strategy is generated, when, and by whom. So, the question of who strategizes, and under what conditions, is the first question we ask.

I learned this painfully when I was coaching the new leader of a major Southern California union on strategy. We met regularly. We often included members of his team. And we would come up with interesting, exciting, and creative strategies. But nothing would ever come of them. After an especially frustrating session, I finally got it. I was imagining strategy *I* could make work. But it was the leader I was coaching who was responsible for making it work, not me. He was the one who had to adapt whatever strategy we came up with to make it work. This was not a matter of intelligence, commitment, or motivation. His experience was not my experience, nor was my experience his. He was accountable in ways I was not. He was the one who had to navigate ever-present political shoals. Strategizing is such a contextualized, creative, and interactive process that it is only done when the campaign is done. Strategizing, like any sustained creative endeavor, is a creature of the creator or creators.

Insiders and Outsiders

An insider may have information needed to strategize, but as we saw in the David-and-Goliath story, it was David, the young shepherd, not one of the seasoned warriors, his brothers, who rose to the occasion and devised the winning strategy. As an outsider, he saw possibilities the insiders, the warriors, could not see, in part because he had to. He recognized the value of his unique resources, was skilled in how to use them, and was aware of his opponent's weakness, his arrogance.

Strategizing thus often requires a combination of insider and outsider perspectives—whether in the same person or in a leadership team. People may be insiders in one way but outsiders in another. In Alabama, Dr. King was an insider in terms of race and religion but an outsider in terms of class, education, networks, and much more.

Personal Motivation

Highly motivated people can strategize creatively, skillfully, and effectively. Experiencing our work as a vocation or a calling motivates us. And motivation, in turn, can encourage focus, concentration, persistence, readiness to risk, and energy. Motivation may move us to do the work to get the knowledge and skills we need to do what we want to do well. People who are intensely committed to solving a particular problem, who are dissatisfied with the status quo, or who experience breaches in their expectations are also more likely to think outside the box.[6]

Motivation also influences strategy with respect to the sources of one's power. If I think my power depends on resources held by my constituency, and if empowering my constituency is one of my goals, I will do what's necessary to sustain constituency engagement. If, alternatively, I think my power depends on resources held by my donors, I will do what's needed to sustain donor engagement. Successes, even small ones, not only can generate more resources. They can also generate greater motivation.

Strategy Teams

Although good strategy is often portrayed as the fruit of a strategic genius, more often it is the work of a good strategic team a good leader has assembled. The leadership team of the Montgomery Bus Boycott, for example, included a seamstress/organizer who rode the buses, a respected local preacher whose congregants rode the buses, an experienced member of the Brotherhood of Sleeping Car Porters who put his learning to work in the community, the leader of an academic women's group at the local Black college, the only Black lawyer in town, and a very young minister of a local church, so new to the community that he did not have enough history for anyone to object to his being there, one M. L. King Jr.

Strategizing in a team can be more creative, well grounded, and motivational than strategizing alone. Innovative thinking is facilitated by encounters with diverse points of view, whether based on the life experience of individuals or diversity of experience within a group. Access to a diversity of salient knowledge not only offers multiple routines from which to choose but also contributes to the awareness of the fact that multiple solutions are possible. Perhaps the most important criterion for a strategy team, then, is that it has a combination of people who have learned, or are open to learning, that there is more than one way to look at things.

Organizing relies on the resources, engagement, and leadership drawn from one's constituency. It is, of course, fundamental that any strategic team include members of that constituency, as well as those who are not members of that constituency.

How Do We Strategize?

Good strategizing often begins with critical reflection on our own assumptions, testing them against our experience, against the evidence, against the perception of others, and against internal contradictions. This can be very frightening even as it can be exhilarating. We see the world through lenses or models shaped by our experiences that both enable and constrain. These lenses enable us to make sense of things, generalize, make choices, draw conclusions, and act. But they can also inhibit our perception, limiting what we see to what we expect to see, and making it difficult for us to learn.[7] Creative thinking requires recognizing our problems as new ones—at least to us—that require new solutions. The Zen practice of *shoshin*—approaching tasks with a beginner's mind—recognizes that openness to new learning can require substantial unlearning.[8]

Obtaining clarity on the facts often requires challenging dominant paradigms or beliefs about how the world works and which typically align with status quo interests. This too calls for the kind of agitation described in the last chapter: surfacing contradictions that people may not have considered or have avoided. The process is uncomfortable, to be sure, but can create the tension needed to break free of the status quo.[9]

Challenging others to consider a different interpretation requires engaging them in critical reflection. Explaining something again and again will change nothing unless the beliefs through which the explanation is filtered are changed as well. While storytelling is an essential tool in tapping into shared values and activating agency, strategizing is not storytelling. Strategizing is about making an argument, about "if-then" hypotheses.

Strategizing well in a team requires intentionally creating a "holding environment," a brave space in which we can learn, treat failure as informative, suspend judgement, ask for help, solve problems, and experience supportive challenge and affirmation. This requires building relationships among participants and their agreement on explicit ground rules and norms of mutual respect that encourage trust, risk taking, learning, and imagination. This was a real strength in the UFW for many years. Our strategy team was diverse in many ways and its members embedded in critical constituencies. Among our nine members were farmworkers, immigrants, citizens; Mexicans, Filipinos, Anglos, and Blacks; Jews, Catholics, and people with no religious affiliation; pastors, a lawyer, women, and men; young people and elders. When we strategized well, and quickly, it was in a spirit of mutual respect, learning, experimentation, and humor. We had a clear decision-making process. And when we didn't strategize as well, we needed time to repair and recover.

When Do We Strategize?

Although strategizing is an ongoing activity, it often begins with strategic planning. A key element of strategic planning is to decide on a specific goal—targeting. Planning can help clarify choices that must be made to begin and in enabling those responsible to arrive at a common vision of where they want to go and how they hope to get there. But a plan is a hypothesis, not a blueprint. As such, paying close attention to the early moments when the rubber hits the road is critically important for discovering false assumptions and missed opportunities. This also requires a capacity to observe what's happening with enough granularity to learn from it. Or as General Eisenhower put it, "In preparing for battle I have always found that plans are useless, but planning is indispensable."[10]

Another very important time for restrategizing is at the midpoint of a project or campaign.[11] Research on organizational culture shows that groups tend to persist as they began, avoiding interventions, until the midpoint, when a realization that less time remains than has elapsed creates a receptivity to fresh analysis (not unlike a midlife crisis). This is the case regardless of whether the project is for three days or three years. By planning for a midpoint evaluation, leaders can take strategic advantage of this natural phenomenon. Groups also tend to reorganize for the endgame, the final stages of the project, when focus on the here and now can be especially critical.

In organizing, the real action is often, as Alinsky put it, in the reaction—by other actors, the opposition, and the challenges and opportunities that emerge along the way.[12] The mindfulness we bring to bear on our choices relative to what we want to achieve can make our response strategic and not simply reactive. An important enabler of this mindfulness is a stance of curiosity rather than fear, as we saw in the chapter on narrative.

Finally, consciousness that we learn not only for the present but also for the future means that a first step in subsequent strategizing is a fresh, clear, and objective analysis of what happened this time and why, win or lose. Although we often describe this debriefing as "pluses, deltas and takeaways" the military calls this "After Action Report (AAR)".

The Strategic Process: Six Questions

Although any multistep process is more useful as a road map than as a blueprint, it can help scaffolding learning. When someone begins learning to drive, a checklist is very helpful, indeed, necessary. But at some point, the person becomes a driver who has mastered the process enough to adapt, innovate, and invent. In Japanese martial arts this is called *shuhari*: *shu* is the master's way; *ha* is the way of adaptation; and *ri*, the way of creation. We ought not to confuse the scaffold with the practice, turning the scaffold into a checklist from which we must not deviate. The following is one way to translate these considerations into a six-step process we can use to scaffold strategizing an organizing campaign. The framework we'll use consists of six questions: (1) Who are my people? (2) What is the change they want? (3) What is their theory of change? (4) What is their strategic goal? (5) What tactics can we use? and (6) What's the timing?

Trying to learn to strategize in the abstract is like trying to learn how to play music without a particular instrument. We will explore each of these questions in the context of the UFW's campaign to win its first real contract (1965/6).

It was February 1966, in Delano, California. Grape workers had been on strike for union recognition for five months. In November, the season had ended with no breakthroughs. A boycott called in December against

Schenley Industries, a major liquor company with 4,000 acres of grapes, had produced no results. So Chavez convened a meeting of leadership at a supporter's home near Santa Barbara to devote three days to figuring out how to move on Schenley, prepare for the spring, and sustain the commitment of strikers, organizers, and supporters. I quote from my notes of that meeting:

> As proposals flew around the room, someone suggested we follow the example of the New Mexico miners who had traveled to New York to set up a mining camp in front of the company headquarters on Wall Street. Farmworkers could travel to Schenley headquarters in New York, set up a labor camp out front, and maintain a vigil until Schenley signed. Someone else then suggested they go by bus to hold rallies across the country, organize local boycott committees, and generate publicity, building momentum for the arrival in New York. Then why not march instead of going by bus, someone else asked, as Dr. King had the previous year? But it's too far from Delano to New York, someone countered. On the other hand, the Schenley headquarters in San Francisco might not be too far—about 280 miles, which an army veteran present calculated could be done at the rate of 15 miles a day, or in about 20 days.
>
> "But what if Schenley doesn't respond?" Chavez asked. Why not march to Sacramento instead and put the heat on Governor Brown to intervene and get negotiations started? He's up for reelection and wants the votes of our supporters, so perhaps we can have more impact if we use him as leverage. Yes, someone else said, and on the way to Sacramento, the march could pass through most of the farmworker towns. Taking a page from Mao's "long march," we could organize local committees and get workers to sign pledges not to break the strike. Yes, and we could also get them to feed us and house us. And just as Zapata wrote his "Plan de Ayala," Luis Valdez suggested, we can write a "Plan de Delano," read it in each town, ask local farmworkers to sign it and to carry it to the next town. Then, Chavez asked, why should it be a "march" at all? It will be Lent soon, a time for reflection, for penance, for asking forgiveness. Perhaps ours should be a pilgrimage, a peregrinación, which could arrive at Sacramento on Easter Sunday.

On March 17, farmworkers began their *peregrinación*, carrying banners of Our Lady of Guadalupe, patron saint of Mexico; portraits of campesino leader Emiliano Zapata; placards proclaiming, "Peregrinación, Penitencia, Revolución"—Pilgrimage, Penance, Revolution—and signs calling on supporters to boycott Schenley. One striker, Roberto Roman, carried a six-foot-tall wooden cross constructed of two-by-fours and draped in black cloth. Timed to coincide with a visit by Senator Bobby Kennedy for the US Senate Subcommittee on Migratory Labor hearings in Delano, the march attracted public attention from the start. Televised images of a line of helmeted police temporarily blocking the marchers' departure evoked images of police lines in Selma, Alabama, the year before. A crowd of more than one thousand welcomed the marchers to Fresno at the end of the first week. Reporters profiled strikers, asking them why they would walk three hundred miles, and analyzed what the strike was all about. The march articulated not only the farmworkers' call for justice but also the Mexican American community's claims for a voice in public life. At an individual level, as Cesar Chavez described it, the march was also a way of "training ourselves to endure the long, long struggle, which by this time had become evident. . . . We wanted to be fit not only physically but also spiritually."[13]

On the afternoon of April 3, as the farmworkers arrived in Stockton, a week's march south of Sacramento, Schenley's lawyer reached Chavez by phone. Schenley had little interest in remaining the object of a boycott, especially as the march's arrival in Sacramento promised to become a national anti-Schenley rally. As a result, just three days before the march would arrive, Schenley signed the first real union contract in California farm labor history. So, on Saturday afternoon, a crowd that had grown to two thousand gathered on the grounds of Our Lady of Grace School in West Sacramento, on a hill looking across the Sacramento River to the capital city that they would enter the next morning. During the Easter vigil service that evening, more than one speaker compared them to the ancient Israelites camped across the River Jordan from the Land of Promise. That night, Roberto Roman carefully rewrapped his cross in white and decorated it with spring flowers. The next morning, barefoot, he bore it triumphantly across the river bridge, down the state capitol mall, and up the capitol steps where he was met by a crowd of ten thousand farmworkers and supporters who launched the farmworker movement.

Question 1: Who Are My People?

The first question an organizer asks is not "What is my issue?" but "Who are my people?" In organizing your people benefit from their own success and only secondarily from your success. Their power will not grow—nor will any power have shifted—unless fundamentally rooted in their commitment of their own resources. People's use of their own resources is what distinguishes a constituency from customers or clients. Organizing is about enabling people to collaborate in developing their own power to solve their own problems. Unless "your people" experience their own agency and the power to act on it, sustained change is unlikely.

So, we start with learning the values, interests, resources, networks, and conditions of our people. As an old union organizer tried to teach us, "Nothing beats sticking close to the people." So, if your people are to be motivated to organize, their motivation will be rooted in their lived experience of the problem—and how it could be different—in their daily lives. The difference between a segregated bus, for example, and a desegregated one. Working with people to do something about climate change becomes far more urgent if about recovery from last year's flood. This is not a time for polling or focus groups but rather for lots of one-on-one meetings. We far too often make assumptions about what people want without asking, only to be surprised they don't show up.

In the UFW case, who were the people? Although the UFW wanted to organize all farmworkers everywhere in the United States, its primary constituency was farmworker families who worked in the table grape industry. Some had joined the UFW before the strike, but most signed up with the UFW only after going on strike. This constituency gradually grew to include farmworkers in other regions of the state and in other crops. In addition, once the strike began, the UFW set to organizing a secondary constituency who did not work in the fields but supported both the strike and the broader movement, which came to be known as "La Causa." This included several young people who came to Delano and volunteered to serve on the picket lines. But most lived elsewhere and included students, union people, community leaders, members of faith communities, members of the Mexican and Mexican American communities, civil rights groups, political liberals, and so on—a network not unlike the constituency for the civil rights movement.

By December 1965, the active core of the organization's primary constituency was the one hundred to two hundred farmworkers and their families who remained in the area after the end of the season, serving full time on the picket lines, managing the food donations, fixing the cars, and otherwise sustaining the strike, now known as "La Huelga." Because of the relatively long table grape season, some lived in the area; others came seasonally; and still others came only at the peak. The core of the UFW leadership team had been a board elected by the members prior to the strike and included Cesar Chavez, Gilberto Padilla, Dolores Huerta, Antonio Orendain, Julio Hernandez, and Roger Terronez. They called the shots in collaboration with the leadership of the Filipino workers affiliated with the AFL-CIO who had started the strike. Chavez was born in the United States near the Mexican border to an immigrant farming family who became migrants when the farm was lost in the Depression. He served in the navy, went to work in a lumber mill, and, from 1952 to 1962, had worked as an organizer of the Community Service Organization (CSO). Padilla, also born in the United States, had worked in the fields before serving in the army and collaborated with Chavez in CSO. Huerta, born in New Mexico and a college graduate, had also worked with Chavez in the CSO but had never worked in the fields. Hernandez, Terronez, and Orendain had all immigrated from Mexico and worked in the fields. This core team also consulted with a set of informal advisors that included two members of the clergy, union allies, political allies, and others. The strategizing thus drew on the salient experiences of a strategically appropriate set of people embedded within both primary and secondary constituencies.

Question 2: What Is the Change They Want/Need?

Developing effective organizing strategy starts with a focus on the change our people really want and need. We may ask first, after doing some relationship building, what do you experience as the "problem"? All our people, some of our people, some more than others? What does it actually look like? Second, what could the world look like if the problem were to be solved; how would your lives be different, specifically? Third, why hasn't anyone solved the problem? Who is deciding how things are? Who is benefiting? Who is losing? And finally, fourth, what would it take to solve the problem? More education? More information? More counselling More data? More power?

For three years before the strike, Chavez and his colleagues had been organizing a farmworkers' association to enable farmworkers to begin building *power with* each other by constructing enough solidarity, interdependence, and trust within the local farmworker community to hold people together when it came to the strike. Farmworker families had many needs: higher wages, access to health care, adequate housing, freedom from abuse on the job, help with social needs like immigration, welfare, traffic tickets, and so forth. The overwhelming belief was that a union could help solve all these problems. But the community also was experiencing the fear, uncertainty, and discrimination that goes with powerlessness. So the initial needs the association addressed were a death benefit, a credit union, help with employment problems, and a newspaper. But the deeper needs evident in these immediate concerns were for the security, dignity, and well-being that could only come with a union powerful enough to make it happen. This would mean challenging the *power over* them held by the growers. Although the strike's wage goal was $1.40 per hour, other goals of health insurance and job security were equally important. The bottom line, however, was union recognition and a multi-year signed contract with the employers that could consolidate the shift in power not only to win but to grow, sustain, and extend that power. As Bob Dylan sang in "It's Alright, Ma," "If you're not busy being born you're busy dying."

Sometimes a community wants what is only one part of a larger change they need. It is not enough to recognize that a community suffers from institutionalized racism. Organizing members of that community to take an active part in solving the problem depends on their plausible belief that their action could yield results. That it could be worth it. If that possibility is rooted in their own experience, so much the better. They own the solution, not someone else. The genius of the Montgomery Bus Boycott, for example, was that it did not claim to be launching an assault on institutionalized racism but rather focused specifically on the condition of riding on a segregated bus. People's anger over the daily disrespect of a segregated bus could be focused on a plausible solution for which people could fight: a desegregated bus. Had the fight been won with a lawsuit, the community might well have benefited but would not have been empowered. Instead, by organizing a boycott, they transformed an individual's dependency on the bus company to get to work into the bus company's dependency on a united community to survive financially. It turned out that everyone did have an individual resource that could be turned into collective power—their feet. The Montgomery Bus Boycott sparked a movement. By using the resources they had to tackle a "first face of power" (the bus) problem, they did so in a way that set the stage for dealing with the second face of power (legalized Jim Crow) as well as beginning to build the power they would need to tackle the "third face of power" (institutionalized racism) and everything in between. We're still working on that one!

Question 3: What Is Their Theory of Change?

A theory of change is a hypothesis that if we were to do this, that would happen, because. . . . Alas, as the example of the two professors shows, this is often the part left out in practice, not only creating a logic gap (lacuna?) between tactics we choose and outcomes we hope for . . . and miracles rarely happen.

Figure 4.3 Then a Miracle Occurs. Copyright © 2005 by Sidney Harris

Sometimes articulation of a theory of change only emerges from analysis of the kind of change really needed—or trial and error—as in the above examples. This is why learning how to learn is such a pivotal leadership practice. Strategizing is inherently iterative, proceeding only rarely in a linear way. The challenge is one of learning how to do something that hasn't been done before—at least in this context, at this time, by these people. Far more useful than being guided by a "best practices" approach—"best" in one context can be "worst" in another—is learning how to devise a practice "best" for this context.

So, what became the theory of change at which strategists of the UFW or Montgomery Bus Boycott arrived? As is so often the case when it comes to organizing, they both arrived at a power theory of change. A power theory of change requires asking: (1) What are our needs? (2) Who holds the resources to meet our needs? (3) What are their needs? and (4) What resources do we have that they need (Figure 1.4).

If our interests are aligned and our resources sufficient, we may choose to create more power "with" each other through collaboration, for example, a credit union or a co-op. But if others hold resources that we need, one source of their power "over" us and our interest's conflict, we must figure out how to use our resources to make it more costly for them to resist the change we seek than to accept it.

In terms of a hypothesis: If we (1) deploy the resources we have in this way in this place at this time, (2) we can affect the needs of others whose resources we need (3) such that it will be more costly for them to deny us access to those resources than to provide them, (4) then we get the resources we need to achieve goals consistent with our interests.

Lest this seem obvious, other theories of change, most of which ignore power, seem more popular in recent years: we can achieve the change we need with better education, more information, transparent information, better data analysis, more robust moral suasion, more compelling storytelling, better access to mental health, more entrepreneurs, a stronger work ethic, more "impact" philanthropy, and so on. Some of these approaches can be useful, but more as forms of support for our people than influencing those holding power them. Based on formal and informal power analysis, these movement strategists decided they would not get the change they needed by trying to persuade those holding power to share it unless it were in their interests to do so. Unless they could find a way to make it more costly (economic, political, moral) for those who hold power to resist change than to accept it, nothing would change. They had to turn the tables on those holding power "over" them to achieve the change they needed.

A good first step is to create a power map. People do this in different ways, but it is about coming up with a way to visualize the connections among all the "actors" with a connection to the problem in term of their own interests and their resources. For example, in the farmworker case, this included growers, labor contractors, supervisors, and landlords, as well as the farmworkers themselves. What did their terms of interdependence look like. The workers depend on the growers for employment, the growers depend on the workers if they are to have anything to sell. Now taking these interdependencies into consideration, you can hypothesize who is likely to have an interest in the change, who is likely to oppose the change, who might be neutral, who might be of potential support, who may be in potential opposition, what role people in the media may have, what role the courts may have, and so on.

Here's one example of what a power map can look like (Figure 4.4). One can start by making a posit for every relevant actor, labeling it with that actor's relevant resources and interests. Then, based on an examination of

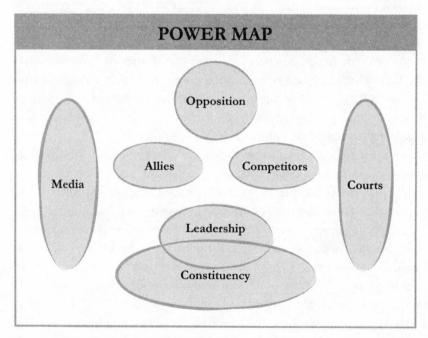

Figure 4.4 Power Map. *Source*: Steve Downer of the Difference

any interdependencies among the actors (who needs whose resources), one can place the posit in the appropriate circle.

At the base is one's constituency—the people who both experience the need for change and whose resources can build the power to create that change. Overlapping the constituency is a leadership team drawn primarily from within the constituency, but which may include others as well (lawyer, researcher, educator, organizer).

Immediately opposite the constituency is the opposition: actors whose interest in maintaining the status quo may be in sharp conflict with those of a constituency in need of change. Particular actors may pass in or out depending on how the campaign evolves.

To the side are actors whose interests may be allied with or in competition with those of the constituency. A neighborhood association, for example, could be allied with an affordable housing group or, if committed to being the only voice of the community, could be a competitor.

And on either side are actors whose resources may or may not be relevant to the campaign, depending on how the leadership chooses to interact with them.

On one side is the legal system, represented by the courts. In some cases, as in the bus boycott, the organizers decided to mobilize the authoritative resources of the courts by filing a suit to desegregate the buses. On the other hand, history is replete with examples of local, state, and federal courts breaking strikes, suppressing demonstrations, and, of course sending people to jail on dubious grounds.

On the other side are the media of communication which on the one hand, may offer a key opportunity to share information, elicit support, and focus attention, and, on the other to publicize vulnerabilities, strengthen the opposition, and, of course, share "fake news." One way to approach this is to see the media itself as an organizing project, building relationships with the journalists, and others. Cesar Chavez's rule was never do something for the press but, rather, skillfully open a window on what you are doing. Rather than give a press conference, he was available on the picket line.

For this analysis Lukes's Three Faces of Power frame work can be very helpful.[14] It was very clear who the winner and the losers were in terms of the first face of power (who wins, who loses): the grower controls access to work, the worker needs access to work. There were many more workers than jobs. Or even more proximately the labor contractor who worked for the grower really did the hiring. Again, more workers than contractors, enabled the contractors to elicit bribes, demand favors, understate wages, and so on.

But if we look at it through the lens of the second face of power—who decides—we see how the growers' exercise power at that level too: funding political candidates, deciding who can be mayor, exchanging favors with the county sheriff, exchanging favors with the local judges, even check the local archbishop from supporting the strikers. Before the strike, farmworkers had no leverage in this domain.

We get an even clearer picture if we try to identify the third face of power— who is benefiting, who is losing, and how these fits into the overall scheme of things. Agricultural workers had no access to federal labor law, as they were excluded in 1935 when it was passed. Most workers were not citizens and had no direct access to political power; many were resident aliens and others had no papers at all. Most farmworkers were people of color barred from influence and access in all the ways race has been institutionalized. And so forth. This analysis, however, is not too distant because it too may reveal points of leverage not accessible at a local level.

Question 4: What Is Their Strategic Goal?

Having done enough of the analysis to have arrived at a possibly functional theory of change, we ask how this theory of change n can enable us focus on specific strategic goals: outcomes that are visible, measurable, each creating new capacity for achieving a larger goal.

Chavez began with a focus on his own people: workers who, like most people, wanted security, dignity, well-being, and a future for their children. Who held the resources needed to address those interests? It turned out the workers themselves did, in fact, have more resources than many assumed that they could combine to create enough power with each other to address some of their interests (loans, for example) And, indeed, the initial farm worker organizing plan was that it would take five years to create a self-supporting association of farmworkers focused on specific benefits: a death benefit, a credit union, and other forms of mutual aid.

But this wouldn't be enough to address their deepest needs When it came to wages, hours, working conditions, and the like, their employers controlled these resources, with some support from local, county, and state government.

Look at what was at stake for the employers: the growers wanted to main-
tain stability and control; they wanted a labor force to harvest the grapes;
they wanted to profit from their sales and to lower costs. Knowing this, did
our constituency hold. resources that could affect their employers' needs or
interests. The farmworkers controlled their labor, their hands, their time,
their skill, their experience, their relationships, their faith, and their cultural
identities.

Finally, the strategic question: How could the farmworkers use these resources to affect their employers' interests enough to cause their employers
to use their resources to respond to our constituency's needs? In other words,
how could the farmworkers make it more costly for the growers to resist their
claims than to accede to them? This led to one of the first ways in which the
UFW turned its theory of change into a specific strategic objective: "If we
withdraw our labor, it will cost our employers more than if they were to give
us what we want, so we will organize a strike for as long as it takes to get
what we want." The UFW strike was the farmworkers' first attempt to use
their resources to affect their employers' interests. But when that wasn't sufficient, the UFW began to identify other resources they could use to impact
their employers, indirectly if not directly. They could call on the American
public, already sensitized to calls for racial justice, to offer economic support
to the strikers. They would learn that they could put political pressure on
the growers through state agencies. They could use the law to fill jails, which
would cost the county money, which would put indirect pressure on local
governments. And they could ask the public not to buy what the employers
were selling.

This is where the secondary constituency comes in, a second set of people
to be organized. In addition to the farmworkers, the UFW began to organize
support committees, first in cities in California, but over time, elsewhere. The
farmworkers, now acting as organizers instead of laborers, could use their
moral authority and cultural affinity with urban supporters to expand their
resource base. These communities could raise money, collect food, and bring
other forms of support to the strikers. But while this support enabled the
picket lines to persist, it didn't increase their wages or improve their working
conditions.

A second major strategic goal then emerged as the strike continued
without clear results: boycott Schenley Industries to cost them enough to
compel them to recognize the union, sign a contract, and improve wages,
hours, and working conditions and, at the same time, show the workers, their

allies, the public—and the growers—that it could be done. This breakthrough came when civil rights activists suggested looking at a boycott. At first, the idea seemed absurd. Table grapes don't carry grower labels, and the season was already over. But the researchers soon learned that Schenley Industries, a New York–based liquor company, owned 4,000 acres of wine grapes in Delano. And Schenley, it turned out, marketed wines and liquors with labels like Cutty Sark scotch. So, starting in November, volunteers were dispatched to major cities to set up picket lines in front of liquor stores, asking customers to shun Schenley. The grape season may have ended, but holiday cocktail parties had just begun.

At the same time, the UFW's leaders focused on the interests of another actor, Edmund G. "Pat" Brown, the first Democrat to serve as California's governor since the 1930s. Brown, who was facing an election, could use his influence on the political, financial, and public interests of the agribusiness industry, its leaders, and their funding; tax policy; water policy; and, more generally, his influence with the broader public.

This was how strategic goals were being crafted, rooted always in a power theory of change and evolving to respond to new obstacles, new opportunities, and new learning. By the time of the meeting of February 1966, described earlier, the UFW's theory of change had focused on a five-year strategic goal to enable farmworkers to build power with each other, based on an analysis that suggested past campaigns had failed because they attempted to strike (mobilize) and organize at the same time. So they began by creating a death benefit, a credit union, and a newspaper: ways to build the solidarity, the sense of hope, and the experience of efficacy that could hold people together in a strike. However, when a rival labor organization called a strike, but only to demand higher wages, the UFW decided to support the strike rather than become strikebreakers. Now the two unions focused on the economic power of workers, as expressed by the strike, and on winning public support for the struggle. The Schenley boycott offered a breakthrough, so the goals could be summarized as winning the boycott, sustaining the strike, and building a support organization rooted in faith communities, the labor movement, political leadership, and the general public.

I turn now to focus on implementation of the campaign goal that came out of that meeting: a march to Sacramento to arrive on Easter Sunday.

The effectiveness of the UFW's strategy lay in finding multiple venues (economic, political, cultural) in which to create the power to make it costly for the employers to resist union recognition. Success came not from persuading the growers of the justice of their cause, the humanity of their workers, or the potential benefits of collaborating with a union. It came from turning resources the farmworkers had into the power they needed to give the growers an interest in recognizing the union.

In selecting a strategic goal on which to focus a campaign, consider the five features of an effective strategic goal:

- Focuses resources on a single outcome that may enable you to achieve greater outcomes.
- Enables your constituency to translate its resources into power, generating greater capacity.
- Leverages your constituency's strength and the weakness of the opposition.
- Is visible, significant, and important enough to motivate your constituency's engagement.
- Is contagious and can be emulated.

The more concrete, imaginable, and specific the goal, the more clearly you, and others whom you hope to engage, can focus your creativity on achieving it. No action will take shape absent motivation. In narrative terms, our strategic goal becomes a critical part of our story of now. We are faced with an urgent challenge, we look for hope we can meet the challenge, and we commit to a course of action, our strategic goal. Hope inspires both in terms of the values in which it is rooted and as a pathway to possibility.

When checking possible goals against these criteria, don't be afraid to brainstorm, come up with outlandish ideas, or change course. Then you must choose. Commit to the goal that you believe is most likely to enable you to mobilize your resources (what you have) in as powerful a way as possible (what you need) to achieve that goal (what you want). There is no perfect choice. This is why strategy is hard. As Cesar Chavez used to say, "It's not so much making the right decision, as it is making the decision that you make the right decision." Once you're satisfied with your strategic goal, you are ready summarize in a single organizing sentence: "We are organizing [who] to [what outcome] through [how] by [when]." This clarity of focus, almost like a DNA, is not meant to oversimplify. But it is meant to clarify so we can use it in many different contexts to strategize with coherence, coordination, and a broad range of learning opportunities.

In the UFW case described earlier, the leadership decided to build a campaign focused on the goal of marching to Sacramento by Easter Sunday. The theory was that the march could publicize the Schenley boycott, put pressure on the governor to intervene, and organize farmworkers across the state to support the UFW, support the strike, and not come to Delano to work when the season resumed. This goal, in turn, was nested with the broader goals of achieving justice for farmworkers by building a farmworkers' union, getting recognition from the employers, making it more costly to the employers to resist than to agree, conducting a successful boycott, pressuring the governor, and building farmworker support. The brilliance of the march as a goal was that it combined the three higher-level measures of impact—achieving the goal, strengthening the organization, and building leadership—within a single very specific goal, thus focusing effort rather than diffusing it, simplifying rather than complexifying. And as an organizing campaign, its impact could be evaluated by asking whether the strategic goal was achieved, whether the union came out of it stronger, and whether leadership was being developed who could deepen and broaden the movement.

Question 5: What Tactics Can They Use?

A tactic is a way in which your theory of change turns into specific activities. Tactics are activities targeted in specific ways and carried out at specific times, through which your strategy becomes real. Strategy without tactics is just a bunch of nice ideas, and tactics without strategy are a waste of resources. The art of organizing is in the dynamic relationship between strategy and tactics, using the strategy to inform the tactics, and learning from the tactics to adapt strategy.

Strategizing involves an ongoing creative stream of tactical innovation and adaptation as circumstances change, opportunities emerge, and reverses are suffered. A laundry list of "what we are going to try" is not a strategy. It is, at best, a list of possible activities. They only become tactics when enacting your theory of change. Channeling possible activities into three or four pathways, such as fundraising, outreach, and research, does not constitute a strategy unless anchored to a specific goal to which you have committed. Once you have a list of possible activities you need to develop a set of criteria to assess them as tactics. Here are a few ideas:

- Make the most of your own resources, as distinct from those of your opponent.
- Operate with the experience of your constituency, outside that of your opponent.
- Choose tactics that unify your constituency while dividing your opposition.
- Choose tactics that are consistent with your values.
- Choose tactics that are fun, motivational, and simple.

The tactical creativity in support of the UFW's strategic goal was perhaps its greatest strength. Framing the action as a pilgrimage, not simply a march, and timing it for Lent gave it a deeply motivational element and rooted it in the faith of the constituency, providing a values-based motivation for the core constituency. Moving outward from the workers themselves, the pilgrimage presented an opportunity to organize local communities, who welcomed the march on the edge of town with a farmworker committee and musicians. The local committee then accompanied the pilgrims through town, always ending up at a park where there would be food, rest, and a rally in the evening, at which local farmworkers would be asked to join in signing the Plan de Delano. In the morning, a priest would lead a Roman Catholic mass, during which the banner of Our Lady of Guadalupe would be handed off to a worker from that town to carry it to the next.

Media tactics included a press center in a VW van that accompanied the march, staffed by a volunteer press person (borrowed from SNCC), and equipped with phones (it was 1966). Stories went out daily as to the progress of the march and special events. The press center hosted journalists who wanted to interview Chavez, interview farmworkers, or come along for the march. This publicity helped create the momentum and scale as the march proceeded north.

As the march progressed, boycott organizers across the country used a variety of tactics to increase the pressure on Schenley with picket lines, interviews, vigils, and fasts. At the same time, negotiating tactics included back-channel talks mediated by a labor leader who had a shared interest in getting it settled, a long association with the company, and wanted to participate in making a historic event happen. Simultaneously, talks were going on with the governor, motivating his engagement and asking him to be at the Capitol to welcome the marchers. Although in the end Governor Brown rejected this request, electing to spend Easter in Palm Springs with his friend Frank Sinatra, this affront to the Latino community may have contributed to his loss to Ronald Reagan later that year.

Question 6: What about Timing?

Campaigns unfold within "time as an arrow." As I discuss further in chapter six, the term was coined by paleontologist Stephen J. Gould, a student of deep time, inspired by the Greek distinction between *kairos*—exactly the right moment—and *chronos*—incremental passage of time.[15] Gould adapted this perspective into what he called "time as an arrow"—the rhythm of change— and "time as a cycle"—the rhythm of continuity. Campaigns start in one place with the goal of ending up in another place: intense focus, high risk, a clear start date, clear ending date, moving from peak to peak to peak, growing the power to overcome resistance and win. In contrast, organizations construct a rhythm of continuity with routines, regular reviews, annual budgets, and so forth.

Given the pace at which campaigns unfold, sensitive to the need for on-going adaptation, scholars of "entrainment" argue the need for a "temporal strategy" by paying attention to the temporal environment in which we op-erate. Time external to the campaign is structured as seasons, semesters, work rhythms, electoral rhythms, news cycles, weekends, holidays, and more. Time internal to the campaign is structured by the need to build momentum by meeting specific goals and to do so at specific times. The campaign time-line also has to recognize the time frame within which one's constituency lives. For example, we ought not to try starting a campaign after the season is half over or schedule a meeting for a weekend when everyone may take their families out of town. Timing a campaign strategically requires situating it within each of these temporal dimensions.[16]

Temporal strategy also requires alignment of the above with the inherent dynamics of a campaign. When is the right time for a kickoff? How much time will it take to reach a first peak? When is it time to make a change? When will participants need time off, even as the campaign moves on? And when, how, and by whom are temporal decisions made?

Momentum requires establishing and maintaining the initiative by expecting that every action you take will produce a reaction to which you have already considered how to respond. It also means never concluding one activity until it is clear how it will lead to the next one. You need to commit your people to what comes next when they are still there together.

It may also be strategic to structure a campaign around a date of inherent significance for your constituency. The UFW wisely chose to align its march with the Lenten Easter season. The clear and deep cultural resonance of the pilgrimage with farmworkers' faith even made the action meaningful to those of other faith traditions. Perhaps it also afforded an educational opportunity for those without a faith grounding. It also created a natural campaign peak for the final week, beginning on Palm Sunday, moving through the Stations of the Cross, Good Friday, Saturday Vigil, and Easter Sunday. Nor was the Easter narrative incidental, as it tells a story of suffering, sacrifice, hope, and redemption.

The timing of the march also tied in with more prosaic, but important, dates in California's political calendar. The Senate committee's decision to hold a hearing in Delano, combined with a special effort to get Senator Kennedy there, provided the perfect opportunity to announce that the march would start the next morning. This tactic turned out to be especially valuable when the Delano police tried to stop the march with a line that resembled the police response in Selma. The image of the police line told a powerful visual story about the connections between what was going on in California and Alabama.

And then there's the sense of timing in dealing with actions and reaction. When I was with the UFW in 1967, we had organized a strike of Giumarra Vineyard, the largest grape grower in the industry. As the strike got hobbled by court injunctions, recruitment of strike breakers, and more, we tried to focus a boycott targeting particularly Giumarra's table grapes. It was hard enough trying to enable consumers to identify whose grapes were whose, but we had had some success following trucks and railcars to identify which stores to picket. Before long, however, the other growers began lending Giumarra their labels, so there was no way to figure out which was which. At first, we did not know how to deal with this disruption to our strategy. Fred Ross saw the opportunity. What if we simply boycotted all table grapes? Then we could tackle the industry as a whole, rather than through piecemeal boycotts, a strategy that gave them the advantage. This insight led to the grape boycott that eventually brought the entire industry under union contract.

The capacity to align our initial strike strategy with the peak of the table grape season not only had an impact on the grower, raising his costs substantially, but it also brought a whole new cohort of workers into the union. So, at the end of the season, in October, when the focus shifted to the cities, we had the people, the leadership, and renewed commitment—and the time—to build local boycott organizations in time to be ready to "stop the grapes" in May at the start of the 1969 season.

Conclusion

In organizing, strategizing combines creativity, analysis, and timing in a very symbiotic and dynamic way. Strategy is rooted in the constituency whose centrality to the strategy is a source of their empowerment. A diverse, informed, and agile leadership team must center the resources, interests, and needs of this constituency in strategizing campaigns that can turn what you have into what you need to get what you want. Effective strategy requires clarity on the overarching change at stake. The why and the how are linked in one's theory of change, which must in turn be based on a solid power analysis. Focusing on a specific goal enables the most strategic use of resources. Achieving clarity as to the goal and the theory of change enables leaders to generate creative, relevant, and motivational tactics within a rhythm of change that is aligned with what's going on both in the world and in the constituency.

If we look back at the UFW campaign, using our three impact criteria— achieving our goal, strengthening our organization, building our leadership— surely it accomplished all three. In terms of goals, the farmworkers won their first contract, the governor got productively involved, and the organizing campaign broke through as a social movement to the public. In terms of capacity, the UFW came out of it far stronger than when it went in, with more members, greater organizing capacity, and lots of learning. In terms of leadership, the campaign developed new leaders in both the farmworker towns and boycott cities, provided opportunities for current leaders to stretch their skills as march coordinators and advance organizers, and allowed the strategic leadership team to test out its ability to move quickly, with focus, follow-through, and communication.

Any campaign that seeks to achieve long-term, meaningful change must have an effective strategy. But strategy without action is all talk. In the next chapter, we turn to the nuts and bolts of action, where change happens.

5

Action

"If you can't count it, it didn't happen!"

I was one of thirty novice organizers packed into a hot, converted tract house living room. Collectively, we had been charged with organizing one thousand farmworkers. Our goal? To win the first union representation election in the history of California agriculture.

The Schenley victory opened the way to a second boycott: the Tree Sweet products of the giant DiGiorgio Fruit Corporation. This, as well as Governor Brown's intervention, moved DiGiorgio to agree to a secret ballot election. The 1.2-million-strong Teamsters Union had allied with the DiGiorgio Fruit Corporation to crush the independent farmworkers' union, then known as the NFWA, led by Cesar Chavez and largely made up of workers of color. This was Delano, California, late August 1966. The table grape harvest was at its peak, and we had thirty days to go until the vote. Every day, we were organizing workers who faced aggressive foremen, threatening bosses, and Teamster thugs.

Each organizer was responsible for organizing a specific number of workers, recruiting a specific number of leaders, and getting support commitments from a specific number of voters—the number of votes we needed to win. We kept track of how many people we tried to get to a meeting and how many came. We asked why those who didn't come, didn't, and why those who did, did. We tracked each worker on a three-by-five file card in a small metal file box.

Cesar had recruited organizer Fred Ross to train us as he had trained Cesar in the 1950s. In charge of the campaign, Fred went person by person. "What are your numbers? Why *those* numbers? What did you learn?" As Fred posted them on the wall for all to see, he asked why good was good, why bad was bad, and what patterns we saw across the whole. It wasn't only about accountability. It was about learning. And if a report included an "I guess" or "it seems," or "about," it was close to a mortal sin. In this way, what could feel like interrogation turned into inquiry: we learned what was working and what wasn't, who was reliable and who wasn't, and how to adapt strategy and tactics given the ever-changing reality of a campaign in which workers had to stand up to threats, firings, and worse.

We understood that we win elections by securing—and delivering—votes. We secure votes by getting commitments. We get commitments by learning each worker's story. God, they say (or the devil), is in the details. Love for the details is a prerequisite for excellence in any craft, including that of organizing.

In the end we won the election: 530 NFWA, 331 Teamsters, 7 No Union.

This approach didn't come easily to me. I had never experienced this intense discipline before my work with the NFWA. I didn't like it. I was cool. I'd earned my chops in Mississippi, where we didn't have to show up for so many meetings, especially right on time, nor did we have to do all this counting. I found an ally in Marcos Munoz, a streetwise farmworker organizer who had learned to survive by knowing a thing or two, even if that didn't include reading and writing. He had no use for Fred's rules either. After a meeting that we didn't want to go to—and boy, had we shown it—Fred came over to us: "Cesar would like to talk with you." Oops. The principal's office?

We sat down with Cesar and Fred. You both have lots of potential, Cesar told us, and you're welcome to stay. "But if you do decide to stay, be clear. Fred is in charge. Fred's rules apply. They apply to everyone. If not, no hard feelings, just good luck, and goodbye."

We decided to stay.

That's when I began to learn organizing as a craft. A few years later, I was managing an organizer who kept losing three-by-five cards. "Those aren't cards you're losing," I explained, "they're people. Each one matters." It helped. Perhaps this was the beginning of what I now call "evidence-based organizing"!

Many years later, I was training a youthful cohort of organizers in the 2003/4 New Hampshire campaign for Democratic presidential candidate Howard Dean. The same age I had been when I learned to count, so did they. A few years later, when I was training organizers in the 2008 Obama campaign, our digital tools had sure improved from the three-by-five cards and the yellow legal pads. But it still came down to the same thing: people working with people . . . again . . . and again . . . and counting . . . and counting . . . and learning . . . and learning. And most critically, knowing what exactly you are counting and why! It's too easy to fall into the trap of the drunk who lost his car keys where his car was parked—a block away from the streetlight under which he was looking for them. When asked why he was searching there, he responded, "It's where the light is."

We have been learning how organizing works. We learned how building relationships lays a foundation for storytelling, the *heart* work, which, in turn, lays a foundation for strategizing, the *head* work, which, in turn, creates a foundation for action, the *hands* work. It is this action work that creates real change. Change happens on the ground, or it doesn't happen.

In this chapter, I focus on action: mobilizing and deploying resources to create real change—and to grow more resources to deploy. Because organizing is about empowering people, the most valuable and abundant resources are those held by people as people: our time, our bodies, our imaginations, and our agency—the capacity to choose, to say no, or to say yes. The challenge then is to mobilize these individual resources and deploy them as collective power. Organizers of the Montgomery Bus Boycott mobilized the individual resource of feet and deployed them collectively as a boycott. Union members contribute dues that can be deployed as hired staff or a strike fund. They can also deploy their time as a strike.

One of the major organizing challenges we face today is the ever-greater reliance on financial resources that come from outside one's constituency rather than on resources from within one's constituency. Today, "Who will fund it?" is often the first question people ask when it comes to almost anything, including organizing. But a focus on fundraising as the first question ("enabling condition") corrupts the craft of organizing, which leads with people as the primary source of power. Instead, too often, power is conditioned on the ability to access the funds of wealthy donors who have colonized civil society with projects that depend on their largesse.[1] This outsized influence of donors shifts the locus of accountability from one's people to one's funders, further eroding the power of people at the heart of organizing.

This chapter discusses how organizers can—and must—meet this challenge, not only to win this or that campaign, but to get democracy itself on track. Motivating people to commit to a shared purpose, turning our commitments into collective action, and turning collective action into power is how we win a campaign to improve a school, elect a president, or fight climate change.

What Is Action?

Action is making it happen on the ground (or online): votes in the ballot box, people at the rally, a union contract signed, a wealth tax passed, schools funded well, housing built, access to health care expanded, the unjustly convicted released, the minimum wage raised, coal power banned, and so on.

Action is about mobilizing and deploying resources. Resource *mobilization* refers to the process of gathering resources, often from individuals. Resource *deployment* refers to the process of spending (or investing) those resources, often collectively. The way resources are mobilized affects how they can be deployed, and the way they are deployed affects how they can be mobilized, as shown in Figure 5.1.

A useful way to think about resources is Albert Hirschman's distinction between economic resources and moral resources.[2] Economic resources deplete with use: spend fifty dollars out of the one hundred dollars that you have, and you'll only have fifty dollars. But moral resources *grow* with use: commitment generates more commitment, trust generates more trust, learning generates more learning, and skill generates more skill.

Because organizers usually must rely on some combination of moral and economic resources, recruiting people and raising money can be built into every activity. In the UFW, we never went anywhere without a can and clipboard. We used both—the can to collect money and the clipboard to sign

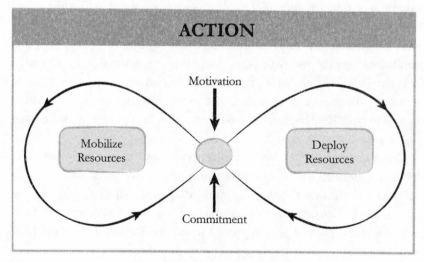

Figure 5.1 Action. *Source*: Steve Downer of the Difference

up volunteers—very extensively on the streets of Manhattan. One day I was walking along, holding a "Boycott Lettuce" sign in one hand and a cup of coffee in the other. Someone passing by said, "I'm with you," and tossed a quarter into my coffee cup.

Organizers fighting for change challenge a status quo with far more abundant economic and political resources. So organizers must not only be resourceful, as I describe in my strategy chapter, but they must also rely on their people's resources. Time, as political scientist Sidney Verba noted, is more widely distributed than money. Tactics that take lots of money—if what you have is lots of people—can severely constrain what you can do. The civil rights movement was resourced fundamentally by the time, commitment, bodies, and courage of its constituency.

When you do need outside money, it matters where that money comes from. The civil rights movement primarily mobilized its financial resources from churches, unions, liberals, four small progressive foundations, and the Voter Education Project, a politically inspired voter registration fund overseen by a team of recognized movement leaders.[3] The movement enjoyed substantial moral, practical, and political alignment among its leaders, its constituency, and its financial supporters. Unions and churches generate their economic resources by bringing people together to create nonmarket value: worship, justice, hope, and community. Funding that depends on the patronage of someone who believes that the millions they made by inventing a new widget—or knowing when to buy or sell it—entitles them to govern civil society is quite another matter.

Deciding to focus on one's constituency is not only about the economics of power. Organizers must develop the capacity of their constituency to lead, strategize, collaborate, and mobilize, not only to generate their own resources but also to practice active democratic citizenship. Outside funding can entrap us in privileging "ownership" over "citizenship": depending on money-based power rather than people-based power.

Although an organization or campaign can mobilize resources in a variety of ways, its center of gravity rests in one of the quadrants depicted in Figure 5.2. If this is in the Inside/People box, then the center of gravity empowers the constituency, becomes accountable to the constituency, and aligns use of resources to the constituency's interest. One example of an organization that can operate in this way is a democratic union. On the other hand, if the center of gravity is in the Outside/Money box, the dependency it can disempower the constituency (unless the constituency is outside), become

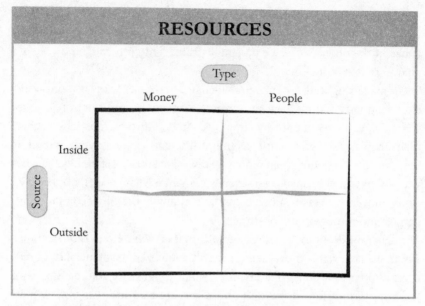

Figure 5.2 Resources. *Source*: Steve Downer of the Difference

accountable to its funders, and limit tactics to those consistent with the interests of its funders.

We need to distinguish the deployment of resources in ways that can generate more resources from ways that simply drain resources mobilized elsewhere. This is one key difference between organizing and mobilizing. In union organizing, for example, the more successful the union, the more members it gets, the larger the dues base, the more leadership it can develop, and the greater its human and financial resources. Similarly, as some community organizations conduct parish renewal work among member churches, their human capacity and financial capacity grow. Grant-based action programs, in contrast, often fail to generate new resources from the work they do, creating a state of perpetual dependency on their funders.

Action is costly in time, effort, and risk. These sacrifices can be widely shared or narrowly held. The more widely shared, the more people have a stake in the outcome. When one or two people do all the sacrificing, they quickly become burned out, while everyone else blames them for whatever goes wrong.

There is no one right relationship between resources and action. But understanding the relationship between resources and action is essential to making mindful choices about how to structure your campaigns and organization to give them a chance to accomplish their purposes, especially when it comes to empowerment of your constituency.

How Action Works: Motivation and Commitment

The more our core resource is time contributed by our people, the more critical is our capacity to sustain motivation and elicit commitment. Since action is ultimately what organizing is all about—changing the world—it's remarkable how often we turn the work of action into a test of how committed we are rather than an opportunity to enhance motivation, deepen commitment, and create opportunities for leadership.

Perhaps you've found yourself in one of the following three situations:

- You've been doing well at recruiting new volunteers, but they only show up to phone bank or to text once or twice and you never hear from them again. How can you keep them coming back?
- You have one person who always runs the tabling operation—or its equivalent—but they're gone for the year. How do you replace them? And, come to think of it, they and a couple of their close friends are the only ones who ever show up to do tabling. Could this be an opportunity?
- Whether it's the check-ins for a conference, getting the food lined up for a celebration, or planning for a hearing, why do I always have to tell everyone exactly how to do these jobs when they ought to know how to do them? People just don't care, do they?

If you've encountered any of these situations, you're struggling with sustaining motivation. You can meet these motivational challenges by designing intrinsically motivational work. When a task is well designed, the people who participate will become more motivated, take more initiative in solving problems, and make a deeper commitment to the work.

When we strategize, we decide on the specific outcomes we need to achieve—and when we need to achieve them—to make the campaign work. For example, our strategy requires that we find ways to give three city council members a greater interest in doing what we want than in ignoring us—or to make it more costly to ignore us than to do what we want. So now we need to organize ourselves to make those outcomes happen.

What specific resources will we ask people to commit: signing a pledge not to eat grapes (for example), signing a petition to the governor, showing up for a meeting, recruiting volunteers for a rally, hosting a house meeting, voting, or something else? A commitment is a specific pledge of the amount of a person's time, money, or action needed to achieve the desired outcome.

It is not whatever a person happens to feel like giving in the moment. When a person says they can't be there for an hour, we may ask, how about half an hour? Can't do that? How about fifteen minutes?

But if it will take an hour for the person to learn what is required, get to work doing it, and they stop before they've gotten good at it, little gets done. What value does this add to our campaign? And what if we need fifty people to show up to a particular meeting to meet a required threshold?

The skill, then, is in matching the needs of your campaign with the motivation of your people. This is the sweet spot for organizing action.

In the above example, only about twenty people ever show up at a city council meeting. So, we've decided that if a delegation of twenty people from each of the three recalcitrant council member's districts showed up, it could be an effective way to kick off our campaign. So how can we organize ourselves to make it happen? What about social media, emails, and texting? These can be useful ways to share information. Will broadcasting an invitation result in twenty people from each district showing up? Not likely. What we need are commitments—commitments we make to each other to be there. So how can I organize this? What if I recruited five people from each district to form a leadership team? And what if each member of the leadership team committed, not only to me but to each other, to commit three more people to join us for a pre-action training session in two weeks? And what if we asked each person, in turn, to make a list of the specific people to whom they would reach out?

Of course, unless people are motivated to fight for the change they need, not much will happen. On the other hand, we too often rely on motivation alone to do the job, without creating the commitment to make it happen—and along the way, launch three leadership teams, working together, to build their own teams. The result, then, is not only sixty people at a council meeting, but new organizational capacity and the new leadership to take it even further—three outcomes, not only one, at best.

So, asking for commitments, protecting them, following up on them, and making good on them is a central function of organizing. Eliciting commitments can be daunting . . . but only if you let it be!

"Will you come to our meeting next Monday?" you might ask. "I'll try," they reply. Great, you think, I got my first one. You put it down as a yes.

Except it isn't a yes. Why not follow up with, "That's fine, but can I really count on you to be there? Yes or no?"

Many people never get there. And in failing to ask for commitments, we are showing a lack of respect for the agency of our constituents to do the work needed to make it happen. Maybe we fear rejection, or maybe even acceptance—which, after all, binds us to the person of whom we have made the ask. Either way, by failing to ask for a commitment we fail to create the tension required to elicit a clear choice. In civic mode, we are not asking people to do us a favor. We are offering those who share our concern an opportunity to do something about it. Their commitment matters.

The key is not in making an *easy* ask but rather in making a *valuable* ask. Some of us believe that the easier the ask, the lower the cost, the more likely the commitment. Is that really the basis on which you decide to what to commit? Here's my one dollar a year, which will solve child poverty. Really? The reality is that we commit—or want to commit—because it's valuable. I am more likely to commit if I believe my contribution will really make a difference, will really matter. When we try to get a commitment by making it easier to say yes, we work against ourselves and our constituents by trivializing the whole effort. Moreover, most of us really do take the commitments we make seriously—which is one reason we avoid making them.

Sometimes we hesitate to ask a committed person for a subsequent or greater commitment. We might think, for example, that if a person commits to giving money, they are less likely to volunteer their time. But it turns out that commitments generate more commitments: once a person makes their first commitment in support of a particular cause, they are more likely to make a bigger commitment in the future! This way of thinking confuses economic resources, which deplete with use, and moral resources, which grow with use.

Social psychologists rely on consistency theory to explain this phenomenon: once we commit, as by signing a pledge, we are more likely to make future choices that are consistent with that one.[4] In other words, someone who signs a petition is more likely to volunteer or give money, and vice versa.

In our grape boycott, you could start by signing a pledge not to buy grapes, then you could volunteer for a shift on a picket line, then you could volunteer to captain a picket line, then you could commit to serving on a local boycott committee . . . all the way up to quitting your job or dropping out of school and joining us full time.

Successful organizing campaigns often incorporate actions that require different levels of commitment, offering people multiple entry points of engagement. The beauty of the grape boycott was that it was an action in which everyone—from a person who shunned grapes in a Florida supermarket to a student who dropped out of school to come to work full time for the UFW, and everything in between—could play a part. At one point in 1975, pollster Lou Harris found that 12 percent of the American public, some 17 million people, were boycotting grapes. The wider the opportunity to contribute, the wider the possible participation, and the more widely distributed the responsibility—and credit—for success. When many people can contribute to the effort, they all can share in its success. It is their victory. This, in turn, creates motivation and a sense of entitlement that facilitates accountability.

There is also a big difference between securing commitments and sharing information as discussed earlier. Broadcasting word of a meeting on social media and asking people for a commitment to attend are not the same thing. Unless organizers and volunteers ask for and obtain commitments to attend—in writing if possible—meeting attendance will depend on chance. This is challenging because we fear rejection, and we fear placing others under obligation because it obliges us as well. Whatever the reasons, it takes courage, training, and dedication to develop a team of leaders who are not afraid to ask for and get commitments. Without this, the action will always remain just a little out of reach.

Finally, there can be a big difference between making commitments and keeping them (unless they were not real commitments in the first place). Many of us say we will be there by 10:00 but instead arrive at 10:15. We say we'll get something done by Thursday but don't finish it until Friday. When we break commitments, even in small ways, the commitment itself begins to mean less for us and for others who are counting on us. Within an organization, failure to honor commitments has an exponentially negative effect. If commitment stops meaning very much for me, when I commit to organizing two house meetings per week with fifteen people at each, am I really going to think that I'll be able to? And if I don't think I can, how hard will

I work toward this goal? Leaders, in other words, need to create a culture of commitment.

Motivation

As an organizer, I had learned certain dos and don'ts of keeping volunteers motivated in the process of mobilizing and sustaining voter registration and petition drives and managing canvassing operations and phone banks. Training, having clear goals, and visible counting helped, as did a little friendly competition.

But I didn't really get it until I was studying with the late Richard Hackman, the distinguished scholar of organizational behavior. Richard introduced me to motivational task design, or how to design tasks so that the motivation to do them well, improve at doing them, and stick with doing them comes from within rather than from extrinsic rewards, like pay, pats on the head, cookies, or medals. Motivational task design entails structuring the work so it becomes intrinsically motivational for those doing it.[5] These ideas were not totally new to me, but this clear articulation of how they interacted with each other enabled me to perform them with craft, intentionality, and excellence. I was surprised to find that the private sector had a far better understanding of how to design inherently motivational work, while sectors that depend on values motivated volunteers remained ignorant. Values-based leaders too often regarded routine tasks as "shit work," assigned it to those of lowest status, and turned them into tests of commitment rather than opportunities for leadership development.

Tasks designed to yield intrinsic rewards are inherently satisfying and produce greater motivation in the form of initiative, learning, and commitment than tasks that only yield recognition, financial, or status rewards.[6] Actions built around tasks that produce greater motivation will create the following experiences for participants:

- **Experienced meaningfulness**: The task is important in the overall scheme of things.
- **Experienced responsibility**: How well the task gets done is up to me.
- **Understood results**: I can see whether I'm doing the work well as I'm doing it.

Organizers can create this experience for participants by designing tasks to have the following characteristics:

- **Task significance**: Does the person experience the significance of the task in terms of its contribution to a valued impact on the world? Does the task matter?
- **Task identity**: Is the person's own contribution, from start to finish, clear in the final result?
- **Skill variety**: Does the task engage a variety of the person's skills, including heart, hands, and head?
- **Autonomy**: Does the person have the space to make competent choices about how to do the work?
- **Feedback**: Are the results visible to the person performing the task as they perform it?

Designing tasks around these characteristics will create the desired psychological states in participants, which leads to positive outcomes for participants and results in positive outcomes for the campaign (Figure 5.3).

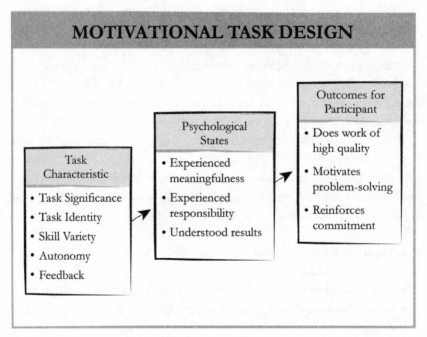

Figure 5.3 Motivational Task Design. *Source*: Steve Downer of the Difference

To see how you put this skill into practice, consider two different ways that you might design a phone bank. It's ten days before an election and early voting has begun. The campaign is trying to nail down voting commitments from less likely voters who are nonetheless believed to be likely to support the campaign's candidate, ballot measure, or cause, if they voted. Given the number of votes needed to win, the number of votes counted, and the number needed to make up the deficit, the goal for this phone bank is to get one thousand commitments in the next four hours. Given the number of volunteers, any given caller would need to obtain at least fifty commitments from a particular part of the city. Molly is the phone bank coordinator, and Ashley is the volunteer.

Scenario 1

Ashley arrives, and Molly greets her volunteer. "Ashley? Thank you so much for volunteering. We need your help. Here's a packet that has all the information: a list of voters, a script, and a way to record results. You can mark their response directly on the list. Just find a spot over there and get started. Good luck. Oh yes, there's some coffee and cookies over there, and the rest room is around that corner. All set?"

Ashley takes her seat, reviews the materials for about ten minutes, and begins to call.

After two hours pass, Ashley puts her phone down and goes up to Molly, telling her, "Sorry, but I have to go. Here's the packet."

Molly replies, "Thanks so much for your help. Just toss the packet over there in the corner with the others. See you next time."

Scenario 2

Ashley arrives. Molly welcomes her: "Thank you, Ashley (it's Ashley, right?). I'm Molly. Thanks so much for volunteering, especially for this shift. I know I don't have to remind you of why winning this vote matters so much for all of us!" She asks why the campaign is so important to Ashley and listens to her answer. Assuming she says anything remotely appropriate, Molly reinforces her response, "Yep. That makes a lot of sense."

After this conversation, Molly provides some background: "We've only got ten days until the polls close, but early voting has already begun. We think we only need another ten thousand votes we can count on. So, we need to nail down five hundred of them here in Springfield tonight. We've assigned you this very important part of town. If you can nail down fifty commits to vote early tonight, with everyone else's work, we should be able to make it. Are you up for that?"

After waiting for a response, Molly moves into the nitty-gritty and hands Ashley a packet. "Can you find the list? Great!" She runs through how it works, consistently asking Ashley to find the relevant information and following up to see if she has questions. Instead of a formal script, she invites Ashley to speak naturally. "Remember, the first thing on the call is to introduce your-self, ask how the voter is doing, respond. Then get to talking points. The idea's not just to read them but to have a conversation about them." When the script does matter, she emphasizes it: "When you're ready comes the ask. Would you read what it says there? Great! That's good. So, when you get your 'yes' click on this link, share anything special, and then you'll be ready to move on."

Molly then directs Ashley to a specific area, "the spot we've reserved for you." She points to the coffee, the cookies, and the restroom. She leaves Ashley, saying, "Thanks, I'll check in in about 30 minutes to see how it's going. And we'll take a break in about 90 minutes, so we get a little rest and see what we've been learning before we get back on the phones. All set? Good luck!"

Molly checks on Ashley after 30 minutes, answers a few questions, asks what she's learning, and notes how well she's done. Over the break, Molly leads a check-in on the numbers and adjusts the plan depending on who's setting an example and who needs support.

At the end of the shift, Molly calls everyone together: "How about a big round of applause for all the good work? Take a look at how we did! Woo! Hoo! We're just two over our goal! Wait a second. Ashley, you got ten. That's three more than anyone else. How'd you do it?" They continue to discuss what worked, what didn't, and what they could do differently.

Molly ends the shift with an invitation to the group: "Before you go, you can see where we need to be, how much we can do if we all show up, so who can commit to tomorrow night? And who will you bring?" Commitments secured, she thanks them and wishes them a good night. "We'll see eight of you again tomorrow! On to victory!!"

* * *

Now let's apply our evaluative criteria on a 1 to 5 scale (see Table 5.1).

In this—admittedly exaggerated—case we can see a clear difference in motiva-tional task design. While most real-life cases would likely generate a score some-where between these extremes of 5 and 25, the point is that you can use these criteria to evaluate your current practice and pinpoint areas for improvement.

Table 5.1 Evaluation of Task Design Scenarios

Criteria	Scenario 1		Scenario 2	
	Characteristic	Score	Characteristic	Score
Task Significance	No context provided. No training.	1	Touched on all key points, goals, and impact; listened; trained.	5
Task Identity	Ashley's interests not recognized at the beginning or end. No interest displayed in her learning. No connection to the final result.	1	Ashley recognized. Clear goal connected to a larger goal, with focus on her preparation. Midpoint check-in; final individual and group recognition.	5
Skill Variety	Read the script, make the call, note the response.	1	Interact with voters, interpret talking points, respond to learning.	5
Autonomy	None	1	Invitation to structure calls based on caller's judgment. Creativity.	5
Feedback	If feedback was available, the caller did not know it.	1	Call progress digitally tracked, visible on ongoing basis, and reviewed after 30 minutes and at the end.	5
Total Score:		5		25

Using these criteria as a diagnostic, we can evaluate participant tasks to determine how motivational they are, redesign them to make them more motivational, and construct them to create a leadership ladder, an opportunity for people to earn greater responsibilities. In these examples, we can clearly see that if the task is designed properly, the phone bank leader can easily identify who's doing well and could possibly do more. Perhaps this volunteer could become a phone bank trainer, a coach, a coordinator, the director of the coordinators, and so on. Any task, properly designed, is an entry point to leadership.

Commitment: The Four Cs
One approach organizers take to getting commitments is called the four Cs: connect, context, commitment, and catapult (Figure 5.4).

Connect. Identify yourself and why you're doing what you're doing and let them know why you're asking them to help. This can be done with a few words.

Context. Be specific about the urgency of the challenge, the plausibility of the hope, and why they matter in achieving a goal about which they care. This can be a story of now.

Commitment. Make the ask as specific as you can to the person you are trying to mobilize. Ask explicitly if you can count on them to do what you're asking. Be very specific about the date, time, and place. Do not be shy. Be certain. And be joyful (if appropriate).

You can use phrases like, "Can we count on you to join us in _____?" Or "Will you join me in doing _____?" Listen carefully to their response.

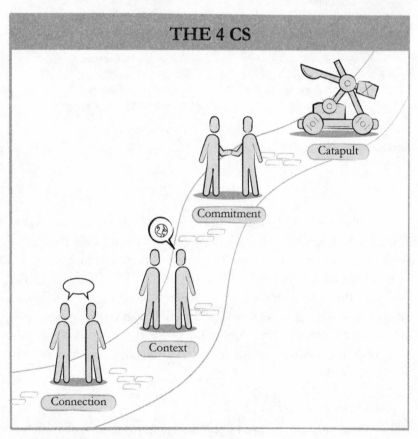

Figure 5.4 The 4 Cs. *Source*: Steve Downer of the Difference

If they say, "Yes! Definitely!" confirm the details. If they say, "Maybe," ask what questions they have and how you can follow up. If they decline, ask why, and give them your contact information in case they change their mind.

Catapult. If someone says yes, then give them the respect of having real work and real responsibility and confirm they have a real plan to get there. You might ask, for example, whether they can bring something to the event (food, posters, etc.), or you might ask them to commit to bringing two people with them. Be sure to ask how the person plans on getting to the event—people with plans are much more likely to attend![7]

To secure the participation of many people, we must delegate the responsibility of securing these commitments to a wide range of leaders or potential leaders. Yet one of the greatest hurdles novice organizers face is finding the courage to ask others explicitly for commitment and to recognize that a no is sometimes better than a maybe. Organizing, after all, is about challenging people to find the courage to make choices consistent with their values. Mobilizing participation through incentives or paying people to volunteer doesn't do this.

Commitments are also made now, or not at all. When you ask someone if they can be at a meeting at 7:00 p.m., and they say yes, get their name and number then and follow up with a reminder call. "I'll try," "I'll do my best," and "Maybe I'll be there" don't count as commitments. The genuine commitments we secure in the moment, then, become an indicator of the outcome we will achieve.

Measurement as Learning: Evidence-Based Organizing

Action must be linked to specific, measurable outcomes with real deadlines. Without clear outcomes, we can evaluate neither success nor failure. If we can't evaluate success or failure, we can't learn for the next time. The absence of clear metrics is one reason volunteer-based work can be perceived as flaky, not reliable, leading people to think that the only way to make the work reliable is to pay for it. After all, they say, "you can't fire volunteers" (except you can) or "you have to settle for what you get" (except you don't). Any serious organizing effort will have to confront this reality if it intends to do real work in the world.

Election campaigns are easier to quantify, in that we must secure a specific number of votes to win. But even in this setting, campaigns often avoid committing to intermediate outcomes. One of the main reasons we may avoid committing to specific outcomes is a fear that failure to reach that goal will diminish the motivation needed to sustain the movement. The cost of avoiding this risk, however, is not only strategic but is also motivational. One of the most important leadership challenges is learning to handle losing. A campaign loss requires narrative interpretation: Does the setback contaminate the enterprise, or does it provide an opportunity for redemption?

Measuring outcomes allows a group to assess, concretely, what is happening and to learn how to improve upon it in what can be a kind of "campaign audit." Assessment allows a group to calculate how it is doing over the course of time. Have we secured as many votes as we had planned to secure at this point in our work? This enables a comparison of one's own outcomes with those of the opposition, or of previous efforts. If we continue at this rate, will we be victorious? What must we do to win? These sorts of comparisons, in turn, allow a group to continue or to alter its course to ensure victory.

Measurement also allows us to learn by making visible who among us is succeeding, who is failing, and why. Who persuaded more people to sign up? Who was not able to persuade as many? What can we learn from this comparison? In other words, how can every organizer perform at the level of the most successful ones?

Similarly, having concrete outcomes allows a group to focus clearly on the specific actions that it must take to produce these outcomes and, in turn, which activities unrelated to the outcome can be eliminated. Without measurable outcome goals, a group can easily lose focus and direction.

Unfortunately, metrics can also be used to assert control, as when a manager decides to fire anyone in the bottom 10 percent, or when an organization makes public statements about who is or isn't good enough. This type of punitive metrics often measures actions that are countable, rather than actions that are valuable. We see this frequently when funders insist on measuring the number of something (phone calls, voter contacts) as a proxy for something else (power, effectiveness).

It is also the case that easily quantifiable measures available digitally can become a kind of ersatz way of measuring outcomes—hyper-analyzed, targeted models—but decoupled from support of the actual ways in which people work with other people.

Total transparency about the use of metrics helps counter the suspicion that numbers are being used to exert control. It's just as important that the constituency sees the numbers being used. For example, Joe's ratio of calls to commitments is very good, especially when compared to Sam's. "So, Joe, describe what you're doing: is it the list, the neighborhood, your pitch, do they already know you? And Sam, describe what you're doing. Oh . . . you haven't gotten the training on how to get commits? Joe, would you give Sam some coaching?" Confronting the reality, probing at what it means, seeing what works and what doesn't, and distancing it from any form of judgment and reprimand can make everyone a learner and a teacher.

Creating measurable outcomes allows us to take control of meeting our goals. Having measurable outcomes—turning out 25,000 votes, for example—lets us focus on something we can control. It becomes a basis for evaluation as well as for learning. Were 25,000 votes in fact enough, as we thought? Or did the other candidate win despite our turning out 25,000? In the future, what should our goal be?

As we discussed in the chapter on strategy, because goals are often embedded within goals, we need to measure our progress on each. For example, in 1990 I worked on the California "Big Green" initiative. To win we would need to identify, recruit, and turn out 75,000 committed voters who only occasionally vote. We would need to kick off the campaign, build the infrastructure to get the job done, and of course turn out these voters on election day.

> **Kickoffs**: On *Saturday, October 20*, mobilize 500 people for seven kickoffs across the state.
>
> **Organizing Peak**: *By November 2,* recruit, train and deploy 1,000 Precinct Leaders to contact 300,000 occasional voters to commit at least 150,000 "green" voters among therm.
>
> **Election Day**: On *November 6*, turn out 75,000 additional "Big Green" voters to the polls.

Of course, each of these outcome goals had several layers of outcome goals embedded within them. For example, how many people needed to be recruited to help turn out the 500 people on October 20? How many of those 500 people needed to assume leadership roles to recruit precinct leaders? How many hours did each of the 1,000 precinct leaders need to work every day to identify their voters?

In the UFW grape boycott, we learned to count grape carloads arriving in a city to evaluate the effectiveness of our local boycott organizing. We learned from asking why one city was more responsive than another. We learned that the effect of the boycott was less to reduce overall grape shipments than it was to reconfigure the market by driving prices down, redirecting grapes, for example, from New York to Dallas. Within each city, we counted the number of customers turned away from a supermarket to calculate the cost we had imposed. This enabled local picket captains, organizers, coordinators, and project directors to experience the impact of their work (or lack of it), learn from it, and strategize ways in which they could become more effective from the bottom up.

In the Obama campaign, we counted the number of volunteers participating in our activities, how many activities were conducted, and who was responsible for which outcome. The intent, however, was not control but learning. Prior to the general election, the Ohio and Pennsylvania teams competed in identifying voters committed to vote for Obama: Barack cheered one state and Michelle cheered on the other.

Organizing physical space to focus on outcomes can help as well—for example, the number of votes secured through phone calls and house meetings can be displayed on a large chart that hangs in the line of sight of anyone who enters headquarters. When you walk through an organizing office, it ought to remind people of what needs to be done, what's important, what things should happen next. The place should have an orienting effect.

Without commitment to clear outcomes, post-action evaluations can't get established as a routine practice. This is routine practice in the military in the form of the After Action Report: a detailed analysis of prior action not for blame but for learning.

Post-action evaluations are a key element in creating a brave space, with the expectation that we must be learning in a regular, ongoing way.

Action in Practice: Contingency, Craft, and Consistency

> Do or do not. There's no try!
> —Yoda, *The Empire Strikes Back*

The world of organizing is a world of contingency—everything can go wrong. Someone forgets to unlock the hall, the sound system is missing a cable, someone forgot to order the chairs, the map got printed backward, half the flyers didn't get printed on time, someone's car has a flat tire, the date was mistranslated in the Spanish version: the list could go on and on. Any human endeavor must deal with contingency. But in a setting where inexperienced people are trying to achieve major tasks, under the pressure of time and with fewer resources than they need—as is typical of most organizing situations—the potential for disaster is always lurking just around the corner. And much of the time, we can't do anything about it.

There are nevertheless contingencies about which we can do a great deal on which we can focus. For example, when asking someone for a specific commitment, asking them to put it in writing improves the odds they will show up. One of the most important aspects of the organizer's craft is to develop the pride of craft discipline to reduce contingencies to a minimum. In this way too structure can create space. As this approach becomes habitual, we can free ourselves to focus on the creative, the innovative, the compassionate, and the hopeful.

Although it may seem intense, the extent to which an organizer can reduce contingency to a minimum is substantial. It is also an investment in making good on time already invested. In a 1974 Bay Area organizing campaign to boycott lettuce, for example, the following is a first-person account of organizing trainer Fred Ross "lovingly" coaching organizer Larry Tramutola on the significance of each detail and the difference getting it right makes. Not unlike learning to create music, excel in athletics, or conduct experiments, this technique is not a way to harass or to blame the organizer. It is a way in which organizers can learn to make the most of their agency to show respect for the work, the people, and oneself.

Pointing to the chart and handing me a colored marker, he told me, "Write down everything you must do each day. Who are you meeting on Monday?" I went over to the butcher paper and wrote down the names and times of the three people that I was supposed to meet that day. Fred continued, "OK, now when are you calling these people to remind them that you are coming to see them?"

Remind them I was coming to see them? "I hadn't thought of that," I told Fred. "Well, write that down," he stated firmly. "Reminding is the essence of organizing." He went over to [the] butcher paper and wrote in the Sunday column: "Make reminder calls to:" Then, he listed the names and phone numbers of the people I was to visit the following Monday.

The lesson continued. "What time are you calling them?" he asked, and before I could answer, he instructed me, "Now write down the time." I did.

But he was not through with me yet. "OK, now on Monday, before you meet with them, you need to call them again, right?" Fred asked. I just nodded quietly while privately thinking that all this reminding and writing down were a bit of overkill. It was only weeks later that I came to understand that these details, and the discipline to put them into practice, are essential to good organizing. At the time, though, I had not learned that for myself, and I certainly did not want to challenge Fred, so I said nothing.

Fred went on. "Good. Now write on the butcher paper the time that you plan to call them, so you don't forget. It is always good to call people right before you visit them, so you don't waste time if they are not there."

"And by the way," he continued, "while you are at the house of one of the people on your list, ask if you can use their phone to call your next appointment. That way they'll see how serious you are," he said.[8]

Of course, Fred practiced what he preached; holding himself responsible for ensuring Larry's success, he held Larry responsible for ensuring that success in making good on their commitments. Larry recalls being coached at the end of each day by Ross:

> We started every call with what I had accomplished during the day. He peppered me with probing questions that demanded thoughtful answers and accountability: "Why did you do that?" "What did you say when he said that?" The interrogation went on for two hours and often longer, as I had to report and relive my successes and failures of the day. Fred asked me one question after another, and unless I was prepared to simply hang up and walk away from what I was doing, there was no escape or relief. But I endured the torment, partly out of pride and partly because I knew Fred was teaching me invaluable lessons about the importance of follow-through and disciplined work.[9]

Good coaches know what questions to ask and know when they are not getting complete answers from those they are coaching. In different organizing situations, there are different questions that are important to ask, and different ways of recognizing when people are bullshitting.

Action in Practice: Motivation and Commitment

Balancing motivational energy and disciplined commitment can be challenging. Focus on commitment can be experienced as trying to quantify,

measure, and "control" motivation rather than as a way to turn motivational energy into the commitment, into the power to change the world. Of
course, the opposite may also be the case: the expressive can be experienced
as interference with the clear strategic logic of commitment. Successful social
movements learn how to cultivate a culture of commitment, learning, and
discipline. At our best, we learned how to do this in the UFW. But cultures
of commitment and discipline, if not about learning, can become seriously
abusive, especially in movements subject to charismatic and authoritarian
leadership structures.

The tools of strategy—targeting, monitoring, and constantly adapting to
ever-shifting realities—do not replace motivation, but they do give it real
leverage. This is the challenge in so many current campaigns whose technological capacity far exceeds anything we imagined at that point in time
but which is no replacement for the motivation rooted in reality. Of course,
motivation without this kind of craft doesn't get it either, any more than it did
back in 1966 when I learned my first lessons about it.

Conclusion

In the introduction to this book, I introduced three measures of impact when
it comes to organizing: the change (our goal), the power (our organizational
capacity), and the people (leadership development). In the context of action,
these measures can be used even more explicitly.

Did we accomplish the goal we set out to accomplish?

Did we pass the law, organize the union, elect the candidate, launch the co-
op, and so on? If we didn't, do we know why? If we did, do we know why? Do
we sustain our effectiveness by measuring visible outputs, analyzing what we
see, and adapting what we do based on what we see?

When a campaign ends, one of the most common behaviors—win or
lose—is to walk away without any serious learning. A commitment to craft,
however, would require asking ourselves: Did we develop metrics to track our
successes and failures? Or did we turn the learning over to the "professionals"
whose interpretation may be a profit-making proposition?

Did we come out of the campaign with greater organizational capacity
than we had at the beginning?

Did we grow stronger as an organization? Did we get better at working
together? Have our people grown more powerful? Can we build on what

we learned? Or do we never want to see anyone connected with this campaign again?

Most electoral campaigns have no interest in building a sustainable organization once the election is over, no matter what the claims (unless they lose). Too often, this is also the case with many advocacy campaigns. In these campaigns as well we need to ask ourselves if we conducted the campaign with an eye to building organizational capacity, or the opposite? Yet for organizing, this outcome is arguably the most important: the transformation of a disempowered community into an empowered community, not only in the conduct of its internal affairs, but also in its ability to influence the shape of the world around it.

Did we recruit, train, and develop the leadership to take our work forward?

Did we develop new leadership motivated to learn, grow, and act? Or did we only exhaust all our old leadership?

* * *

We next turn to the ways to structure the interaction of relationship building, storytelling, strategizing, and action in our work with each other in both campaigns and organizations.

6

Structure

"I resign!"

I was among some 150 youthful SNCC organizers packed into the social hall of Gammon Theological Seminary in Atlanta, Georgia, for the December 1965 staff meeting. We all gasped as Bob Moses, the highly respected director of the Mississippi Summer Project, announced his resignation. His last name was no longer Moses, his father's name, he said. Now he was Bob Parris, his mother's name. We were stunned. What just happened? What did it mean? What now?

Since the end of the Summer Project, SNCC had been struggling not only with heightened tensions over race, gender, and size but also with strategic direction after the defeat at the Democratic National Convention in Atlantic City. The small, intimate, consensus-governed, mostly Black, direct-democracy SNCC had ballooned in size, become more diverse (more white), and developed much more organizational complexity. At the center of it all was the Mississippi Summer Project, the project Bob had led since 1961.

SNCC was rich in committed, creative, and purpose-driven leadership—Jim Foreman, John Lewis, Ruby Doris Robinson, Stokely Carmichael, and others—but Bob had been a unique point of stability, bridging Black and white, inside and outside, novice and experienced. Without agreed-upon rules, practices, or processes—without clear structure—Bob's move plunged SNCC into a painful loss of direction, endless meetings, acute internal divisions, increasing racial tension, and frustration.

My experience in the UFW, on the other hand, revealed how much we could achieve with clear, if far-from-perfect, decision-making, accountability, and learning—one reason I stayed for sixteen years. With a clear structure, one campaign after another could add up. The energy of change created the power of continuity.

But this too came to an end, at least in part due to structural failure. We had failed to construct intermediate levels of power, like a regional local union, between the hundreds of local ranch committees and an eight-person national board led by Cesar Chavez. Without this level of leadership, accountability, and distributed power, the organization was ill equipped to survive the tragic political paranoia that in the mid-1970s gripped Chavez and sent the entire organization into a tailspin.[1]

My experience at SNCC taught me the dangers of a radical diffusion of power. My experience with the UFW taught me the dangers of a radical concentration of power. It turns out that we cannot rely on even the most virtuous of individuals to stay on mission in the absence of virtuous institutions.

What Is Structure?

When we join others in making a commitment to where, when, and for how long we will meet, we create structure, from the Latin "to build." By building structure, we can reduce future uncertainty and conserve creative energy by building a predictable space in which we can coordinate, collaborate, innovate, and organize the work we need to do to achieve shared goals.

Most of us do expect to honor our commitments (one reason we may be reluctant to make them), and we expect others to honor theirs. And because we are far from perfect, we also need to agree on how to hold ourselves and each other accountable. When we build structure, we invest it with the authority of legitimate rules, processes, and procedures with which we can govern ourselves. The greater the number of people trying to work together, the greater their need for shared, accessible, and transparent rules, processes, and procedures.

We create space by creating structure. The alternative is not liberty but chaos. But not all structures are created equal. Some structures can be used to constrain more than to enable. They resist change, tolerate stagnation, and court collapse. Other structures can be used to enable more than they constrain. Do they facilitate authoritative participation, collaboration, and dissent? Do they facilitate responsiveness to change, assure equitable accountability, and prevent concentrating too much power in too few hands? Because change is a constant, we can more usefully think of structure, like strategy, as more of a verb than a noun.

In this chapter we will focus primarily on how authority is structured. Interacting with the authority structure, however, are two other dimensions of structure: how resource flows are structured and how the work itself is structured (Figure 6.1). In addition, informal social networks interact with all three.

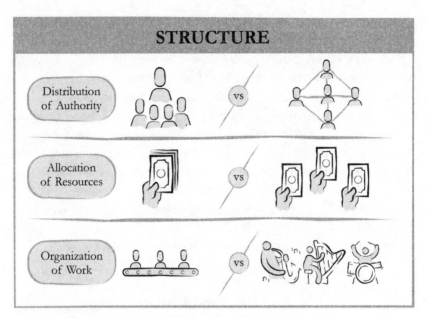

Figure 6.1 Structure. *Source*: Steve Downer of the Difference

We considered the significance of resource flows in the prior chapter: do resources come from the inside or the outside, and are they principally money or people? When one is trying to understand how an organization works, the power dynamics may have more to do with how resource flows are structured than with anything else. For example, although authority may be equally distributed among members of a board, if one member represents a unit that contributes 40 percent of the budget, far more than any other, this will amplify the power of his or her voice, no matter the formal equality. In the UFW, one of the tensions was whether contracts could be won based on each worker's resource of his or her labor, often in the form of a strike, or on resources contributed by supporters in the form of purchasing power, usually a boycott, access to which was controlled by the central leadership of the union.

The way work itself is structured also matters. Is it designed more like an assembly line, supervised by a single foreman, in which each person does their prescribed, often repetitive task? Or is it designed more like a team, requiring interdependent collaboration? I saw this very clearly in Salinas Valley in the difference between an hourly compensated hoeing crew, each hewing to his or her row, with one supervisor. The lettuce harvest crews, on the other hand, were paid by an amount per box, divided among a crew of twenty-five. The crew then decided how to distribute the pay among the "trios" of two cutters and one packer, a closer for every two trios, and a loader for every six or so. When it came to holding the power, the lettuce crews, far and away, had the most solidarity, coherence, and mutual support.

And finally, an informal structure with impact is that of the relationships among persons within the organization: did they go to the same prep school, did they come from the same town in Mexico, did they belong to the same neighborhood gang, do their kids go to the same school, or are they simply friends whose families hang out together? In fact, in the absence of clear formal authority structures, it will often devolve into opaque interpersonal relationships.

Structuring the practice of democracy is what this chapter is about.

Four Structural Tensions

In the months immediately following Trump's election, Americans banded together in groups small and large to express their outrage with the administration's policies. Seven years later, many of these groups have disbanded, not so much due to expected opposition but more likely overcome by structural challenges, organizational dysfunction, and insecure funding. Only rarely did they scaffold leadership development, commit to robust forms of self-government, establish deep membership financial support, or become effective voices in regional or national decision-making, including the choice of their own leadership. Although many conceived of themselves as national in purpose, too often they devolved into local groups, capable of making authoritative claims neither regionally nor nationally. Nor could they hold state or national entities with which they were associated accountable. Nor could their state or national entities hold locals accountable. Without structures for peer organizational learning, local groups missed opportunities to learn from each other's failures and successes. The result minimized local, state, and national capacity for power building in the name of individual liberty, local autonomy, or resistance to bureaucracy. Some groups survived to become for-profit firms or nonprofit firms dependent on major donors. There are exceptions, mostly at the local level. Some owed their effectiveness to volunteers who belonged to a church, a union, a PTA, a soccer league, or another remnant of Tocqueville's great free schools of democracy. Others may have been trained in the 2008 Obama campaign. And still others, organized in the Alinsky mode, have built long-lasting community organizations, rooted mostly in local parishes, synagogues, and mosques, launched long before Trump and each of which tackles diverse "issues" that can contribute to growing the power of the organization.[2] They remain almost exclusively local, barred from political action and unable to engage power structured at the state or national levels. Few are governed by leadership accountable to a membership base that neither elects nor funds them, most dependent on donors, large and small.[3] The truth is that claims we make to justice or policy have little clout without a vision of the organization or institution we are building to sustain growth of the power our constituency needs. Winning a single campaign—or even a series of them—is a good thing. But only rarely does winning a campaign shift the balance of power: wins are too easily reversed, promises not lived up to, and control reverts to the hands that held it before. Deep change requires organizing the sustained power to win it, keep it, and grow it. In the UFW, we knew we were building a union, so every individual campaign, won or lost, could contribute to that objective. Over the years many strikes had led to short-term wage increases but not to the sustained power needed to change the rules of the game. Organization enables people to transform individual interests into common interests, individual resources into collective power, and short-term wins into long-term power.

So a major challenge has been more focus on issues and campaigns than on power and organization. Although SNCC was a "band" of organizers engaged in numerous campaigns, the campaigns, in many cases, were about building powerful locally rooted organizations: the Mississippi Freedom Democratic Party, Lowndes County Freedom Organization, and others. In fact, SNCC could be quite critical of campaigns led by Dr. King, who would arrive in town, stir things up, and leave few remnants behind. In the UFW as well, I led many campaigns, but the project there too was to build an organization strong enough to sustain, grow, and expand the power of its constituency: a farmworkers' union.

Democracy is a way to structure collective authority rooted in the equal worth of each person's voice in concert with others. It is, in the words of Charles Taylor, an effort to govern ourselves rooted in commitment to equality, solidarity, and freedom.[4]

Given the reality of cultural, racial, ethnic, generational, economic, and religious conflict, pluralism in terms of identity, interests, and values democracy requires political structuring that affirms individual and minority rights within governance by the many. This is particularly challenging in the United States, because the nonrepresentative and anti-majoritarian features of our Constitutional structure—the Senate, first-by-the-post elections, gerrymandered and noncompetitive districts—make it possible for a relatively homogeneous minority to dominate a far more heterogeneous majority.[5] It isn't just a matter of crossing the aisle. As James Baldwin is said to have observed, "We can disagree and still love each other unless your disagreement is rooted in my oppression and denial of my humanity and right to exist."

For those committed to democracy, the development of an experiential, moral, or values-based narrative—or identity—within which these kinds of differences can be situated can be one way to address this challenge. Relationship building can also contribute. But neither shared narrative nor relationship building is sufficient in the absence of organizational structures that enable people to work together, make decisions, coordinate action, and hold themselves accountable.

The structural challenge is to design a way that legitimate decisions can be made in the name of the whole community, based on the equal authoritative value of each person's voice and enacted in ways that both respect each person's voice and can get things done.

For example, we may hear each person's voice when we decide to build a new school. We may deliberate with each other in a process in which each voice has equal value, after which we may decide by a majority vote. Who then is responsible for getting the school built? All of us? Let's say we commit to building the school with our own hands. What if some people are more able than others? Many of us lack the requisite skills, or we can't take off work. Most likely we would select—or already have selected—one person or a small team who accepts responsibility to make it happen. Do we continue to take votes on every step they take, or have we delegated to them the authority to do what must be done to get it done, including holding us accountable to the commitments we make, in return for which they accept responsibility for getting the school built, subject to the approach we had decided to take? Similarly, when we commit to a campaign, do we expect to vote on every strategic choice those who hold responsibility for leading the campaign must make?

We may all participate in robust debate about whether to take the hill, but we structure ourselves differently when it comes to actually taking the hill. This is one of the dilemmas of a commitment to self-governance: When does authority flow from the bottom up, and when must it flow from the top down or, if you prefer, from the outside in or from the inside out?

When we create any structure, democratic or not, we must tackle four core dilemmas (Figure 6.2). How can we facilitate change and enable continuity? Whom do we include and whom do we exclude in what decisions and what actions? How do we sustain the diversity to facilitate inclusion, creativity, and accountability and simultaneously ensure the unity that enables focus, coordination, and collective action? How can parts participate in constructing a whole greater than a sum of the parts? And how can a whole facilitate development of strong parts? In this chapter we explore tensions inherent in the structuring of democratic collective action: change and continuity, inclusion and exclusion, unity and diversity, and parts and wholes.

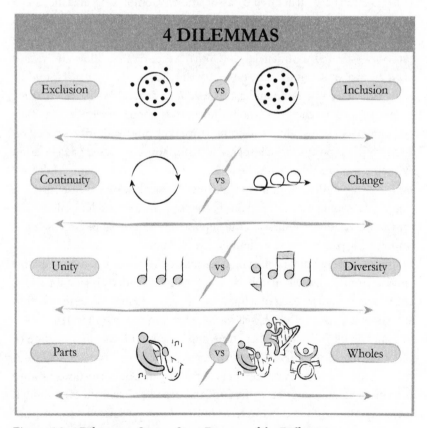

Figure 6.2 4 Dilemmas. *Source*: Steve Downer of the Difference

Change and Continuity

Organizing is usually about change, but organization requires continuity. Organizing a campaign requires urgency, focus, capacity building, and adaptation. It moves from a status quo condition to a future and different condition. Organization requires predictability, stability, and coherence. It is about turning new conditions created by a campaign into the capacity for a sustained exercise of power. Sustained vitality, relevance, and effectiveness require adaptation driven by new voices, experiences, and learning. Continuity requires predictable ways to hear these voices, respond to these experiences, and engage in learning.

Continuity: Organization

For purposes of this book, I distinguish between organizations structured as firms and those structured as associations. Complex organizations can be distinguished by whether authority flows from the top down or from the bottom up. Businesses, nonprofit firms, and bureaucracies structure authority—as well as financial and other resources—to flow downward from an owner, set of owners, donors, or boards to top managers, middle managers, and workers. Complex organizations do not have members. They have customers or clients to whom they market goods or services, and they hire employees whose time and compliance they buy. Authority is based on ownership (property),[6] with leaders exercising authority based on delegation by their superiors. Firms may be inclusive and even participatory, but they are not democratic. Although both forms of organization have politics, the coin of firm politics is authority itself, that is, palace or insider politics. The coin of associational politics is the support of membership. Organizing— empowering people—is about building associations.

Unions and civic and professional association's structure authority to flow upward from individual members who elect local leaders, regional leaders, and national leaders, each of whom is authorized to make decisions within their domain. Authority is based on membership (people). Elected leadership may work full time or part time and may recruit or hire full-time or part-time administrators who provide services and/or organizers who recruit, equip, and coordinate members to participate. Authority flows upward as to basic rules, choice of leadership, and broad policy. And even though authority usually flows downward or outward as to programs, projects, and campaigns, in the past, financial and membership resources flowed upward.

This changed in the last thirty to forty years, as professionals could use communication technologies to generate both money and members directly from a center that distributes these resources downward. What had been a bi-directional flow of authority and resources made leading an association far more challenging than managing a firm.[7] The fact that resource flows are far less bi-directional has made sustaining the democratic character of many associations significantly more problematic as well. Yet it is associations, not firms, that have always been our "great free schools of democracy."

Religious, political, and advocacy groups, as well as social movements more generally, structure themselves in both ways. The Roman Catholic Church, for example, structures authority to flow top down, like a firm, perhaps guided by the subsidiarity principle that decision-making be delegated down to the lowest level practical but is very active in motivating participation as well as significant resources from the bottom up. Many Protestant churches, Muslim mosques, and Jewish congregations, on the other hand, structure authority and resources to flow from the bottom up, like an association, guided by the federal principle of delegating authority upward. As a membership-based organization that derives its funds from members and elects its membership at the local, state, and national levels, the NRA operates as an association. Ironically, in most community organizations, no matter how hard the staff works to engage them, those they call their "base" do not elect leadership, hold staff accountable, pay for the organization, or govern themselves.

To the extent that a membership association aspires to make an impact (even a local impact), it often requires reaching beyond the local, and it will grow larger, become more geographically diffuse, acquire more assets, engage in tasks of greater complexity, try to preserve more lessons from its past, and try to extend its horizons further into the future. This is also known as "getting to scale" and requires and facilitates greater complexity in authority structures, routines of practice, and resource configurations. Operating this kind of organization requires commitment of more—and different—resources, energy, and leadership.

This phenomenon puts associations at risk of falling victim to what sociologist Robert Michels described as the "iron law of oligarchy": the operations side can take over the policymaking side. As more resources are devoted to the organization itself, the goals of the organization may transform into sustaining the organization itself as a goal. This is especially problematic if, as it grows, the organization's work grows more specialized and requires more full-time elected or appointed staff. As such, the staff may compete for organizational resources, using its control over resources to insulate itself from membership accountability.[8]

Further, a kind of elective affinity may come into play to the extent that this organizational tension reflects conflicts in our own feelings about stability and change. On the one hand, our curiosity, sense of adventure, and desire to learn may draw us to innovate. On the other hand, our need for predictability, proficiency, and stability may cause us to fear innovation. Although most of us experience both kinds of pull, some of us are drawn more to the innovative, evangelical, and experimental, while others are attracted to the stable, predictable, and proficient. The fact that people with different dispositions converge in different parts of an organization creates the possibility of either constructive synergy or organizational fragmentation.[9]

This challenge can become acute in membership associations. An association that successfully grows its membership creates the constituency most inclined to resist investing organizational resources in further growth. The issue becomes particularly acute in that control over organizational resources falls naturally into the hands of those stabilizing the organization to a greater degree than those growing it—into the hands of bishops, in other words, rather than missionaries. It is therefore essential to build in strong accountability mechanisms at both the individual and the organizational levels from the beginning.

Change: Campaigns

We build organizations to enable continuity, but we launch campaigns to create change. If we structure an organization to remain responsive to its constituency, support ongoing renewal, invite dissent, and sustain capacity for unified action, we structure campaigns to deploy people for a limited period by focusing on achieving a particular outcome. Organizing requires both forms of structure.

Our word "campaign" comes from the French *campagne*, the word for field, and that came to describe an army's process of taking the field. Campaigns are not designed to last. They are designed to win. They are a very focused, intensive, deadline-driven stream of activity, launched on a particular day to achieve a particular goal at a particular time by winning a particular battle. The winner then gets either to impose welcome change or to have resisted unwelcome change.

A campaign is structured strategically as an unfolding narrative or story. It begins with a foundation period (prologue), starts crisply with a kickoff (curtain goes up), builds slowly to successive peaks (act 1, act 2), culminates in a final peak determining the outcome (denouement), and is resolved as we celebrate the outcome (epilogue). Our efforts generate momentum not mysteriously, but as a snowball. As we accomplish each objective, we generate new resources that can be applied to achieve the subsequent greater objective. Our motivation grows as each small success persuades us that the subsequent success is achievable—and our commitment grows.

Campaign timing is structured in clear phases, with a peak climaxing each phase—a specific day when your whole campaign will deploy its full current capacity to cross a qualitative threshold, the result of which will be a whole new level of capacity. In organizing, our first major peak may be when we focus most of our effort on turning people out from across the region to kick off the campaign. Happily, many actually show up. The region is divided into five districts, so we can pull together the people who came from each district. We can then support them in organizing their own team in each district, each of which can organize their own kickoff. And so forth.

After each peak, your staff, volunteers, and members need time to rest, learn, retrain, and plan for the next phase. Often organizations say, "We don't have time for that!" This is a mistake. Campaigns that don't take time to reflect, adjust, and retrain end up burning through their human resources—treating them more like "resources" than like "humans" and becoming more and more reactionary over time.

When it comes to authority, most campaigns are strategically led from a center. Whether centered on a neighborhood, city, state, national, or global campaign, strategic focus matters. Yet good strategy requires an overview of the whole (from the mountaintop) with a nuanced view of the local (down in the valley). Wise campaigns combine leadership from a center not only with information gathered locally but with local strategic leadership as well. The effectiveness of the campaign on the ground may depend on local leadership with the responsibility—and authority—to organize their own turf, adapting to local nuance, constraint, and opportunity. This tension is more easily managed if a campaign is local, but a very similar tension can play out between neighborhood leadership and that of a city as a whole. The key is to structure a campaign in a way that connects the information needed, the skills required, and the authority to decide what is right in the right locations.

We must also distinguish between the far more common mobilizing campaigns than organizing campaigns. A mobilizing campaign usually concentrates authority at the center, based on whatever form of information is available to the center (often digitally mediated, like polling or modeling) and what control is accessible. At times, control goes all the way down to the script a local volunteer can use to speak to a particular voter, whether digitally or in person (message control). The volunteer is a messenger delivering a prescribed message and not an organizer, even if the campaign calls the messenger an organizer.

An organizing campaign requires that authority be much more widely distributed so that decisions can be made about how to proceed based on information only locally accessible. The 2008 Obama campaign structured itself at state, regional, local, and even polling-place levels because the campaign leadership understood that developing trained, committed, and responsible local leadership could maximize voter turnout. Authority then was nested all the way up—at the precinct, region, district, city, state, and national levels—with coaching, training, accountability, and support available at every level. Consequently, the campaign invested in the development of more civic capital than anything before or since.

So where does the democracy come in? Does everyone vote on campaign strategy? If so, who is included in "everyone"? Who is responsible for making the strategy work? Does everyone decide their own local strategy even if it is a regional, state, or national campaign?

One way to look at this is to ask how widely distributed authority is throughout the campaign structure. For example, one could argue that a team structure is more "democratic" than a single leader structure in the way it creates interdependence and distributes responsibility—and the authority to go with it.

Another way to look at it is to ask, Who decided to do the campaign in the first place? Was it an organization? Was it a democratic association in which authority is rooted in the participants, or a democratic association in which authority is rooted in the organizers? Was it an NGO—a type of firm—in which authority is rooted in a self-selected board? Did the decision not come from an organization at all, but rather from a wealthy funder or candidate?

In other words, the place to look for democracy may not be in the campaign itself, but rather in the structure of the organization that decided to launch the campaign and that may benefit from it. And this brings us back to the tensions associated with inclusion and exclusion.

Inclusion and Exclusion

Whose voices are heard? Whose voices count? Anyone who shows up at a meeting? The founders and their friends? People who commit to obligations in return for voice and the rights and benefits that come with it: citizens, members, dues payers? People appointed by a board. People chosen to speak on behalf of a whole. Chosen or elected? By whom?

In democratic associations, the first question is, who is a member? Who gets the right to authoritative voice in the commons in return for commitments the commons require? Individuals acquire such rights as choosing leadership, deciding on policy, and so on, in return for accepting such obligations as paying dues, honoring norms, respecting legitimate decisions, and attending meetings. In this way, individual interests can be transformed into common interests and individual resources into collective power.

Economist Albert Hirschman described this arrangement as the promise of voice in return for loyalty.[10] No collective can survive based on rights alone: show up whenever, participate when you like, respect decisions if it suits. In the absence of voice, Hirschman argues, exit is the only option if things don't go your way. Exit is how markets work. The difference between the two highlights how political decisions about common interests differ from the way markets transform individual preferences into narrowly efficient, if not just or wise, outcomes. Consumers enter a marketplace at will, exercise their preferences, and exit. But these are mechanisms of transaction, not of commitment, combination, and politics. Obligations give us an interest in making the community work, even when it is difficult and when we disagree with it. Constituents enter into a relationship with each other, accept responsibility for the whole, and get access to the power that grows with it.

Who is in and who is out? And who decides who is in and who is out? Every act of inclusion also excludes: at the moment we define our bounded in, our "us," we also define a bounded out, our "not-us." On the one hand, boundaries may limit our capacity for inclusion. On the other hand, a community—or, for that matter, a marriage, a family, or any other kind of group—without boundaries is not a community. The question, then, is not whether we bound an organization, but rather how we bound it that gives it an identity shared by those who participate in it.

We need bounding to create trust among the members, as organizational behavior scholars Kenwyn K. Smith and David N. Berg articulate:

For a group to develop the critical internal relationships so that it can become an entity worthy of being trusted, it needs to have the trust of its members and the assurance they will stand by the group through the bad times and the good. The paradox of trust can be represented by the conundrum of a cycle that depends on itself to get started: for trust to develop in a group, members must trust the group and the group must trust its members, for it is only through trusting that trust is built.[11]

Clear boundaries as a key component of organizational structure empower members to understand and embrace the responsibilities that come with membership. Amorphous structures create situations in which members experience confusion, and sometimes resentment, about what they're being asked to do. When I, as a member, confuse the commitments that I have chosen with bureaucratic obligations that are imposed upon me by someone else, I've made a serious mistake. I have confused the responsibilities of membership in a multitiered organization that delegates authority upward with the burdens of a top-down organization that delegates control downward. The less clarity and transparency an organization has about its structure, the more likely members are to experience the kind of confusion that creates organizational dysfunction.

In democratic organizations, each of us—or our representatives—can participate in and decide on the structure to which we will commit: the rules, processes, and procedures that enable us to work together, including boundaries for participation and decision-making.

Unity and Diversity

Diversity is an asset when it comes to strategizing, learning, inclusion, and collaboration; it helps us avoid groupthink. But once we have decided on a course of action, we need unity in carrying it out. Deep-rootedness in diverse local communities can be a source of real strength, but coordination in the pursuit of common regional or national goals can be a source of real power. Diversity of experience, skill, and perspective can be a vital resource when we form a team, but unity of shared purpose is required for that team to become functional.

Without knowing who is in a group, the cycle of trust—which is difficult to begin, even with organizational boundaries in place—is even more difficult to set in motion. Bounding an organization also entails setting norms for the organization. While norms will develop naturally whether we set them explicitly or not, we are better off being explicit. As social psychologist Richard Hackman explains, we must set norms explicitly to counter human tendencies that lead to unproductive organizational work:

> A first ordinary tendency is our disposition to react to whatever captures our attention and demands a response, rather than to actively scan our environment for less obvious problems and opportunities that may call for nonstandard actions. . . .
>
> A second human tendency . . . is our understandable impulse to have harmonious interactions with others, to be approved rather than rejected by our teammates, and generally to keep anxieties as low as possible.

Third, as a group sets explicit norms to approach its work proactively and agrees on "the outer-limit boundaries of what behaviors are acceptable," it can effectively counter these tendencies.[12]

Unity is the source of a membership association's power because it is through combination that associations acquire the resources they can deploy to create the power they need. At the same time, diversity is often the most critical source of an association's creativity, accountability, and ability to learn. As social psychologists have learned, the more homogeneous a group, the better it can be at taking the hill, but the more diverse a group, the better the decisions it will make about whether to take the hill in the first place.[13]

Dissent, in other words, can be associated with better decisions, but poorer performance. Unanimity can be associated with better performance, but poorer decisions. Too much unity (such as groupthink) can stifle an organization by destroying its responsiveness to its constituency and its capacity for renewal. If an association fragments into factions, each of which views its interests as the interests of the whole, it loses the capacity to discern the common interests that make combination possible, let alone the capacity to translate those interests into the effective mobilization and deployment of resources.

Dissent is critical for decision-making processes, but dissent on its own can be divisive and lead to scapegoating within an organization. A group needs to be able to receive negative feedback about its processes to learn and grow, but the message may feel like an assault on the group's norms. The bind is that the group may elect not to listen to the very things it needs to hear. Instead, it may choose to reject the carrier of the message so that it does not have to deal with the message, treating the concerns as "belonging" to the person expressing them rather than seeing this as an integral part of the group itself.

Parts and Wholes

Groups that find success typically desire growth. The campaign worked: Let's do another one! The neighborhood chapter made city hall listen: Let's build citywide! While scaling up offers the thrilling possibility of making change at scale, growth creates another set of tensions about the relationship between parts and whole that leaders engaged in democratic practices must ultimately confront.

Although exclusively local groups may operate as single entities, many associations or movements find they must coordinate their efforts across localities or at regional, national, or international levels. Until the 1960s, this challenge was often addressed through the formation of three-tiered, federated structures that linked local, state, national, and, in some cases, transnational efforts.[14] This form persists in unions, some faith communities, and membership organizations like the Sierra Club. But many individuals and movements have, especially in recent years, come to view this structure as bureaucratic, controlling, and stifling.

The challenge is how to harmonize local units with regional and national strategy and regional and national strategy with local units to enable the trans-local coordination, learning, and mutual support needed to win. Although many view decentralized local organizations as democratic and responsive (good), and the trans-local and centralized as oligarchic and unresponsive (bad), local groups, too, can become oligarchic and unresponsive, and national groups, democratic and responsive.

Political scientist E. E. Schattschneider, writing about political conflict, argues that widening participation by linking groups across localities is a way to amass the power one needs to accomplish organizational goals (by pooling resources, creating a broader strategic venue, etc.). Additionally, geographical growth facilitates accountability—both to one's constituency and to the broader goals on behalf of which one organized in the first place. Schattschneider claims that elites try to localize conflict, while insurgents try to broaden the arena of conflict—they can access more allies, more diverse resources, and more observers who can be mobilized for support. Trans-local organizations can moreover create venues within which local elites can be held more accountable. We seem to forget this reality with a focus on the virtues of local direct democracy over those of representative democracy.[15]

This argument builds on that of James Madison in Federalist Paper No. 10, where he argued that large democracy is preferable to small democracy because it is harder for a single faction to take control, turning the common interest into factional interest. Traditionally, corruption in the United States was far more common at the local and state levels than at the national level (although the Trump administration did its best to catch up).[16] Organizationally, the greater the degree of local autonomy, the more vulnerable the organization is to oligarchy, not at the top but at the bottom. As such, it contributes to the fragmentation of organizational resources as each local group becomes a Madisonian faction, seeing its own interest as the interest of the whole. The whole can then become reduced to the lowest common denominator, less than the sum of the parts, rather than more.

This phenomenon grows out of the ways that associational members form their interests—their preferences. A carpenter working in commercial construction in San Francisco, with only a local organizational affiliation, may understand her interest entirely as a local carpenter. But if she also belongs to an organization that links all the San Francisco building trades, she may learn to see her interest more as a building tradesperson, not only a carpenter. If that unit, in turn, links people who work in the building trades with other working people in the area, it may turn out that she also has shared interests with other working people—such as transportation costs, access to health benefits, and so forth. This realization makes broader mobilization possible. And if this new grouping is also affiliated with a political party or other political grouping that links working people with others in a similar economic situation but who earn their incomes differently, common interests may emerge in public schools, parks, and other public facilities. Associations with which we affiliate not only represent our interests; they may shape our understanding of those interests as well. And the more interdependent we understand ourselves to be, the more broadly we can construe our interests to be as well.

Meeting this challenge is one version of the challenge that faces all democratic organizations: designing ways in which legitimate decisions can be made rooted in the equal value of each person's voice and enacted in ways that can get the job done. The goal is to create a structure that can assure authoritative participation, accountability, and effectiveness.

Unless our decision-making process is coupled with our getting-things-done process, and both are accountable to the membership, nothing may happen. For this to work, local groups, like individuals at local levels, must have a legitimate voice in decisions made at regional or national levels. At the same time, each person's responsibility of loyalty must be clear when it comes to acting on those decisions. Unfortunately, a common default position seems to offer each local group the autonomy to do what it will do, even though this will cripple trans-local strategy, learning, and development. Usually, though, once these local groups are launched, the larger organization loses interest in facilitating training, coaching, and other aspects of sustained development. Or the local groups respond to resist national bodies they experience as trying to impose illegitimate regional or national programs on the local group. The former is a formula for frustration, diffusion of effort, and failure; the latter, for ongoing conflict, resistance, and resentment.

The problem of parts and wholes is an organizational version of the strategic dilemma discussed in chapter 4: effective strategizing can occur only when the overview of the context from the top of the mountain is combined with the intimate view of context in the valley. One is not right, nor the other wrong. They are two perspectives that, when linked, transform the power of both on their own. Local groups that insist they can see the whole truth of the situation, or national groups that insist they can see the whole truth of the situation, are both missing the true picture. In concert with others, local leadership can compare practices, coordinate work on common challenges, and place their local experience within a broader statewide or national frame of reference.

Examples of the relationship among local control, accountability, and a broader mission can be found the labor movement. Unions structure themselves in a variety of ways, one metric of which is their degree of local, often craft-based, decentralization and regional, often industry-based, centralization. Examples of highly decentralized unions include the building trades, craft unions, and others that traditionally operated in local labor markets in which they could assert control by organizing highly skilled workers. These unions typically had very large locals, operated autonomously, and paid a very small per capita to their national organizations, which were typically governed by a national board dominated by the leaders of the large local unions.

In contrast, the industrial unions that organized employees of companies operating across multiple localities such as autos, rubber, or steel tended to be more centralized. These unions could often only assert control in local labor markets by leveraging the influence they had in places where they enjoyed political support to organize other places where they did not. In the auto industry, for example, the UAW was able to use the leverage it held in Michigan, where it had conducted effective sit-down strikes without interference from a friendly governor, to organize other states where the politics or labor market conditions were far less friendly. These unions typically had locals of diverse sizes, organized into districts or regions or departments within which they had to collaborate to arrive at common positions, paid large per capita dues to their national organizations, and were governed by a board dominated by leaders elected on a regional or national basis. As a side note, the more radical socialist unionists also favored this form of centralized industrial organization to develop greater working-class consciousness and solidarity.

Which form is more oligarchic? Which is more corrupt? Which is more adaptive? Which is most democratic? What is the role of leadership and organizing with respect to these structures.

Both forms are vulnerable to oligarchic take over in the absence of robust mechanisms of internal accountability, and internal organizing. Incumbents tend to use the resources to which they, as incumbents, have access to do what they need to do to remain incumbents. As the Mexican saying goes, "entre menos burros, mas elotes"—the fewer the donkeys the more the corn. Michels famously identified this challenge as the "iron law of oligarchy"— full time officials, elected or not, sooner or later put their own interests, for the "good" of the organization itself, ahead of those of their members.[17] Lipset further clarified the structural dimension of this problem as not simply a matter of "bad people."[18] Margaret Levy also identified conditions under which members are unlikely to challenge incumbents, whether corrupt or radical: having built enough bargaining power to deliver for them.[19] Even though accountability mechanisms may exist, members may not want to take advantage of them.

In reality it takes **both** good leadership and organizing to put the accountability mechanisms to work . . . not so different from what it takes to make any democracy work. Structure may well be necessary but is insufficient for making a democracy work.

Although there have been notable oligarchic abuses in national unions, especially if members and weaker or strategically dependent locals rely on national economic, political, and strategic resources to function. For example, the Teamsters in the Jimmy Hoffa era or the United Mine Workers in the Tony Boyle era.[20]

Local large autonomous local unions are perhaps more vulnerable to oligarchic power grabs because it is all local: the work, the people, the bosses, the courts, the media, the golf courses, etc. Corruption of large locals became endemic, for example, in UNITE HERE, the hotel, restaurant, and culinary workers union, including locals "mobbed up" by the Mafia. Only an aggressive disciplined, strategic, and sustained internal organizing campaign, led by the national union could begin to take them back in the 1970s and 1980s.[21] National unions not controlled by large locals can, at the very least offer support, intervention, and reform, along the lines of SEIU's efforts in the 1980s and the 1990s.[22]

National unions and local unions can run as effective democratic organizations. But without the leadership and organizing to use the accountability structures it won't happen. Both can become oligarchic in the absence of such leadership, not to mention the structural tools with which to work.

Some of the most effective democratic unions are hybrids. These organizations figured out how to integrate the centralizing features that can afford more bargaining strength, educational resources, and political influence— and the "distributed" features of local and regional engagement and representation.

The United Auto Workers (UAW) can be a case in point. Since the 1940s the UAW, in the tradition of Walter Reuther, was a progressive, honest, and powerful hybrid union—at the local, regional, and national level.[23] The collapse of automobile manufacturing the more recent years of recovery only increased the gap between management profit and workers' earnings and benefits tied to concessions made in the 1980s. So in 2020 autoworker Shawn Fain began to organize Unite All Workers for Democracy, an internal union reform caucus organization that seized an opportunity created by US Labor Department anti-corruptions. They won a structural change in how national officers are chosen. Instead of election by convention delegates it would be vote of the entire membership. They the organized the vote needed to win, organized support for long overdue contract improvements, which turned into support for a remarkable strike, and they won.[24]

So here's the point. They're interdependent. Democratic structural features can make it possible. Leadership organizing can make it happen.[25] They can also make for a more powerful union.[26] And so, it is for making democracy work.

In sum, it's not all about "centralized" structure or "local" structure, but their integration that can offer the best means of integrating parts and whole, give insurgents room to maneuver, create broader strategic venues, create opportunity for broader understanding of common interest, and minimize oligarchic control. But all this only makes it more or less possible. It takes leadership and organizing to put it all together and make it happen.

Three Ways to Manage Tensions

Tensions are inevitable, even necessary, in democratic organizing, but they need not derail a movement. We can devise diverse strategies to manage the tensions—if we acknowledge them—that come with balancing continuity and change, inclusion and exclusion, and unity and diversity. Among these are distributing responsibility, facilitating collaboration, and preserving dissent (Figure 6.3).

Distribute Responsibility

An organization committed to leadership development and wide participation is better equipped to engage with change on an ongoing basis than an

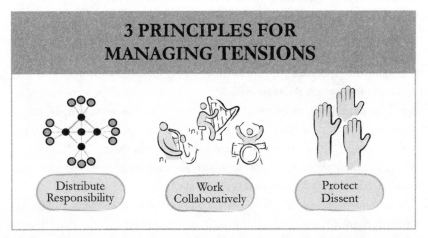

Figure 6.3 3 Principles for Managing Tensions. *Source*: Steve Downer of the Difference

organization that walls its leadership off in a tight circle of control. Sustained commitment to identifying, recruiting, and developing new leaders, and to finding new ways to engage one's members more broadly, requires organizational leadership to respond to new currents, new ideas, and new challenges. Wide participation can also ensure ongoing responsiveness to the need for change, albeit within a framework with substantial continuity.

Similarly, openness to bringing in new people and broadening participation confronts leaders with the challenge of how to engage different kinds of people, people with different backgrounds. At the same time, openness creates venues within which members can express their concerns, be heard, and see evidence of organizational responsiveness. The more extensively responsibility is shared among the leadership and membership of an association, the more the parts come to understand—and play a part in—the whole, and the more the whole must understand about the interests and resources of the parts.

This is all very good, but what are the consequences of taking this approach for organizational performance in general? In membership associations, the more widely we share responsibility for organizational results, the greater interest the members acquire in the common effort and the more resources they will commit to its success. It may be more efficient to get five people to spend the whole day collecting signatures in a city, but it may be more effective to get ten teams of five to spend one hour each getting signatures in their own neighborhoods. Similarly, scholars of work organization have shown that distributing responsibility, or "vertically loading" jobs, can increase motivation and—by extension—productivity.[27]

Second, distributing responsibility not only empowers an association by engaging the resources of more people. It also empowers more people within the organization because they hold the resources needed to do the work. The more members share the responsibility for doing the work, the more getting the work done depends on their cooperation. And the more cooperation it requires, the more resources that can make accountability real are placed in more hands. If only five people can do all the work, theirs are the only resources needed to get the job done, which means they may be the only ones with the power to exercise real accountability.

When an organization's work depends not on resources generated by the efforts of many people but on resources generated by a single fundraiser, who holds power within the organization? Have you ever been in a meeting where you start hearing about what the funders will support and won't support, and why we need to do this or that so we can get the money—all, of course, interpreted by the person responsible for raising the money? No matter how democratic the formal structure of an organization, if one person's resources make the whole thing possible, that person will have the say. This is why effective democratic leadership rests on a solid practice of delegation—a practice that we focus on in our discussion of leadership.

Action entails cost but can also promise recognition. The more widely shared the cost—or sacrifice—the more people have a stake in the outcome. If one or two people do all the sacrificing, they quickly burn out, while everyone else blames them for whatever goes wrong. Similarly, when many people have an opportunity to contribute, they can also claim a share in success. It is their victory, not someone else's. This, in turn, creates motivation and a sense of entitlement that facilitates accountability. The wider the opportunity to act is, the wider the participation, the responsibility, and the capacity to hold leadership accountable will be.

It might not be surprising that we may resist distributing responsibility or widening participation to the extent that it threatens our control.

Facilitate Collaboration

Establishing collaborative work practices within an organization—for instance, teams, group deliberation, evaluation, peer learning, and so on—can help address the challenges of balancing change and continuity. This practice overcomes a critical barrier to ongoing adaptive change in the form of an isolated leadership that resists open evaluation.

Similarly, collaborative work practices help us manage the tension of unity and diversity. Leading a unified organization requires more than defensive maneuvers to avoid divisive factions. When done proactively, work can be designed to require greater interdependence, thus requiring more collaboration. One of the dangers of professionalizing an organization is that we may minimize interdependence. Instead of relying on a team of volunteers (and their inefficiencies), we hire someone to do their job. But something is lost with this choice. Whom does this empower within the organization? Whom does it disempower?

Effective collaboration depends on skilled leadership, a chief art of which is learning to blend the unique capacities—and deficits—of different people. This, of course, goes to the tensions around diversity and unity. Work

assignments are the result of a negotiation between the actual persons—
their personalities, their experience, their talents, and their difficulties—and
the roles they are needed to play. If everyone were the same age, race, and
gender and had the same skills, life experience, and so forth, their "power
with" would remain limited because of so little opportunity for productive
interdependence. We can't lift a table if we all lift the same corner at the same
time. But if we each lift our own corner, we can. The trick is to match the right
people with the right corners.

Effective collaboration also requires continuity. Richard Hackman offers
this anecdote:

> NTSB [National Transportation Safety Board] staff combed the agency's da-
> tabase to identify the circumstances under which aircraft cockpit crews are
> most likely to get into trouble. They found that 73 percent of the incidents
> in the NTSB database occurred on the crew's first day of flying together, and
> 44 percent of those took place on a cruise very first flight.

Hackman explains why flights get safer when flight crews work in familiar
teams: "They learn who is especially knowledgeable or skilled about which
aspects of the work and thereby build the team's capability to actually *use*
what members know and know how to do."[28]

Productive collaboration, then, is the result of harmony, not homogeneity. This is what it means to construct community based on difference. The
idea is to create a star team, not to be a star player. A coach begins with the
common interest a team has in winning. But it only becomes a winning team
if the coach learns how to combine the unique strengths and weaknesses of
each player. The team then has an interest in remaining a team.

Dissent Is Not Disloyalty

The capacity of an organization to respond to its constituency, their needs,
and the world of change in which we are living requires accountability.
Democracy grows out of a claim that leaders may lead in the public interest not because they are virtuous, but because the public has the power
to hold them accountable. Accountability (as in electoral competition)
is also a mechanism that requires democratic leaders to respond to new

circumstances, new constituencies, new challenges. For democratic organizations, responsiveness and renewal are thus directly linked with the legitimacy of dissent. Accountability only works when linked to the open debate of different points of view.

A loyal opposition not only holds leaders accountable but can become an agent of change by giving voice to alternatives that can stimulate an adaptive response. For this to work, however, requires a rich diversity of perspectives. This requires learning how to manage difference—neither denying it nor accepting it as absolute. The legitimacy of dissent requires agreed-upon ways we can continue collaborating, even when we disagree. This requires decision rules—rules that allow us to make decisions, move forward, and get work done, even if everyone doesn't agree. Formal procedures for debate, discussion, voting and evaluation can help by depersonalizing disagreements. *Robert's Rules of Order* may still have its uses.

Leaders can nurture a culture that values difference by affirming the single voice that the rest of the group tries to drown out, rather than joining the chorus. Learning to deliberate in ways that affirm our commonalties while protecting dissent can transform our diversity into an asset, which can aid us in realizing and acting upon our common interests. It is equally important to learn to celebrate in ways that affirm both the distinctiveness of our identities and the communality of our organizational undertaking.

Dissent can undoubtedly be uncomfortable. Dissent, however, is a fundamental source of learning, accountability, and the capacity of democratic associations to respond to change.

Meetings, Actions, Celebrations

When it comes to practice, the complex tensions just described are evident in the only three kinds of activities that organizations actually do: meet, act, and celebrate (Figure 6.4). *Meetings* are where much of the shared head work gets done in the form of deliberation, decision-making, learning, information sharing, and evaluation. They can also be excessive, especially when used to avoid challenging action. *Action* is the hands work: providing the service, organizing the march, recruiting new members, and researching critical information. *Celebration* is the heart work: sustaining commitment, honoring values, recognizing contributions, and affirming relationships.

Figure 6.4 Meet, Act, Celebrate. *Source*: Steve Downer of the Difference

Ask yourselves to what extent distributed responsibility, facilitated collaboration, and respect for dissent are evident in your meetings, your actions, and your celebrations.

Meeting

While many meetings can take place between two individuals or small groups (indeed, some must), an association only really comes to life as a group of people assembled in a room (or on Zoom) deliberating about what they are doing together, sharing what they have been learning together, and engaging with the challenges they are facing.

How does distributing responsibility work in a meeting? How much effort is made to turn people out? Who participates in the planning team for the meeting? Who speaks in the meeting and what do they have to report on?

How about working collaboratively? What is the role of committees? How are committee reports handled? Is any collaborative work done in the meeting, like brainstorming? In large meetings, are groups from different locations identified by signs, symbols, or colors? And how is all the new information coming from participants integrated?

What norms have been established to establish that dissent is not disloyalty? Is there a role for a devil's advocate? How is debate structured? Are there rules of respect in place?

Acting

The second thing organizations do is act—conduct programs, run campaigns, provide services, and so on.

How does distributing responsibility work in acting? How widely has the responsibility for mobilizing participants been spread? Has responsibility for turnout been pushed all the way down, or only for sharing information? Are there teams? Team captains?

How about working collaboratively? How was the action planned? Who participated? Are there regular evaluations? Who participates? Are participants identified by their local group, their role in the organization, a symbol or logo?

What norms have been established to establish that dissent is not disloyalty? What procedures exist for people with complaints to have them heard? Does the leadership look for opportunities to act on suggestions voiced as dissent?

Celebrating

Finally, organizations celebrate their narrative, their successes, their setbacks, and their milestones.

How does pushing responsibility down and broadening participation work in celebrations? Is it a catered meal or a potluck? Are professional entertainers hired or are members called upon to contribute? Who does the decorations? Who cleans up?

How does working collaboratively come into play? The whole way a celebration is planned, the way committees do their work, and how the event itself is conducted can be an opportunity for widespread collaboration, or you can just hire a professional event manager, if you have the money. But how about a talent show? And singing? Who will lead it? Will you open and close with a prayer, a poem, a reflection?

How does understanding that dissent is not disloyalty help celebrations? Think creatively about how to honor different points of view, different perspectives, and different angles on what is being celebrated.

Conclusion

Successful organizing—and practicing democracy as such—requires structuring. As Jo Freeman reminded us, whenever people get together with any interest in the future, they will structure themselves intentionally or not, consciously or not, and transparently or not.[29] The real question is not whether to structure but how to structure and how to embrace structure as a critical element of the organizing craft.

Structuring is not easy, any more than writing a constitution is. We create structure by committing to the ground rules by which we will govern ourselves. The ground rules really matter, in that they determine how we decide, how we hold ourselves responsible, how we resolve conflict, and how we facilitate change. In addition to ground rules, structure requires an agreed-upon shared purpose and clear roles.

In a recent version of my organizing class, we focused on how the structuring of leadership teams interacted with the development of plausible strategy. Of twenty-seven teams, only four failed to develop plausible strategy. Each of those teams had notably failed to create a viable structure. Not every well-structured team came up with great strategy, but they learned. The dysfunctional teams got nowhere.

In sum, building powerful civic associations poses important challenges that only come fully into play as we begin to succeed. The responsiveness, relevance, and continued vitality of our associations depend in great part on how we learn to manage the dilemmas of change and continuity, in-clusion and exclusion, unity and diversity, and parts and wholes. We have suggested three practices that can help: distributing responsibility, working collaboratively, and recognizing that dissent is not disloyalty. Keep us posted.

7

Developmental Leadership

In the book of Exodus, chapter 18, we meet the prophet Moses (Nebi Musa) as he is taking a break. Having brought his people out of Egypt, he is exhausted. His father-in-law, Jethro (Nebi Shaib), a Midianite priest, arrives suddenly with Moses's wife, Zipporah, and their two children, Gershom and Eleazar, in tow. This is the family Moses left behind when he was called to his mission in Egypt. When Jethro asks Moses how it's going, Moses complains about how hard it has been. Jethro then invites him to join him in praising God for having blessed him.

The next morning, Jethro goes to work with Moses as he starts his task of judging the people. Moses sits on the ground as people gather around him, towering over him with questions, claims, and demands. Jethro intervenes: "This is not good for you. And it is not good for the people. It will exhaust you both." He urges Moses to step back, select one man among each ten whom he judges to be "capable, God-fearing, and honest," educate him in the law, and authorize him to lead the others. Jethro, in other words, urges Moses to select, train, and delegate. Then, Jethro says, select one among these ten to do the same and so forth, until Moses can work directly with only ten people. This step will transform his life and that of his people. Moses acts on the plan immediately.

It's one thing to get good advice. But it's quite another to act on it quickly, especially if we ourselves are the source of the problem. Why did Moses put himself in this situation in the first place? Was he hungry for power? Why do we often wind up in the same spot? Was it maybe that he cared so much about getting it right that he couldn't risk someone else getting it wrong? Sound familiar?

Recall that Jethro's encounter with Moses in this story begins with Jethro reminding Moses that he is more than the leader of his people. He is a father. He is a husband. He is blessed by God. By restoring Moses's relationship with his family and with his God—sources of identity that transcend his work, giving him the courage to let go—Jethro enables Moses to risk giving up enough control to empower himself and his people.

Are you willing to give up enough control to let others lead so that you can develop the power you need to achieve your goals? Developing a leadership-rich organization depends on your answer to that question. As one of my students put it, the test of good leadership is not how many hats you can wear at the same time. It is how many people you can enable to wear hats.

An organizer's job is to identify, recruit, and develop leadership who can identify, recruit, and develop more leadership, who can identify, recruit, and develop more leadership in a cascade of leadership.

Why Developmental Leadership?

Powerful organizing requires the sustained development of leadership. Having defined leadership as accepting responsibility for enabling others to achieve shared purpose, previous chapters focused on five specific leadership practices critical to the practicing of democracy: relationship building, storytelling, strategizing, action, and structuring. The reason developmental leadership concludes this book rather than starts is because as a practice, it doesn't stand apart but is at the center of each of the practices described in previous chapters. Presenting developmental leadership here is an attempt at integration. It is also a reminder that this book is about what people can do together. That begins, however, with at least one person saying, "Yes, we can!"

Here, I focus the developmental dimension of the collaborative and distributive forms discussed in the last chapter. While fundamental to organizing, this approach can also be useful in domains where the value being created is the fruit of values-based motivation, collaboration, and sustained learning: healthcare, education, and the arts and culture, to name a few.

We are wise to distinguish authority from leadership. Authority describes the legitimacy of certain rules and of the power of those responsible to enforce those rules. Legitimacy grows out of compliance with agreed-upon practices as well as cultural beliefs. Organization is a way to formalize authority relations—people's rights and their obligations—among the participants. Bureaucracies structure authority as a set of rules according to the dictates of a manager. Markets structure authority as a set of rules according to which people make enforceable contracts based on their individual resources. Civic associations usually structure authority democratically, in that leaders are chosen by and accountable to the constituents they serve. Exercising leadership in a civic, especially voluntary, setting can require more skill than in other settings because it depends more on persuasion than on command.[1]

Most of us have been in situations where those with authority have not earned their leadership but try rather to compel cooperation based solely on their access to the power to dominate others. Cultures have institutionalized beliefs about who is authorized to lead, and who isn't, that may bar certain kinds of people from the opportunity to earn leadership. Leaders who develop under these conditions constitute a challenge to conventional ideas of authority. Once again, we see that leadership and authority are not the same thing.

Finally, we distinguish leaders from activists. Hardworking activists show up every day to staff the phone bank, pass out leaflets, and put up posters, making critical contributions to the work of any volunteer organization. This is not the same, however, as engaging others in doing the work of the organization. Effective leaders turn activists into leaders who can in turn activate others, but the process takes time and intentionality.

Because leadership is so important to organizing, we must make sure our constituency has the leadership it needs. Structure is important, but ultimately the effectiveness of organized people—especially in social movements or civic associations that try to bring people together, facilitate their mutual understanding, and enable them to act together on common interests—depends more on the depth of their leadership than on the efficiency of their systems.

Effective developmental leadership is built right into the work. A long-standing debate in the field of executive education is about the value of off-site training when it comes to sustained change. At the conclusion of any quality workshop, participants often experience a glow as they reflect on their new discoveries and dream of new possibilities. But it is often also the case that, after a limited time back on the job, old behavioral patterns return because nothing has changed in the structures of work that produced the old patterns in the first place. In other words, unless the work is structured in such a way as to develop newly desired practices, off-site executive training can only be of limited value in transforming managerial culture. The same truth applies for leadership practices in organizing.[2]

In this chapter we focus on ways to approach developmental leadership systematically. But like most things, these practices are most effective when used strategically. Particularly good organizers always have their antenna on alert for the one with the "sparkle in their eyes." The one who asks more questions, good questions, and learns from the responses, perhaps generating his or her own. The one who has people; that is, they're interacting with others as part of their MO, not as their acolytes but as their collaborators, their teammates. The one who takes pride when one of his mentees shines, rather than reacting as if they take the light away from him. Good organizers also have a plan. Hmm . . . this spot will be opening soon and it looks like Maria might be able to take it on . . . or it looks like David is stuck where he is. I wonder what would enable him to take the next step . . . Maybe Omar would be perfect to pair him up with. And so on.

Take a look at the leadership quotient of your organization. How many people hold real leadership responsibility? Is there one leader on whom everyone else depends, linked to that leader like spokes to the hub of a wheel? Or is no one linked to anyone else because there are no leaders, or because everyone is a leader? Or are some people always leaders and others always followers? Is the organization leadership rich, or is it leadership poor?

Developmental leadership requires a systematic commitment to identifying, recruiting, and developing the capacity of constituency-based individuals, teams, and communities in building the power needed to achieve the group's larger goals. Developing leadership doesn't happen with the depth or at the scale it needs to without intentionality. And without developing leadership, it is too easy to end up like the person in the image: all the arrows point at you, or they point nowhere.

Why Leadership Teams?

How can we structure the development of leadership committed to developing more leadership? Get started by asking yourself what kind of leader you want to be should be, and what you look for in others.[3]

Sometimes we think the leader is the person everyone goes to, like the "I'm the leader!" approach. But what does it feel like to be the leader in the middle, with all those arrows coming at you? And if you're not the leader, what does it feel like to be an arrow trying to get through? What happens if the leader in the middle drops out?

On the other hand, some of us question the whole concept of leadership. Shouldn't everyone be considered a leader? Is leadership really necessary? Isn't it repressively hierarchical? Why do we need this kind of structure at all (Figure 7.1)? Can't we just come together?

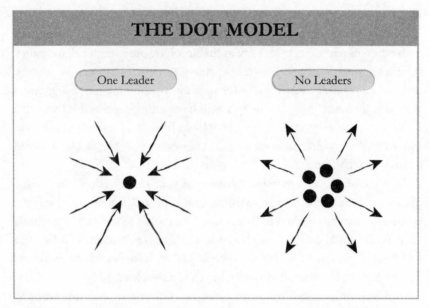

Figure 7.1 The Dot Model (previously appears in chapter 1 as Figure 1.8). *Source*: Steve Downer of the Difference

Sometimes, against the odds, this approach works. But who's responsible for coordinating everyone? And who's responsible for moving the whole group forward when you can't reach a decision?

Since neither "I'm the leader" nor "we're all leaders" creates the conditions for effective democratic organizing, what are the alternatives? One option is building an interdependent leadership team that enables people to practice collaborative leadership on behalf of a shared purpose. Like a soccer team or a string quartet, each team member may lead with a particular practice (strategy, storytelling), function (data, communications), or constituency (downtown, the eastside, etc.), even if one of the roles is that of the captain, first violin, or coordinator. A well-designed team can also put the unique assets of each individual to work. Launching a leadership team creates strategic capacity: the ability to strategize with the creativity, salient information, and agility to produce more vibrant, situated, and engaging strategy than any one individual could create alone.

Despite the mythology of a lone alpha leader, most movement leaders led with teams: Moses, Aaron, and Miriam in Exodus; Jesus and his twelve disciples in the New Testament; the Buddha and his first sangha; the Prophet and his companions in the Qur'an. In the Montgomery Bus Boycott, Dr. King, Ralph Abernathy, Rosa Parks, Jo Ann Robinson, and E. D. Nixon operated as a leadership team.

The sooner you can begin working with a team, the sooner your "I" can become a "we" of an organization. You can structure a regular rhythm of meeting, decision-making, accountability, and learning that enables real progress. No one can build a real organization of five hundred people by recruiting them all on their own. Instead, you build it by recruiting people willing and able to commit to building it with you. If you can't recruit them, it may be that they don't need you.

In the Obama campaign, the field structure enabled layers of leadership teams at all levels of the campaign. A state leadership team could coordinate regional leadership teams, who could coordinate volunteer neighborhood leadership teams. Although not always realized in practice, the idea was that people on teams at each level could focus on a shared mission and strategize together about how to fulfill that mission. This structure could create multiple points of entry for volunteers, real opportunities for learning, access to sustained coaching, and the actual responsibility for leadership.[4]

Why, then, doesn't everyone work in leadership teams?

Many leaders have only experienced dysfunctional teams. Perhaps a leader has never actually worked within what Richard Hackman called a real team at all. Perhaps the team was not structured to enable constructive conflict, lacked accountability measures, rarely learned from its mistakes, or let the work fall entirely on one person or on no one at all.

More specifically, they—or you—may have found yourself in a situation like the following:

- You are in a team meeting. But it's unclear who you can count on to step up, take responsibility, and get the work done. Two or three people often wind up doing all the work, which means that no matter how hard you work, you can't get it all done.

  Whenever you need to decide, you always seem to be missing some crucial piece of information, skill, or set of relationships.
- You talk and talk and talk, but when it's all over, you realize that each person had a different idea of the outcome you were talking about.
- When you get stuck, you have nowhere else to turn for help. You help each other as much as you can, you may contact another volunteer leader, but it's not clear where you can go for expert advice.

In the face of so many bad experiences, it's tempting to throw up our hands in defeat: "I'll just do it on my own," we may conclude. "I hate meetings, just tell me what to do," we say. "I don't want any responsibility; just give me stamps to lick."

There's just one problem: your group can't ever become powerful enough to do what you need to do if you can't even work together as a self-governing leadership team. By drawing on the craft of team design, you can create conditions that increase the odds your team can work together successfully.

Launching Leadership Teams

Organizing is a craft. Leadership is a craft. Organizing a leadership team is a craft. We have learned a lot about how to do this in practice, based especially on the work of Richard Hackman: bounded, stable, and interdependent leadership teams that operate with a shared purpose, clear norms, and well-defined roles, with access to able coaching, are more likely to get results than teams that lack these structures.[5]

Three Outcomes of an Effective Team

An effective team has three clear goals and objectives, ultimately setting the organization up for future success. A successful team:

- *Accomplishes the goals for which it is responsible:* effective organizing enables groups to achieve their goal—pass the law, win the election, launch the credit union, make beautiful music, and so on.
- *Operates in ways that make it better as a performing unit over time:* effective organizing creates more collective capacity; stronger and/or deeper organization; new competencies; greater solidarity—not as a side benefit but as *the* core purpose.
- *Contributes to the learning and well-being of individual members:* effective organizing enables the development of leadership, not as a side benefit, but as a core purpose.

One may fail to achieve the goal yet wind up with a stronger organization, more power, and the ability to try again. Alternatively, one may achieve the goal but wind up with a weakened organization, as in "I never want to see anyone involved in this campaign again" (a result of a scorched-earth approach). Focusing on the second and third outcomes along with the first inherently brings a longer term or more strategic perspective to choices about how to go about achieving the first goal.

Three Conditions for an Effective Team

An effective team is bounded, stable, and diverse.

When a team is bounded, it is clear who is on the team and who is not on the team. It is clear how new people can join the team and how people can leave the team.

People sometimes object that these conditions are downright wrong—no one should ever be excluded from anything. But a bounded team is not exclusionary just because it has clear expectations about what is required of those who serve, what the criteria of selection are, and why it has decided to operate the way it does. Consider teams that actually get things done: a basketball team, an airline cabin crew, a string quartet. How do you think it would work if anyone who showed up was on those teams? Why not bring that same principle to the work of social change?

When a team is stable, people commit to clear terms of engagement: regular meetings, a regular length of time, regular terms of service. The team is not a revolving door, with members never knowing who will show up.

Some organizers object that stability is unrealistic. People have busy lives. They can't always show up for meetings. Life happens. All of this is true. But we all make choices as to our commitments if we are to honor them, to feel good about ourselves, and to feel valued by others. Team commitments must be as clear as possible from the beginning, so I can have some idea of what I'm getting into and what is expected of me. When only half of the team shows up and half of the meeting is used to bring those who didn't show up last time up to date, a process repeated at meeting after meeting, too much time is wasted.

People who want to participate can contribute in many other ways besides serving on a leadership team, or any team for that matter. They may provide expertise when needed. They may participate in public events. They may share good ideas with a team member. But a person who can't or won't follow through should not accept the responsibilities that go with serving on a leadership team. Those who do accept membership on the leadership team, moreover, need to feel that the costs of accepting that responsibility are worth it: the motivation must be strong (the cause really matters), the experience of making a difference real, and the opportunity for growth significant.

When a team is diverse, its members can contribute the range of skills, talents, viewpoints, and constituencies needed to accomplish their goals. In this way, leadership can be understood not as a one-person-who-is-good-at-everything job. On the contrary, it is a job that requires the interdependent strength of many.

Some leaders object that they just don't have access to the appropriate diversity of skills, talents, viewpoints, or constituency. For a leadership team, the most salient forms of diversity are rooted in their constituency's identity: young, older, old; those who work at home, at the office, both places, neither, who are retired; which neighborhoods; degrees of wealth; race; ethnicity; religion; and so forth. The unique skills or experience that a person brings to a team also matters, especially if the interdependence is to be real. This is not a one-size-fits-all approach to team diversity, but when there is agreement on shared purpose or core values, the more diversity the better.

Three Decisions for an Effective Team

An effective team has established a shared purpose, clear ground rules or norms, and interdependent roles.

When a team has a shared purpose—a what, who, and how—it is rooted in the shared values, interests, and resources of its members: *what* is our common goal, *who* are our people, and *how* (through what kinds of activities) will we get it done.

Without a shared purpose, every decision relitigates what our purpose really is. Or we assume our version of the purpose is everyone's version of the purpose. In bureaucratic organizations, a superior may simply assign a purpose to a team. Self-governing leadership teams, on the other hand, must accept responsibility for deciding on a purpose themselves, even if their purpose is nested within broader organizational goals. And it is work they must do.

Recently, with my colleague Abel Cano, I was asked to work with members of an emergent movement of community labs, based at MIT, whose leadership wanted to define a shared purpose. Their proposal was to survey their members; gather data on values, interests, and resources; and turn it over to an algorithm capable of convergent and divergent processing. Voila! Out would come their shared purpose. Although I'm intrigued by the potential of digital technology, I had to point out this would be the shared purpose of the algorithm, not the shared purpose of their people. If their people were to own a shared purpose, they would have to do the work: hear each other, learn with each other, debate their differences, identify their commonalities, and come to an agreement for which they would be responsible. Aggregating many individual preferences is not the same thing as engaging with each other to come up with a whole that can be greater than the sum of its parts.

One way we've learned to do this is to ask each member of the team to write one sentence in which they describe how they see the goals, constituency, and activities of the team. Each person is then asked to read their sentence out loud. A facilitator notes key words on a poster or screen in one of three columns: goal, constituency, and activities. The facilitator then leads the group first in synthesizing what is shared and clearly differentiating what is not. The group can then hear arguments as to the differences and decide. Then they write a second round of sentences, which usually produces more convergence. After a similar exercise as before, the facilitator tries to focus the group on where the most energy and other key elements seem to be shared. The facilitator chooses the sentence closest to the whole. Rather than wordsmithing the sentence, the facilitator asks its author to come up with a proposal. The reason this works is that we usually begin our discussions of shared purpose from our differences rather than our commonalities. We may all care for the natural world, but I'm for whales, you're for trees, and a third person is for dealing with carbon emissions. That sets the context for our work. In contrast, the process I've described begins by identifying areas of convergence, which then become the context of our work. This approach makes resolving our differences less arduous: after all, in the previous example, we're all for saving the environment.

When a team has established norms for decision-making, honoring commitments, managing conflict, and respecting time, it has accepted responsibility for self-governance. Norms are not just rules. They are explicit expectations about how you will work together, how you will make decisions, how you will manage your time. What are things you will always do, and what are the things you will never do? And how will you correct yourselves if you fail?

Perhaps a team's most important norm is how the team will make decisions. Effective decision-making can be supported through a stepwise process of defining the problem, establishing criteria, brainstorming possibilities, synthesizing ideas, formulating options, evaluating options against the criteria, and deciding. Some prefer deciding by vote; others, by consensus; others, by delegating the decision to an individual.

Norm-setting is an exercise in self-governance for which the team must take responsibility. If these ground rules are not clear from the beginning, every substantive debate can easily turn into a process debate, leading to irresolution, anxiety, and frustration. Norm-setting is a constitutional moment, the only moment in which consensus is required if the team is to move forward. Taking the time to do this is an investment in the health, effectiveness, and future of the team.

Norm-setting often involves explicitly setting aside a regular time for meetings, learning, and coaching. Regular team meetings can become the eye in the hurricane, a source of order at the core of what can feel like a chaotic enterprise. But this time must be sacred. When I was coordinating the organizing for Nancy Pelosi's first campaign for Congress in 1987, I looked for an opportunity to establish this practice. We had just begun our daily coordinators' meeting when someone came running into the room shouting, "Nancy's on the phone! Nancy's on the phone! She's got to talk to you right away!" All eyes turned to me. Was our time really sacred, or not? "Please tell Nancy that we're in our coordinators' meeting," I said. "I'll call her as soon as we're done." "But, but, but," came the response. Again, "Please tell her I'll call her as soon as we're done." A big sigh of relief. From that point on, we never had any problem sticking to our daily meeting.

Norms only really exist in practice. Norm violations that have no consequences redefine the norm. We agree to meet at 10:00. Someone wanders in at 10:30. No one says anything, instead looking down at their feet. A new norm has been created: roll in by 10:30.

Some members of a team resist the idea of a norm correction. It is a way a team can share responsibility for accountability, rather than assigning policing to one member who has to take all the heat. A correction need not be onerous or burdensome; you don't need to assess a huge fine every time someone is late. The best norm corrections are often humorous. If someone is late, perhaps they need to do a ten-second dance to a song of their own choosing. Correcting norm violations is not about public shaming. It is about reminding others about the responsibility of respecting our own commitments.

When a team uses interdependent roles to organize its work, each member has responsibility for their own share of the leadership work needed to achieve the goal. Role requirements need to be clearly described. Even though roles are likely to evolve during a campaign, roles must be set in the first meeting. The idea is to match needs with abilities, rather than making role assignments a popularity contest, a test of who has the most power, or a test of meeting criteria other than those most relevant to the particular responsibility.

When roles are designed to be interdependent, everyone has a stake in everyone else's success. Team members speak up when they need help, and they get it. No one works in a silo that's secretive to others. And everyone swarms to the need. A team of diverse identities, experiences, and resources brings more to the table than a homogeneous team. To the extent that leadership teams define the same basic roles across levels and locations, they facilitate parallel role-based online learning, peer coaching, and adaptation.

Leadership teams often struggle with deciding whether to design roles based on function or on constituency. But if one's mission is organizing, roles are better defined by constituency: the west side of town, the east side of town, the colleges, and so on. In this way, each leadership team member can own responsibility for their own constituency, which they organize by building relationships, developing leadership, coaching the campaign, and so on. This basic structure can be supplemented with functional roles especially suited for event management, such as the data person, the media person, the training person, the fundraising person, the special events person, and so on. This approach works well for organizing an event but not for organizing a community. Depending on the size of the campaign and the team, these roles may be combined with functional roles, but any functional structure will dilute the focus on organizing. By extension, a team responsible for a particular function, like data management, could build their own data management team.

One caution is that the work of the team will necessarily prioritize the concerns of its members. When I was leading a statewide campaign in California, my team included a coordinator for the Bay Area, another for San Diego and Orange County, another for the rest of the state, and three for Los Angeles, which was subdivided into three regions. Why did LA have three? Three times as many voters lived in LA than in any one of the other areas, and I wanted to be sure that reality would be reflected in our meetings. We also had a person handling administration, another for press, media, and so on. In this way, our leadership team structure managed to simultaneously fulfill functional roles and represent the constituency to the greatest extent possible.

* * *

The decisions that must be made to structure an effective and collaborative leadership team can be stressful. Inevitably, people will disagree over goals, responsibilities, norms, and procedures. A lesson we have learned from launching leadership teams all over the world is the importance of launching with the heart as well as the head and hands. Finding ways to celebrate, to build an emotional connection, can be a way to restore emotional harmony to the team after what may have been a moment of contentious debate.

Every team needs a name, so why not start with brainstorming possible team names? Some suggestions will be descriptive—Green Team—while others will be values-based—Just Organizers—while others draw on shared jokes or cultural experiences—Justice Jedis or 7 Deer Dancing or the Love Gas Station. The creativity, humor, and consensus building involved in choosing a name begins to create the experience of a shared identity rooted in values shared by the team.

A team chant takes this one step further, often producing lots of laughter, loss of self-consciousness, healthy humbling (but not humiliating), and creativity. Chants have also included elements of dance; the most creative I've seen was in an organizing workshop in Beijing. People can move around after what may have been a long day. And team members perhaps not as engaged in the head and hands work may really flourish here, finding new ways to contribute to the team as well. It's fun, it's expressive, and it works.

Distributed Leadership: Getting to Scale

So far, this chapter has focused on collaborative leadership teams as a core organizational structure. These teams, however, form the core of a far greater distributed leadership development process. One way organizations can begin distributing leadership is for each member of the core leadership team to accept responsibility for organizing their own leadership team.

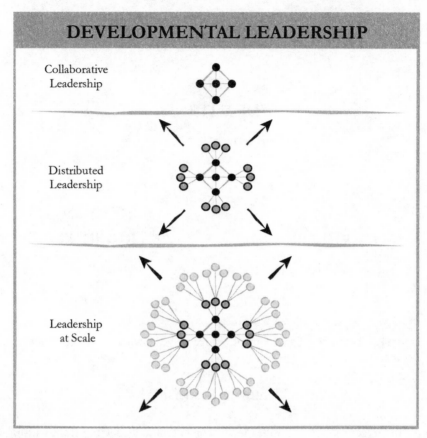

Figure 7.2 Developmental Leadership (previously appears in chapter 1 as Figure 1.9). *Source*: Steve Downer of the Difference

Each member of those teams can, in turn, build their own team and on and on. Because of the team structure that radiates from the center out, many organizers describe this approach to leadership development as creating a snowflake or snowflaking out. We now turn to how to build your snowflake out (Figure 7.2).

Developmental leadership, if it is to be real, must be structured in a spirit of risk-taking, learning, and adaptation. Leadership development—like any form of trust—involves risk. You may delegate to the wrong people, and they may let you down. But as Moses learned from Jethro, if you fear delegating, you will stifle growth in the power of your organization. You can increase the odds of success by building practices designed to identify, recruit, and develop leadership systematically into the work you do each day (Figure 7.3).

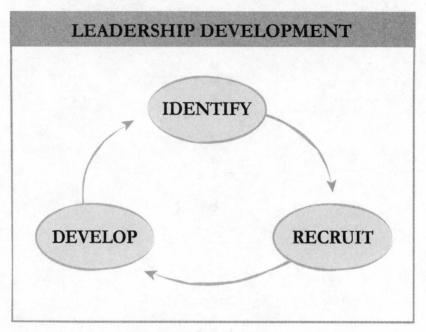

Figure 7.3 Leadership Development. *Source*: Steve Downer of the Difference

Identifying Leadership

An organizer's job is to find leadership or potential leadership from within their constituency, leaders who can identify, recruit, and develop others. Here, leaders need to be aware of their own cultural biases, as we have all absorbed culturally specific lessons about who is and isn't a natural leader. Leaders should also realize that some people may want to identify themselves as leaders based on little more than their own self-confidence. So it is important to identify leadership based on the evidence.

I recall one experience in the farmworkers, getting started in a new town. My colleague and I were confronted by three people who claimed to be the leaders of the community. "Great," we said. "How about getting twenty or thirty community members, especially the most active, so we can meet them tonight?" How many do you think showed up? Zero. Not even the three leaders. This is what the farmworkers called leadership "de los dientes pa'fuera"—from the teeth outward.

Sometimes in these situations, it eventually became clear that the de facto leaders were biding their time, waiting for more information to judge for themselves whether they should put themselves—and the people who rely on them—at risk. Sometimes the individuals who had earned the least respect, built the fewest relationships, and are the most eager for outside support were the ones who showed up first. If you misidentify these folks as existing leaders, you can end up orienting your organizing effort around those least representative of the people you hope to organize.

So how do you identify leadership? Leaders are people committed to change, open to learning, in relationship with others, and able to accept responsibility for the hard work of organizing. They are not RPs—the "real people" campaign consultants sometimes conjure up to legitimate their candidates. They are people who step up to form the backbone of an organizing campaign. They must be people whose candor you can trust, to whom you can delegate real responsibility, and on whose commitments you can count.

Based on their experience, do others look to them as leaders? Do they turn out the people for the meeting? Do they get the petition signatures? Do they pose challenging questions? Identifying leadership is a process of looking at the facts, at deeds, not words.

Recruiting Leadership

We only develop good judgment about who to recruit by taking risks, making choices, experiencing success and failure, and learning from the whole experience. And even then, we will still be surprised. The more experience we can draw on, the better the judgment we can develop—if we are paying attention. There is no rule book, but if you fear making bad choices, you cannot learn to make good choices.

Here are some questions you might ask yourself: How do you select to whom to delegate? How do you know who the right person is? How can you find out ahead of time? How do you know when a person is ready for a big job? Do you select them because they are available, or do you select them because they are the right person to do the job? Do you select them because you know from past experience that they will know what to do, because they look like they will know what to do, or because they could—and want to—learn what to do? Do you select them because you heard they were good? Where did you hear that? Who told you? Should you believe them? How do you know? As you can see, there are lots of questions that need to be asked.

Risking small failures early in a campaign helps avoid big failures later. When you risk learning to delegate, you also learn to judge who may come through and who won't. It is wise to learn this lesson when something small is at stake—say, a small meeting instead of a monster rally. Quantifiable goals, regular reports, and ongoing evaluation processes enable leaders to detect failure and success early on so that they can become learning opportunities for everyone. "So, Mary, why did that work so well?" "So, Sam, what happened there? What could you have done differently?"

As in any beginning, there will be successes and failures because you are still learning. It may even be unclear what the right way is when you begin a new project. You can turn this fact to everyone's advantage if you can find the courage to risk sharing responsibility with others for outcomes you care about.

Developmental Leadership

Sustained and systematic leadership training—or formation—is a key component of leadership development. It can clarify expectations, build your members' confidence in accepting leadership roles, and express the value you place on leadership, competence, and learning.

Initial training sessions can onboard new people, enroll them into an organizing culture, and enable them to build relationships with each other. You can also use trainings to introduce core practices, develop teaching skills, and launch new leadership teams. This is how we used our two-and-a-half-day Camp Obama training sessions in 2007 and 2008. At the first one, held in a sound stage in Burbank, California, in July 2007, we hosted more than two hundred volunteers selected from among those who had applied online. They arrived Friday afternoon as individuals but left Sunday afternoon as members of leadership teams. Each had committed to specific goals, including the goal of recruiting at least twenty people to come to their first meeting back home. We introduced them to the five leadership practices (relationship building, storytelling, strategizing, acting, and structuring) and equipped them with basic technical skills (how to use voter files, media, digital skills, etc.). The training enabled them to take responsibility for clear goals within their congressional district, including developing more leadership teams within their district, ultimately down to the precinct level.

Launching leadership with an initial training is thus not just about learning everyone's name, filling out forms, reviewing a manual, and giving out assignments. It is about introducing people to the concepts, skills, and values that can create a foundation for individual and organizational development.

Ongoing periodic training can scaffold further development, enable learners in one session to become teachers in a subsequent session, support improvement in practice as well as adaptive innovation, and provide a venue in which newly salient practices can be introduced.

In the 1988 Democratic Presidential GOTV campaign in California, we hired three hundred organizers to organize 14,000 precincts. We built a multitiered structure led by a five-person core leadership team, seven regional field directors, forty-two coordinators, and about seven organizers per coordinator. Each organizer then had to build their own multitier volunteer organization to deploy GOTV teams in some three hundred precincts on Election Day. As the campaign unfolded, we had to retool—and remotivate—as each new phase arrived. We started with weekday training of regional directors, adapting the plan alongside them; they would retrain their coordinators, and the coordinators would retrain the organizers, who would then relaunch their volunteer teams in a weekend event. This, alas, was in the era of yellow legal pads, WATS unlimited-use phone lines, and lots and lots of printing. How much better (and cheaper) the whole thing could be done today using online tools like Zoom, which enable face-to-face training with large groups, breakout groups, and zero travel.

The point is that we found a way to combine leadership development, training, and action at some depth on a large scale. Although this effort was not enough to swing the California of 1988 into the blue column, it did result in almost a refounding of the California Democratic Party. It's a prime example of how even a losing campaign can be used to develop a more powerful organization.

Structuring Developmental Leadership into the Work

Successful developmental leadership requires structuring it into the work: opportunities, responsibilities, and accountability. You've established leadership teams and have begun cultivating practices for developing distributed leadership. These are important and necessary steps. But developing leadership isn't something that happens just once in the life of an organization.

Opportunities

Developmental leadership requires structuring opportunities for people to earn their leadership. Since followers create leaders, leaders can't appoint themselves, nor can you appoint them. But you can create opportunities for people to accept leadership responsibilities and support them as they learn how to fulfill these responsibilities. If you had to get the word out for a meeting, in the days before social media, you could get three or four friends to help you pass out leaflets in a strategic location on a campus, worksite, or neighborhood. Or you could recruit two or three people from each residence hall, shop, or precinct to accept responsibility for recruiting five people each. People learning to motivate others to commit to coming to the meeting creates an opportunity for them to earn leadership, even though it requires greater investment of time and effort at the front end.

This process isn't so different for social media. You can rely on Facebook or an equivalent to spread the word. Or you can build a team to reach out to recruit specific people to show up, not unlike the teams Sunrise built to get out the vote for the 2020 presidential election.

Responsibilities

Developing leadership is not about assigning tasks. It is about offering opportunities to accept responsibility. It is the difference between asking, "Would you make these fifty phone calls telling people about the meeting?" and, "Would you take responsibility for getting ten people to come to the meeting?" In the first, you give them a script and tell them what to do. In the second, you give them tools that allow them to figure out how to fulfill their commitments.

When you delegate tasks, you risk turning a person into a yo-yo: go do this, come back for what's next, go do that, come back for what's next. The person is helping you fulfill your responsibility. But if they have accepted responsibility for something, the person takes it and runs with it. Your role is to help them meet their responsibility. In a December 2022 article, civic journalist Micah Sifry described this as the difference between "entaskment" and empowerment.[6]

When you're looking for someone to take responsibility for something, don't try making the responsibility easier, and easier, and easier . . . until there's nothing left. The challenge for leaders is in learning to motivate people to accept the level of responsibility needed to get the job done. When a person has accepted responsibility, the motivation for the work follows. Keeping others motivated, keeping yourself motivated, and getting the work done all depend on accountability, recognition, and coaching.

Accountability

Responsibility is only real if the person is clearly accountable for the responsibility they accepted. Accountability must be regular, specific, and timely. The point is not to catch someone doing something wrong and punish them for it. Rather, it is to learn what kind of results they are getting so that everyone can learn from them.

If someone is having trouble, we need to learn why so that we can figure out what to do about it. If someone is successful, we need to learn why so that we can try the same thing in other places. Without accountability, the most important learning we can do over the course of a campaign—systematic reflection on our own experience—is impossible. You cannot expect a person to take responsibility without authority. If you want someone to take the responsibility to get ten people to a meeting, hold that person accountable, provide training, and offer support, but then give them the authority to do what they've been asked to do. If you see or hear of them making a mistake— or think you can do it better—go directly to them, not around them. Do not take care of it for them. This is really a matter of basic respect.

If you think about it, these guidelines are not that different from the advice Jethro gave Moses some three thousand years ago: Choose people of good character, provide them with education, and give them real responsibility.

Developmental Leadership as Coaching

The understanding of leadership with which I began this book is "accepting responsibility for enabling others to achieve shared purpose under conditions of uncertainty." We then focused on organizing as a form of leadership that asks, first, who are my people; second, what is the change they need; and, finally, how can they turn resources they have into the power they need to secure that change. We then dove into learning five practices with which we can do this. There is one more practice, however, with which we can operationalize "enabling others" to excel at all the rest: coaching.

Sustained leadership development requires ongoing and consistent coaching. Formal training sessions only scaffold learning. Real learning grows along with real practice in the field. Traditional on-the-job learning methods, such as, "Throw them in the water and see if they sink or swim" or "Follow me around, kid, and see what I do," mostly test leaders' survival skills. This is not coaching. Coaching offers support before, during, and after leadership challenges, allowing leaders to receive constant feedback on their development. I learned by working with a coach who helped me to prep before the meeting, observed me (without intervening) in the meeting, and debriefed me in the coffee shop after the meeting. In the UFW, Fred Ross did this for me—not day in and day out, to be sure, but enough times that it helped me build preparation and critical reflection into my own learning. Through that process, I learned how I could begin to coach others.

Coaching is a direct intervention in an individual's or team's work process to help them improve their effectiveness. It is useful whenever we are working to enable others to build their own capacity to act. While contexts vary, the process is very similar.[7]

Coaching to Overcome Three Key Challenges

My mother, who was an educator, early on taught me that the root for education in Latin, *educare*, refers to bringing out, not putting in; to elicit a person's capacity, not to infuse them with advice. We coach others to improve their effectiveness. Coaching is not about giving advice, preaching, making judgments, or telling someone what to do. It facilitates learning to the extent that it enables people to find the wherewithal to overcome three common forms of challenge—motivational, educational, or strategic—that inhibit performance:

- **Motivational** (heart) coaching is required to enhance effort. Whether the person fears failure, lacks confidence in their own efficacy, or lacks commitment, the individual lacks the motivation to take the risks needed to learn, to put in the hours needed to practice, or to put in that last ounce of energy needed to cross the threshold.

- **Educational** (hands) coaching is required to enhance acquisition of information or skills. One may not have critical data needed to do the job, the skills required, or the experience to make good judgments.
- **Strategic** (head) coaching is required when someone has the information and the motivation but doesn't know where, when, and how to use that information in this particular context to get the desired result—that's a strategic challenge.

Learning to distinguish among these challenges—and how to intervene successfully—requires learning how to ask questions, how to listen with both the head and the heart, and how to support with both affirmation and challenge. Coaching is not all about praising people for strengths, criticizing them for weaknesses, or telling them what to do. It requires learning to identify a person's strengths and their weaknesses to ally with—or mobilize—the strengths to overcome the weaknesses. Although some coaching may be corrective (telling the other person what to do), most coaching, especially leadership coaching, is developmental (enabling the other person to learn what to do).

Coaching as a practice is most reliable if built into a regular schedule, not on an as-needed basis. If regular, coaching builds learning right into the work. Both the coaches and the quality of the work itself improve. If coaching only happens when needed, people may be reluctant to ask for help to the extent that it signals they don't know what they are doing. In reality, not asking for help when you need it signals you truly don't know what you're doing. But it may take a while to establish this norm. At the same time, if one is summoned for coaching, it can feel a little bit like getting called to the principal's office. All these situations can be avoided by incorporating coaching into the routine.

How Coaching Works: The Five-Step Process

Coaching requires learning how to use three methods to implement five steps. The three methods are to ask questions, listen (head and heart), and support (affirm and challenge). This approach to coaching appreciates the fact that the coachee most often has all the information needed within, but that information has not yet been articulated—put into words. The coach then applies each of the three methods across five steps (Figure 7.4).

1. Observe: What do I see and hear?
Listen very carefully, observe body language, and ask very focused, probing questions to satisfy yourself that you get the problem. It may take time to get the facts straight. But if you don't understand the problem, you can't help your coachee solve it. Don't be shy about asking specific stubborn questions. This process can help the coachee articulate just what the problem is in a way they may not have before. This process is not only about getting information but about enabling the coachee to articulate what he knows but may not know that he knows.

2. Diagnose: What is the problem?
Getting the diagnosis right really matters. For example, if an organizer is struggling with strategy and you focus on getting them to try harder, the result will only be frustration—or vice versa.

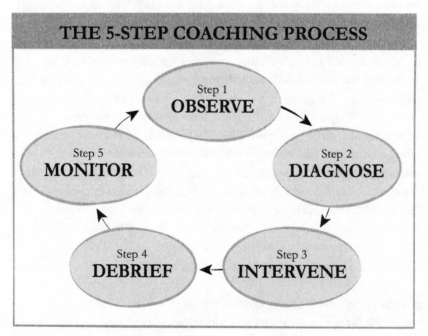

Figure 7.4 The 5-Step Coaching Process. *Source*: Steve Downer of the Difference

Is the challenge **motivational** (effort/heart)? Is the individual struggling because they are not putting forth enough effort? Is she not trying hard enough because she's embarrassed? Is he quitting too soon because of frustration or fear?

Is the challenge **educational** (information/skills/hands)? Is the individual struggling because he lacks the skill to execute effectively? Are they getting interference from other habits? For example, someone well versed in marketing-speak may not know how to tell an authentic story. Is it something you could model, or role play with them?

Is the challenge **strategic** (strategy/head)? Is an individual who is motivated and has the skills struggling how to use these skills in this particular context (e.g., an urbanite in a rural area, an immigrant in a nonimmigrant community)? Does he understand the concepts or underlying principles clearly? Has she not thought it through carefully? Are the goals not achievable? Does the strategy make sense?

3. Intervene: What do I do?

Once you think you've figured out what the problem is, don't just tell the coachee what you think she should do. Find out what she thinks she should do. Ask questions that enable the coachee to see the problem, that allow you to see how the coachee sees the problem and how she could discern a way to solve it. Get the coachee's views out on the table. The appropriate intervention depends on the diagnosis.

If the challenge is **motivational**, you can encourage and exhort—you can do it! Offer a kick in the pants (with love). Help the person confront their fear, embarrassment, or other emotions that may get in the way of their ability to risk acting, persevering, or trying new things. Communicate with empathy, hope, and affirmation of the coachee's self-worth. Model courage and emotional maturity in your own behavior. Confess fear and explain how you move toward it, rather than away from it.

If the challenge is **educational**, you can model the behavior and invite the coachee to imitate you to get the feel of the activity. You can break it down into small parts and invite the individual to try one part at a time. Offer three or four different practice exercises and observe which ones work best for that person. Suggest others with whom the person can practice or suggest ways to figure out where to find the missing information.

If the challenge is **strategic**, you can work through a specific example with the person, asking questions to guide the strategic process. Then reflect on the process itself, asking them to describe how it worked. Ask questions about how the individual is thinking about the practice: Why did you choose that tactic? Offer your observations, asking how the person might think about it differently: At that point, were there other options? What might they have been? Why did you choose the one you did? Offer feedback on what you are hearing, asking if that describes the situation and, at the same time, offering possible reframing of it. Use silent reflection and self-diagnosis: Why don't you take a moment to think through what you believe is working and not working and let's talk about that?

4. Debrief: What did the coachee learn?
Ask your coachee to summarize their takeaways from the session. Commit to next steps and decide when you will check back in. What went well? What are you challenged by? What are some possible solutions? What are your goals or next steps?

5. Monitor: How can I continue to support the coachee?
Schedule periodic check-ins to support your coachee in integrating this new or revised solution into their regular practice. Find out from the coachee how the situation has changed. Assess whether the diagnosis and intervention were successful. Celebrate success!

Table 7.1 The Do's and Don'ts of Effective Coaching

Effective coaching is	Effective coaching is not
Showing up and being present to another person's experience, and listening with both your head and heart.	Being so prepared that you work out all the answers for the coachee before you even hear or observe their challenges.
Helping the coachee explore and make sense of their challenges and successes, and what they learned from it all.	Falsely praising of the coachee or only focusing on their strengths because you do not want to hurt their feelings.
Helping the coachee find solutions to challenges.	Solely criticizing the coachee.
Asking questions that both support and challenge the person you are coaching.	Telling the coachee what to do.

In organizing campaigns, new people are usually trying to make new things happen under new conditions, so ongoing learning is essential. Performance feedback, especially on early failures, is critical not only for adapting strategy but also for leadership development. Coaching is a far better option than either micromanagement (telling someone exactly what to do . . . all the time) or hands-off management (sink or swim). Coaching can best be done as part of ordinary leadership practice by embedding it in the work itself. Peers can coach one another with sufficient training in both the coaching and the particular practice itself.

Conclusion

Developmental leadership is at the heart of what makes organizing work. It is is not only about enabling others to achieve shared purpose under conditions of uncertainty; it is also about enabling others to enable others to enable others. This is how we build the capacity we need at the scale—and with the depth—we need to create the change that we want. It's the kind of micro work that is required to achieve macro results. It's valuable not only for the goals it makes possible in the future but also because it enriches individual and collective human agency in the present. And if not now, when?

Conclusion

Where We've Been

In writing this book, I've tried to share what I've been learning about how the leadership, organizing, and action to practice democracy are rooted in five core practices of building relationships, storytelling (heart), strategizing (head), acting (hands), and structuring. By developing leadership skilled in these practices to organize at scale, we can create the power we need to shape a better world. But this book is not an organizing model, nor is it a manual or a blueprint. Rather, rooted as it is in my own learning journey, it may suggest ways in which you can embark on your own learning journey; it is, and always will be, an adaptable work in progress.

Each of these five practices is grounded in capabilities we all have. By making explicit what many of us know implicitly, we can turn these capabilities into powerful craft. These practices are people-centric, not issue-centric. They are not specific to solving the problems of immigration status, criminal justice, global warming, or the dysfunctional school down the street. This book is an invitation to join others in learning practices that can improve the odds of getting real outcomes, growing stronger, and developing leadership. Change and continuity are usually in tension with one another, yet the continuity in our practices, if put to work, can yield real change. The focus here, then, has been on exploring the value of these practices and learning them well enough that you and others can use them to become effective, creative, and generative leaders and organizers.

All five practices are rooted in values fundamental to the practice of democracy. They are based on the belief that all people can learn (head), grow (heart), and shape (hands) their own destiny in concert with others—and that everyone ought to have access to the emotional, material, and cognitive scaffolding they need to do so. We can use these practices to enact individual and collective agency in response to challenges anchored in experiences of self-worth, solidarity, and hope as opposed to self-doubt, isolation, and fear. This approach to organizing respects the diverse cultural, religious, and political traditions in which we all grew up, as well as the responsibility to adapt or transform those traditions based on who we are, when we are, and where we are. This common ground is one reason people of such diverse cultures, regions, and institutions find the approach so useful—not as a blueprint but, in the words of Samar Dudin, as a road map.

The one certainty we can count on is change. Each of the five practices includes a commitment to sustained learning, learning what works and why, what isn't working and why. In this way we can improve, adapt, and innovate as we change, our communities change, and the world changes. As I noted in chapter 4 when learning Japanese martial arts, *shuhari*, one begins by learning the master's way (*shu*), then adapting that way as needed (*ha*), before finally creating one's own way (*ri*), which can, in turn, be shared with others. We can treat what has come before as a resource on which we can draw to shape what is to come, instead of as a bulwark against it.

* * *

Where do we go from here?

Since the 1970s, we have created a political economy in which the interests of the many, who work, are subordinated to the interest of the few, who own. In the United States, we've allowed a trifecta that links economic structures that facilitate the accumulation of wealth at the top; electoral processes that have become almost entirely monetized; and a civil society dependent on the largesse of many of the same people benefiting from all the rest, but in philanthropic form. This operates within a Constitutional structure that grows less representative of America every day. In the response to the global financial crisis of 2008, those who held the economic, political, and military power decided to protect investors (owners, banks, and markets) rather than the people (citizens). The "many" lost their homes, lost their jobs, and lost their hope, while the "few" racked up billions in salaries, bonuses, and capital. And even as the COVID-19 crisis brought every kind of inequality into vivid relief, creating a unique opportunity for reform, the wealthy prospered amid the unparalleled suffering borne by those whom class, racial, gender, educational, and professional difference excluded from the favored circle of protection. Ironically, the most disruptive reaction to the status quo—the people with pitchforks—has come from the right, not from the left, and it has come as an attack on democracy itself. Characterizing itself as a reaction to rule of the elite, which in too many ways it has been, it revives a far older and more traditional racism, nationalism, patriarchy, and fundamentalist religion, spiked by a fresh dose of populism that threatens a more humane and demo-cratic future for America and the world.

This is the challenge that demands our response. It will require overcoming the divisions, elitisms, and confusions of those with whom sharing values, an interest in change, and hope for a better future is not enough. This will require going back to the basics. The work starts with each other—with people: with the relationships we can build; the stories of our shared values; the resourcefulness to turn our assets into more rather than our deficits into less; the courage to act on what we can, without which nothing can change, including ourselves; and the wisdom to structure our interactions with each other to effectively include the many, not the few.

This is the hope I experience in the people I meet and have the privilege of working with every day, whether online or off. These are people like the twenty or so young people I met with in summer 2022 in Tunis, where I had gone for a Leading Change Network staff retreat. The young people in ques-tion had completed an online organizing class in Arabic led by my friend and colleague Nisreen Haj Ahmad in Amman. We met in a cultural club in the medina (old city) of Tunis. With the help of my Arabic-speaking colleagues and friends, the session was still going strong when the cultural club in which we were meeting threw us out after two-and-a-half hours. What had held the group's attention? The participants were riveted by hearing each other's stories, learning who they were organizing with, what they were fighting for, and, most of all, witnessing the hope rooted in their shared experiences, faith, and sense of possibility.

Their hope was not a hope based on the coming of a political savior or the enforcement of a perfect ideology or the mirage of joining the global elite. In fact, they were deeply disappointed with the limited change produced by their revolution more than a decade ago. But while they were disappointed, they were not cynical. They still believed change was possible, and they were dedicated to making it so, together. In my workshops, and now in this book, I am attempting to offer them the best support I can in doing that work in the time that we have together.

In the United States, real challenges to the status quo—the kind of chal-lenge we need if people who work are to retake their power from those who own property—have often come in the form of social movements. These movements, whether fought for temperance, abolition, women's suffrage, agrarian reform, labor reform, progressivism, civil rights, environmentalism, gender equity, or even conservatism, have combined personal, community, and political change. They have linked local organization to state and national strategy, and they have fought to put their values in place. Movements emerge from the efforts of purposeful actors (individuals or organizations) to respond to conditions they experience as unjust. They also emerge in response to opportunities to assert new public values, form new relationships rooted in those values, and mobilize political, economic, and cultural power to translate these values into action.

Movements differ from fashions, styles, or fads in that they are collective, strategic, and organized.[1] They differ from interest groups in that they not only reallocate goods, but they also redefine them. Not content with winning the game, movements try to change the rules.[2] When movements succeed in expanding the equality of voice, they strengthen democracy. When they narrow equality of voice, they weaken democracy.

We are again in a movement moment. People of all ages—and especially young people—are calling for societal responses to the climate crisis, racism, xenophobia, socioeconomic inequality, the housing crisis, transphobia, gun violence, and more. Our challenge is linking social movement energy with organizational capacity to transform it into political, economic, and cultural power. This in turn depends on our capacity for leadership, organizing, and action.

This is what the craft of organizing is all about. Organizers recruit, train, and develop leadership, build a constituency with that leadership, and enable this constituency to turn their own resources—time, energy, imagination, money—into the power they need to effectively pursue their goals. Although organizing is rooted in our everyday capacity for relating to each other, it is also a craft that requires training, learning, and coaching to bring intentionality, skill, and purpose to the work. It is not about providing services to dependent *clients* or marketing products to paying *customers*. It is about bringing individuals together to form constituencies able to exercise their individual and collective voices. Recall that "constituency" derives from the Latin *con* (with) and *stare* (stand): people who can stand together, learn together, work together, and win together.

Organizing people only begins with solving immediate problems—like making sure your candidate gets the most votes or putting up a stop sign. It is about doing this and, *at the same time,* developing the leadership, organization, and power to take on structural challenges in the long run. Organizing is not about fixing a *bug* in the system like offering a "safety net." It is about transforming the cultural, economic, and political *features* of the system. I got hooked on organizing in the civil rights movement because the process showed me how people could find the resources within themselves and each other to create the power they needed to change the institutions responsible for their problems in the first place. That is what healthy democracy requires. And in the words of American poet Langston Hughes, "Let America be the dream the dreamers dreamed— . . . The land that never has been yet—And yet must be—the land where every man is free. . . ."

Will you join us?

Notes

Acknowledgments

1. Special thanks to Charlie Hale, Dean of Social Sciences at UCSB, for generous support.

Introduction

1. See Brueggemann, *The Prophetic Imagination*.
2. Branch, *Parting the Waters*; Robinson, *Montgomery Bus Boycott and the Women Who Started It*.
3. Takaki, *Strangers from a Different Shore*; Starr, *Americans and the California Dream, 1850–1915*; Starr, *Golden Dreams*; McWilliams, *North from Mexico*.
4. What would become the United Farm Workers began as the Farm Workers Association (FWA) then became the National Farm Workers Association (NFWA). When the NFWA merged with the Agricultural Workers Organizing Committee of the AFL-CIO, it became the United Farm Workers Organizing Committee AFL-CIO (UFWOC). In 1973, having been recognized by the AFL-CIO as a fully chartered union, it became the United Farm Workers (UFW). Hereafter the organization will be referred to as the UFW, its last and current name.
5. Levitsky and Ziblatt, *How Democracies Die*; Snyder, *On Tyranny*.
6. Lessig, *They Don't Represent Us*; Levitsky and Ziblatt, *Tyranny of the Minority*.
7. Meyer and Tarrow, *The Resistance*.
8. Tooze, *Crashed*.
9. MacLean, *Democracy in Chains*.
10. Brown, *Undoing the Demos*.
11. Sheingate, *Building a Business of Politics*.
12. Ganz, "Voters in the Crosshairs."
13. Fisher, *Activism, Inc.*; Walker, *Grassroots for Hire*; Han, *How Organizations Develop Activists*.
14. Putnam, *Bowling Alone*; Skocpol, *Diminished Democracy*.
15. Anderson, *Private Government*.
16. Tufekci, *Twitter and Tear Gas*.
17. Mazzucato, *The Value of Everything*; Sandel, *What Money Can't Buy*.
18. Tufekci, *Twitter and Tear Gas*.
19. Freeman, "The Tyranny of Structurelessness."

20. MacLean, *Democracy in Chains*; Reich, *Just Giving*; Brown, *In the Ruins of Neoliberalism*; Skocpol, *Diminished Democracy*.
21. Hirschman, *Exit, Voice, and Loyalty*.
22. Mazucatto, *The Value of Everything*.

Chapter 1

1. See, for example, Andrews et al. "Leadership, Membership, and Voice"; Baggetta, Han, and Andrews, "Leading Associations."
2. Ganz and Lin, "Learning to Lead: A Pedagogy of Practice."
3. Ganz et al., "Crafting Public Narrative to Enable Collective Action."
4. Freire, *Pedagogy of the Oppressed*.
5. McKenna and Han, *Groundbreakers*.
6. Addams, *Twenty Years at Hull-House with Autobiographical Notes*, 65–88.
7. On relational power, see Emerson, "Power-Dependence Relations." See also Battilana and Casciaro, *Power for All*.
8. Francis (pope), *Fratelli tutti*, §119, §214.
9. Ober, *Democracy and Knowledge*.
10. Tufekci, *Twitter and Tear Gas*.
11. Verba, "The Citizen as Respondent."
12. Hirschman, *Exit, Voice, and Loyalty*.
13. Gould, *Time's Arrow, Time's Cycle*, 10–15.
14. Ganz and McKenna, "Bringing Leadership Back In."
15. Hackman and Wageman, "A Theory of Team Coaching."
16. Schlozman, *When Movements Anchor Parties*.

Chapter 2

1. Putnam, *Bowling Alone*; Francis (pope), *Fratelli Tutti*.
2. Taylor, *Sources of the Self*.
3. Marx, "The Commodity," in *Capital*.
4. Polanyi, *Great Transformation*.
5. Tocqueville, *Democracy in America*, 553.
6. Skocpol, *Diminished Democracy*, 12–13.
7. Olson, *Logic of Collective Action*.
8. Brown, *Undoing the Demos*; Turkle, *Alone Together*; Francis (pope), *Frateli Tutti*, §43, §105; Sandel, "What Isn't for Sale?"; Rodgers, *Age of Fracture*.
9. Putnam, *Bowling Alone*.
10. Gecan, *Going Public*.
11. See Tocqueville, *Democracy in America*.
12. Ober, *Origins of Democracy in Ancient Greece*; Aristotle, *The Athenian Constitution*.

13. Chambers, *Roots for Radicals*, 74.
14. Granovetter, "The Strength of Weak Ties."
15. GBIO, "About GBIO," https://www.gbio.org/about-gbio.html.
16. Williams, "Boston Interfaith Organization to Celebrate 10 Years of Service."
17. Burt, "The Power of an Organized Citizenry and Coalition Politics: The 1949 Election of Edward R. Roybal to the Los Angeles City Council."
18. Levy, *Cesar Chavez: Autobiography of La Causa*, 92.
19. McKenna and Han, *Groundbreakers*.
20. McKenna and Han, *Groundbreakers*.
21. Class sessions include lecture, discussion, role-playing, chatting, and polling. As of spring 2023, I've had the opportunity to work directly with 2,280 online student practitioners, each leading their own organizing project, in some 119 countries.
22. Tufekci, *Twitter and Teargas*; Han, *How Organizations Develop Activists*.
23. McAdam, *Political Process and the Development of Black Insurgency*, 2.

Chapter 3

1. Martin Luther King Jr., "I've Been to the Mountaintop," Memphis, TN, April 3, 1968.
2. Peterson, *Maps of Meaning: The Architecture of Belief*.
3. See Bruner, *Actual Minds, Possible Worlds*.
4. Thanks to narrative psychologist Dan MacAdams for this distinction (what *is* in the world and what *is good* in the world), personal email.
5. Reber, *Implicit Learning and Tacit Knowledge*.
6. Ganz et al., "Crafting Public Narrative Toward Collective Action: A Pedagogy for Leadership Developments"; Cohen-Chen et al., "The Differential Effects of Hope and Fear on Information Processing in Intractable Conflict."
7. Pascal, *Pensées*, Section IV, Of Means of Belief, #277, page 29.
8. Marcus, *The Sentimental Citizen: Emotion in Democratic Politics*.
9. Alinsky, *Rules for Radicals*.
10. Walzer, *Thick and Thin*; Polletta, *Freedom Is an Endless Meeting*.
11. Scott, *The Moral Economy of the Peasant*.
12. Scott, *Weapons of the Weak*; Gamson, *Talking Politics*.
13. Nussbaum, *Anger and Forgiveness*.
14. Martin, *How We Hope*.
15. Dr. Bernard Steinberg on Maimonides, *Mishneh Torah*, Kings and Wars 12, Knowledge 7, and Repentance 5.
16. Keltner, *Awe*.
17. Nussbaum, *The Therapy of Desire*; West, *Democracy Matters*.
18. McKee, *Story: Substance, Structure, Style, and the Principles of Screenwriting*.
19. Rizzolatti, Fogassi, and Gallese, "Neurophysiological Mechanisms Underlying the Understanding and Imitation of Action"; Stephens, Silbert, and Hasson, "Speaker-Listener Neural Coupling Underlies Successful Communication."
20. Aristotle, *Poetics* 6.

21. Tulving, "Episodic Memory: From Mind to Brain."
22. Taylor, *Sources of the Self*.
23. Bruner, *Acts of Meaning*, 83.
24. March and Olsen, "The Technology of Foolishness."
25. Polletta and Jasper, "Collective Identity and Social Movements."
26. Shakespeare, *Henry V*, act 4, scene 3.
27. Heaney, from "The Cure at Troy" (1990).
28. Martin, *How We Hope*.
29. McAdams, *The Redemptive Self*, 3, 81–100.
30. Scott, *Domination and the Arts of Resistance*.
31. Vygotsky, *Mind in Society*.
32. Croft's narrative is available as a video online at https://www.youtube.com/watch?v=lymvc5d6qxY.
33. Meeropol, Abel. "Strange Fruit." Performed by Billie Holiday. 1939. On *Billie Holiday's Greatest Hits*. New York, NY: Columbia Records. Vinyl recording.

Chapter 4

1. See Tillich, *Love, Power, and Justice*.
2. Jenkins and Perrow, "Insurgency of the Powerless: Farm Worker Movements (1946–1972)," 249.
3. See Mintzberg, *The Rise and Fall of Strategic Planning*.
4. This story is also the starting point for my 2009 book, *Why David Sometimes Wins: Leadership, Organizing, and Strategy in the California Farm Worker Movement*.
5. I discuss this in greater length in my book *Why David Sometimes Wins*.
6. Thomas Kuhn makes this point persuasively when he points out that "paradigm shifts" in science have often originated with arrivals from other disciplines or younger or newer scholars less committed to the taken for granted view. Kuhn, *The Structure of Scientific Revolutions*.
7. For research on these dynamics: Rick Busselle, "Schema Theory and Mental Models"; Michael Shayne Gary et al., "Enhancing Mental Models, Analogical Transfer, and Performance in Strategic Decision Making."
8. Suzuki, *Zen Mind, Beginner's Mind*; Gopnik, "Why Adults Lose the 'Beginner's Mind.'"
9. Kegan and Lahey, *Immunity to Change*.
10. Speech at National Defense Executive Reserve Conference in Washington, D.C., on November 14, 1957.
11. Gersick, "Pacing Strategic Change."
12. See Alinsky, *Rules for Radicals*.
13. See Levy, *Cesar Chavez: Autobiography of La Causa*, 207.
14. See Lukes, *Power: A Radical View*.
15. See Gould, *Time's Arrow, Time's Cycle*.
16. Hall, *The Dance of Life*; Gersick, "Time and Transition in Work Teams."

Chapter 5

1. Reich, *Just Giving*; Ganz and Reyes, "Reclaiming Civil Society"; Giridharadas, *Winners Take All*.
2. Hirschman, "Against Parsimony."
3. Dobson, *Freedom Funders*.
4. Festinger, *A Theory of Cognitive Dissonance*; Aronson, "Dissonance Theory: Progress and Problems."
5. Hackman and Oldham, "Motivation through the Design of Work: Test of a Theory."
6. Deci and Ryan, *Intrinsic Motivation and Self-Determination in Human Behavior*.
7. Hackman and Oldham, *Work Redesign*; Hackman, *Leading Teams*, 22–25.
8. Tramutola, *Sidewalk Strategies*, 39.
9. Ibid.

Chapter 6

1. Kramer, "Political Paranoia in Organizations."
2. Greater Boston Interfaith Organization is one example, now in its twenty-fifth year, as is the California Faith in Action Network.
3. Exceptions include Isaiah, a statewide community organization based in Minneapolis, now operating within its structural design since its founding with adaptations that have facilitated its dynamic, innovative, and effective work. Sunrise is in the midst of its own radical restructuring as a 2.0 version. The DSA (Democratic Socialists of America) has been adapting its inherited traditional membership base democratic structure in light of a radical demographic shift in its membership combined with explosive growth. And MoveOn sustained itself almost entirely on funding by their own members.
4. Taylor, "Degenerations of Democracy."
5. Lessig, *They Don't Represent Us*; Levitsky and Ziblatt, *Tyranny of the Minority*.
6. Anderson, *Private Government*.
7. Wilson, *Political Organizations*.
8. Michels, *Political Parties*; Lipset et al., *Union Democracy*.
9. Mintzberg, *Mintzberg on Management*.
10. See Hirschman, *Exit, Voice and Loyalty*.
11. Smith and Berg, "A Paradoxical Conception of Group Dynamics," 641.
12. Hackman, *Leading Teams*, 108–9.
13. Hackman, *Leading Teams*.
14. Skocpol, Ganz, and Munson, "Nation of Organizers."
15. See Schattschneider, *The Semi-Sovereign People*.
16. See Grossman, *Political Corruption in America*.
17. Michels, *Political Parties*.

18. Lipset et al., *Union Democracy*.
19. Ahlquist and Levi, *In the Interest of Others*.
20. Sloane, *Hoffa*; Hume, *Death in the Mines*.
21. Conversations by the author with HERE unions officials, Vincent Sirabella, Miguel Contreras, and John Willhelm (1980–1991).
22. Conversations by the author with SEIU union officials including Andrew Stern, Mary Kay Henry, Eliseo Medina, and others (1984–2005).
23. Lichtenstein, *The Most Dangerous Man in Detroit*.
24. Scheiber, "Why the UAW's President Has Taken a Hard Line."
25. Weil, *Turning the Tide*.
26. McAlevey, *Raising Expectations (and Raising Hell)*; *No Shortcuts*; *A Collective Bargain*.
27. Hackman and Oldham, *Work Redesign*; Deci and Ryan, *Intrinsic Motivation and Self Determination in Human Behavior*.
28. Hackman, *Leading Teams*, 55.
29. Freeman, "The Tyranny of Structurelessness."

Chapter 7

1. See Weber, "The Types of Authority and Imperative Coordination"; Wilson, *Political Organizations*; Burns, *Leadership*; Bennis, *On Becoming a Leader*; Heifetz, *Leadership without Easy Answers*.
2. See Hackman, *Leading Teams*; Salas et al., "The Science of Training and Development in Organizations."
3. Our approach to leadership teams is strongly rooted in Richard Hackman's work on "real" teams. My colleague Ruth Wageman and I adapted this approach to self-governing teams in our work with the Sierra Club, which, in turn, we introduced to the Obama campaign in 2007. See Ganz and Wageman, *Sierra Club Leadership Development Project*.
4. McKenna and Han, *Groundbreakers*.
5. Hackman, *Leading Teams*.
6. Sifry, "If the Movements of the Last Decade Are Done, What Comes Next?"
7. Hackman and Wageman, "A Theory of Team Coaching."

Conclusion

1. Ganz, "Leading Change."
2. See Schlozman, *When Movements Anchor Parties*; Foner, *The Story of American Freedom*.

Bibliography

Addams, Jane. *Twenty Years at Hull-House with Autobiographical Notes*. New York: Macmillan, 1910.

Alinsky, Saul D. *Rules for Radicals: A Practical Primer for Realistic Radicals*. New York: Random House, 1971.

Ahlquist, John S., and Margaret Levi. *In the Interest of Others: Organizations and Social Activism*. Princeton, NJ: Princeton University Press, 2013.

Anderson, Elizabeth. *Private Government: How Employers Rule Our Lives (and Why We Don't Talk about It)*. Princeton, NJ: Princeton University Press, 2017.

Andrews, Kenneth T., et al. "Leadership, Membership, and Voice: Civic Associations that Work." *American Journal of Sociology* 115, no. 4 (2010): 1191–242.

Aronson, Elliot. "Dissonance Theory: Progress and Problems." In *Theories of Cognitive Consistency: A Sourcebook*, edited by R. P. Abelson et al., 5–27. Chicago: Rand McNally, 1968.

Baggetta, Matthew, Hahrie Han, and Kenneth T. Andrews. "Leading Associations: How Individual Characteristics and Team Dynamics Generate Committed Leaders." *American Sociological Review* 78, no. 4 (2013): 544–73.

Battilana, Julie, and Tiziana Casciaro. *Power for All: How It Really Works and Why It's Everyone's Business*. New York: Simon and Schuster, 2021.

Bennis, Warren. *On Becoming a Leader*. 1989. Reprint, New York: Basic Books, 2009.

Branch, Taylor. *Parting the Waters: America in the King Years, 1954–63*. New York: Pan Macmillan, 1989.

Brown, Wendy. *In the Ruins of Neoliberalism: The Rise of Antidemocratic Politics in the West*. New York: Columbia University Press, 2019.

Brown, Wendy. *Undoing the Demos: Neoliberalism's Stealth Revolution*. Cambridge, MA: MIT Press, 2015.

Bruggeman, Walter. *The Prophetic Imagination*. Philadelphia: Fortress Press, 1978.

Bruner, Jerome. *Acts of Meaning: Four Lectures on Mind and Culture*. Cambridge, MA: Harvard University Press, 1990.

Bruner, Jerome. *Actual Minds, Possible Worlds*. Cambridge, MA: Harvard University Press, 1987.

Burns, James MacGregor. *Leadership*. New York: Harper and Row, 1978.

Burt, Kenneth C. "The Power of an Organized Citizenry and Coalition Politics: The 1949 Election of Edward R. Roybal to the Los Angeles City Council." *Southern California Quarterly* 85, no. 4 (Winter 2003): 413–38.

Busselle, Rick. "Schema Theory and Mental Models." *The International Encyclopedia of Media Effects* (2017): 1–8.

Chambers, Ed. *Roots for Radicals: Organizing for Power, Action, and Justice*. New York: Bloomsbury, 2003.

Cohen-Chen, Smadar, Eran Halperin, Roni Porat, and Daniel Bar-Tal. "The Differential Effects of Hope and Fear on Information Processing in Intractable Conflict." *Journal of Social and Political Psychology* 2, no. 1 (2014): 11–30.

Deci, Edward L., and Richard M. Ryan. *Intrinsic Motivation and Self-Determination in Human Behavior*. Berlin: Springer Science & Business Media, 1985.

Dobson, Sean. *Freedom Funders: Philanthropy and the Civil Rights Movement, 1955–1965*. Washington, DC: National Committee for Responsive Philanthropy, 2014.

Emerson, Richard. "Power-Dependence Relations." *American Sociological Review* 27, no. 1 (1962): 31–41.

Festinger, Leon. *A Theory of Cognitive Dissonance*. Stanford, CA: Stanford University Press, 1962.

Fisher, Dana. *Activism, Inc.: How the Outsourcing of Grassroots Campaigns Is Strangling Progressive Politics in America*. Stanford, CA: Stanford University Press, 2006.

Foner, Eric. *The Story of American Freedom*. New York: Norton, 1998.

Francis (pope). *Fratelli Tutti*. Encyclical Letter, October 3, 2020. https://www.vatican.va/content/francesco/en/encyclicals/documents/papa-francesco_20201003_enciclica-fratelli-tutti.html.

Freeman, Jo. "The Tyranny of Structurelessness." *Berkeley Journal of Sociology* 17 (1972/73): 151–64.

Freire, Paulo. *Pedagogy of the Oppressed*. New York: Seabury Press, 1970.

Gamson, William A. *Talking Politics*. New York: Cambridge University Press, 1992.

Ganz, Marshall. "Leading Change: Leadership, Organization, and Social Movements." In *Handbook of Leadership Theory and Practice*, edited by Nitin Nohria and Rakesh Khurana, 527–68. Boston: Harvard Business Press, 2010.

Ganz, Marshall. "Voters in the Crosshairs." *American Prospect*, December 19, 1994.

Ganz, Marshall, Julia Lee Cunningham, Inbal Ben Ezer, and Alaina Segura. "Crafting Public Narrative to Enable Collective Action: A Pedagogy for Leadership Development." *Academy of Management Learning & Education* 22, no. 2 (2023): 169–90.

Ganz, Marshall, and Emily S. Lin. "Learning to Lead: A Pedagogy of Practice." In *Handbook for Teaching Leadership: Knowing, Doing, and Being*, edited by Scott Snook, Nitin Nohria, and Rakesh Khurana, 353–66. Los Angeles, CA: SAGE, 2011.

Ganz, Marshall, and Elizabeth McKenna. "Bringing Leadership Back In." In *The Wiley Blackwell Companion to Social Movements*, edited by David A. Snow, Sarah A. Soule, Hanspeter Kriesi, and Holly J. McCammon, 185–202. Hoboken, NJ: Wiley-Blackwell, 2018.

Ganz, Marshall, and Art Reyes III. "Reclaiming Civil Society." *Stanford Social Innovation Review* 18, no. 1 (2019): A6–A9.

Ganz, Marshall, and Ruth Wageman. *Sierra Club Leadership Development Project. Pilot Project, Report and Recommendations*, May 8, 2008, http://marshallganz.usmblogs.com/files/2012/11/LDP-Final-Report.pdf.

Gary, Michael Shayne, Robert E. Wood, and Tracey Pillinger. "Enhancing Mental Models, Analogical Transfer, and Performance in Strategic Decision Making." *Strategic Management Journal* 33 (2012): 1229–246.

Gecan, Michael. *Going Public: An Organizer's Guide to Citizen Action*. Boston: Beacon Press, 2002.

Gersick, Connie J. "Pacing Strategic Change: The Case of a New Venture." *Academy of Management Journal* 37, no. 1 (1994): 9–45.

Gersick, Connie J. "Time and Transition in Work Teams: Toward a New Model of Group Development." *Academy of Management Journal* 31, no. 1 (1988): 9–41.

Giridharadas, Anand. *Winners Take All: The Elite Charade of Changing the World.* New York: Knopf, 2018.

Gopnik, Alison. "Why Adults Lose the 'Beginner's Mind.'" *New York Times: The Ezra Kline Show,* podcast, April 16, 2021.

Gould, Stephen Jay. *Time's Arrow, Time's Cycle: Myth and Metaphor in the Discovery of Geological Time,* vol. 2. Cambridge, MA: Harvard University Press, 1987.

Granovetter, Mark. "The Strength of Weak Ties." *American Journal of Sociology* 78 (1973): 1360–80.

Grossman, Mary. *Political Corruption in America: An Encyclopedia of Scandals, Power, and Greed.* Millerton, NY: Grey House, 2008.

Hackman, J. Richard. *Leading Teams: Setting the Stage for Great Performances.* Cambridge, MA: Harvard Business Review Press, 2002.

Hackman, J. Richard, and Greg R. Oldham. "Motivation through the Design of Work: Test of a Theory." *Organizational Behavior and Human Performance* 16, no. 2 (1976): 250–79.

Hackman, J. Richard, and Greg R. Oldman. *Work Redesign.* Reading, MA: Addison-Wesley, 1980.

Hackman, J. Richard, and Ruth Wageman. "A Theory of Team Coaching." *Academy of Management Review* 30, no. 2 (2005): 269–87.

Hall, Edward T. *The Dance of Life: The Other Dimension of Time.* New York: Anchor Books, 1983.

Han, Hahrie. *How Organizations Develop Activists: Civic Associations and Leadership in the 21st Century.* New York: Oxford University Press, 2014.

Heifetz, Ronald A. *Leadership without Easy Answers.* Cambridge, MA: Harvard University Press, 1998.

Hirschman, Albert O. "Against Parsimony: Three Ways of Complicating Some Categories of Economic Discourse." *Economics and Philosophy* 1, no. 1 (1985): 7–21.

Hirschman, Albert O. *Exit, Voice, and Loyalty.* Cambridge, MA: Harvard University Press, 1970.

Hume, Brit. *Death in the Mines: Rebellion and Murder in the United Mine Workers.* New York: Grossman, 1971.

Jenkins, J. Craig, and Charles Perrow. "Insurgency of the Powerless: Farm Worker Movements (1946–1972)." *American Sociological Review,* 42, no. 2 (1977): 249–68.

Kegan, Robert, and Lisa Lascow Lahey. *Immunity to Change: How to Overcome It and Unlock Potential in Yourself and Your Organization.* Boston: Harvard Business Press, 2009.

Keltner, Dacher. *Awe: The New Science of Everyday Wonder and How It Can Transform Your Life.* New York: Penguin, 2023.

Kramer, Roderick M. "Political Paranoia in Organizations: Antecedents and Consequences." In *Research in the Sociology of Organizations,* vol. 17, 47–88. Bingley, UK: Emerald Group Publishing, 2000.

Kuhn, Thomas S. *The Structure of Scientific Revolutions.* Chicago: University of Chicago Press, 1962.

Lessig, Lawrence. *They Don't Represent Us: Reclaiming Our Democracy.* New York: HarperCollins, 2019.

Levitsky, Steven, and Daniel Ziblatt. *How Democracies Die.* New York: Crown, 2018.

Levitsky, Steven, and Daniel Zibatt. *Tyranny of the Minority: Why American Democracy Reached the Breaking Point.* New York: Penguin Random House, 2023.

Levy, Jacques E. *Cesar Chavez: Autobiography of La Causa.* New York: Norton, 1975.

Lichtenstein, Nelson. *The Most Dangerous Man in Detroit: Walter Reuther and the Fate of American Labor.* New York: Basic Books, 1995.

Lipset, Seymour Martin, Martin A. Trow, James S. Coleman, and Clark Kerr. *Union Democracy: The Internal Politics of the International Typographical Union.* Glencoe, IL: Free Press, 1956.

Lukes, Stephen. *Power: A Radical View.* London: Macmillan, 1974.

MacLean, Nancy. *Democracy in Chains: The Deep History of the Radical Right's Stealth Plan for America.* New York: Penguin Books, 2018.

March, James G., and Johan P. Olsen. "The Technology of Foolishness." In *Ambiguity and Choice in Organizations,* 69–81. Oslo: Universitetsforlaget, 1979.

Marcus, George E. *The Sentimental Citizen: Emotion in Democratic Politics.* University Park: Pennsylvania State University Press, 2002.

Martin, Adrienne. *How We Hope: A Moral Psychology.* Princeton, NJ: Princeton University Press, 2014.

Marx, Karl. "The Commodity." In *Capital: A Critique of Political Economy,* vol. 1, 125–63. New York: Vintage Books, 1981.

Mazzucato, Mariana. *The Value of Everything: Making and Taking in the Global Economy.* New York: Public Affairs, 2018.

McAdam, Doug. *Political Process and the Development of Black Insurgency, 1930–1970.* 2nd ed. Chicago: University of Chicago Press, 1999.

McAdams, Dan P. *The Redemptive Self: Stories Americans Live By.* New York: Oxford University Press, 2006

McAlevey, Jane F. *Raising Expectations (and Raising Hell): My Decade Fighting for the Labor Movement.* New York: Verso Books, 2012.

McAlevey, Jane F. *No Shortcuts: Organizing for Power in the New Gilded Age.* New York: Oxford University Press, 2016.

McAlevey, Jane F. *A Collective Bargain: Unions, Organizing, and the Fight for Democracy.* New York: Ecco, 2020.

McKee, Robert. *Story: Substance, Structure, Style, and the Principles of Screenwriting.* New York: Regan Books/HarperCollins, 1997.

McKenna, Elizabeth, and Hahrie Han. *Groundbreakers: How Obama's 2.2 Million Volunteers Transformed Campaigning in America.* New York: Oxford University Press, 2014.

McWilliams, Cary. *North from Mexico: The Spanish-Speaking People of the United States.* New York: Greenwood Press, 1968.

Meyer, David S., and Sidney Tarrow. *The Resistance: The Dawn of the Anti-Trump Protest Movement.* New York: Oxford University Press, 2018.

Michels, Robert. *Political Parties: A Sociological Study of the Oligarchical Tendencies of Modern Democracy.* 1911. Translated by Eden and Cedar Paul. New York: Hearst's International Library, 1915.

Mintzberg, Henry. *Mintzberg on Management: Inside Our Strange World of Organizations.* New York: Free Press, 1989.

Mintzberg, Henry. *The Rise and Fall of Strategic Planning: Reconceiving Roles for Planning, Plans, Planners.* New York: Free Press, 1994.

Morone, James. *Hellfire Nation: The Politics of Sin in American History.* New Haven, CT: Yale University Press, 2004.

Nussbaum, Martha. *Anger and Forgiveness: Resentment, Generosity, Justice.* New York: Oxford University Press, 2016.

Nussbaum, Martha. *The Therapy of Desire: Theory and Practice in Hellenistic Ethics.* Princeton, NJ: Princeton University Press, 1994.

Ober, Josiah. *Democracy and Knowledge: Innovation and Learning in Classical Athens.* Princeton, NJ: Princeton University Press, 2008.

Ober, Josiah. *Origins of Democracy in Ancient Greece.* Berkeley: University of California Press, 2007.

Olson, Mancur. *The Logic of Collective Action.* Cambridge, MA: Harvard University Press, 1965.

Pascal, Blaise. *Pensées.* New York: E. P. Dutton & Co., 1958.

Peterson, Jordan B. *Maps of Meaning: The Architecture of Belief.* New York: Routledge, 1999.

Polanyi, Karl. *The Great Transformation: The Political and Economic Origins of Our Time.* New York: Beacon Press, 2001.

Polletta, Francesca. *Freedom Is an Endless Meeting: Democracy in American Social Movements.* Chicago: University of Chicago Press, 2004.

Polletta, Francesca, and James M. Jasper. "Collective Identity and Social Movements." *Annual Review of Sociology* 27, no. 1 (2001): 283–305.

Putnam, Robert. *Bowling Alone: The Collapse and Revival of American Democracy.* New York: Simon and Schuster, 2001.

Reber, Arthur S. *Implicit Learning and Tacit Knowledge: An Essay on the Cognitive Unconscious.* New York: Oxford University Press, 1993.

Reich, Rob. *Just Giving: Why Philanthropy Is Failing Democracy and How It Can Do Better.* Princeton, NJ: Princeton University Press; 2018.

Rizzolatti, Giacomo L., Leonardo Fogassi, and Vittorio Gallese. "Neurophysiological Mechanisms Underlying the Understanding and Imitation of Action." *Nature Reviews Neuroscience* 2 (2001): 661–67.

Robinson, Jo Ann Gibson, and David J. Garrow. *The Montgomery Bus Boycott and the Women Who Started It: The Memoir of Jo Ann Gibson Robinson.* Knoxville: University of Tennessee Press, 1987.

Rodgers, Daniel T. *Age of Fracture.* Cambridge, MA: Harvard University Press, 2011.

Salas, Eduardo, Scott I. Tannenbaum, Kurt Kraiger, and Kimberly A. Smith-Jentsch. "The Science of Training and Development in Organizations: What Matters in Practice." *Psychological Science in the Public Interest* 13, no. 2 (2012): 74–101.

Sandel, Michael J. "What Isn't for Sale?" *The Atlantic*, April 2012.

Sandel, Michael J. *What Money Can't Buy: The Moral Limits of Markets.* New York: Farrar, Straus and Giroux, 2012.

Schattschneider, E. E. *The Semi-Sovereign People: A Realist's View of Democracy in America.* New York: Holt, Rinehart and Winston, 1975.

Scheiber, Noam. "Why the UAW's President Has Taken a Hard Line." *New York Times*, October 26, 2023.

Schlozman, Daniel. *When Movements Anchor Parties: Electoral Alignments in American History.* Princeton, NJ: Princeton University Press, 2015.

Scott, James C. *Domination and the Arts of Resistance: Hidden Transcripts.* New Haven, CT: Yale University Press, 1990.

Scott, James C. *The Moral Economy of the Peasant: Rebellion and Subsistence in Southeast Asia.* New Haven, CT: Yale University Press, 1977.

Scott, James C. *Weapons of the Weak: Everyday Forms of Peasant Resistance.* New Haven, CT: Yale University Press, 1985.

Sheingate, Adam. *Building a Business of Politics: The Rise of Political Consulting and the Transformation of American Democracy*. New York: Oxford University Press, 2016.

Sifry, Micah L. "If the Movements of the Last Decade Are Done, What Comes Next?" *The Connector*, December 20, 2022.

Skocpol, Theda. *Diminished Democracy: From Membership to Management in American Civil Life*. Norman: University of Oklahoma Press, 2003.

Skocpol, Theda, Marshall Ganz, and Ziad Munson. "A Nation of Organizers: The Institutional Origins of Civic Voluntarism in the United States." *American Political Science Review* 94, no. 3 (2000): 527–46.

Sloane, Arthur. *Hoffa*, Cambridge, MA: MIT, 1991.

Smith, Kenwyn K., and David N. Berg. "A Paradoxical Conception of Group Dynamics." *Human Relations* 40, no. 10 (1987): 633–58.

Snyder, Timothy. *On Tyranny: Twenty Lessons from the Twentieth Century*. New York: Duggan Books, 2017.

Starr, Kevin. *Americans and the California Dream, 1850–1915*. New York: Oxford University Press, 1973.

Starr, Kevin. *Golden Dreams: California in an Age of Abundance, 1950–1963*. New York: Oxford University Press, 2009.

Stephens, Greg J., Lauren J. Silbert, and Uri Hasson. "Speaker-Listener Neural Coupling Underlies Successful Communication." *Proceedings of the National Academy of Sciences* 107, no. 32 (2010): 14425–30.

Suzuki, Shunryu. *Zen Mind, Beginner's Mind: Informal Talks on Zen Meditation and Practice*. Boston: Shambhala, 2006.

Takaki, Ronald. *Strangers from a Different Shore: A History of Asian Americans*. Boston: Little, Brown, 1989.

Taylor, Charles. "Degenerations of Democracy." In *Degenerations of Democracy*, by Craig Calhoun, Dilip Parameshwar Goankar, and Charles Taylor, 18–47. Cambridge, MA: Harvard University Press, 2022.

Taylor, Charles. *Sources of the Self: The Making of the Modern Identity*. Cambridge, MA: Harvard University Press, 1989.

Tillich, Paul. *Love, Power, and Justice: Ontological Analyses and Ethical Applications*. New York: Oxford University Press, 1954.

Tocqueville, Alexis de. *Democracy in America*. 1835/1840. Chicago: University of Chicago Press, 2000.

Tooze, Adam. *Crashed: How a Decade of Financial Crises Changed the World*. New York: Penguin, 2018.

Tramutola, Larry. *Sidewalk Strategies: Seven Winning Steps for Candidates, Causes, and Communities*. Austin, TX: TurnKey Press, 2003.

Tufekci, Zeynep. *Twitter and Tear Gas: The Power and Fragility of Networked Protest*. New Haven, CT: Yale University Press, 2017.

Tulving, Endel. "Episodic Memory: From Mind to Brain." *Annual Review of Psychology* 53, no. 1 (2002): 1–25.

Turkle, Sherry. *Alone Together: Why We Expect More from Technology and Less from Each Other*. New York: Basic Books, 2011.

Verba, Sidney. "The Citizen as Respondent: Sample Surveys and American Democracy. Presidential Address." *American Political Science Review* 90 (1996): 1–7.

Vygotsky, Lev. *Mind in Society: The Development of Higher Psychological Processes*. Cambridge, MA: Harvard University Press, 1978.

Walker, Edward T. *Grassroots for Hire: Public Affairs Consultants in American Democracy.* Cambridge: Cambridge University Press, 2014.

Walzer, Michael. *Thick and Thin: Moral Argument at Home and Abroad.* Notre Dame, IN: University of Notre Dame Press, 1994.

Weber, Max. "The Types of Authority and Imperative Coordination." In *From Max Weber: Essays in Sociology*, edited by Hans Gerth and C. Wright Mills. New York: Routledge, 2013.

Weil, David. *Turning the Tide: Strategic Planning for Labor Unions.* Acton, MA: Xanedu Publishing, 1994.

West, Cornel. *Democracy Matters: Winning the Fight against Imperialism.* New York: Penguin, 2004.

Williams, Christine. "Boston Interfaith Organization to Celebrate 10 Years of Service." *The Pilot*, May 16, 2008. http://www.thebostonpilot.com/article.php?ID=6283.

Wilson, James Q. *Political Organizations.* 2nd ed. Princeton, NJ: Princeton University Press, 1995.

Name Index

For the benefit of digital users, indexed terms that span two pages (e.g., 52–53) may, on occasion, appear on only one of those pages.

Subject Index

For the benefit of digital users, indexed terms that span two pages (e.g., 52–53) may, on occasion, appear on only one of those pages.

Tables and figures are indicated by an italic *t* and *f* following the page number.